THE SPIRIT OF SOLESMES

SR MARY DAVID TOTAH is a Benedictine nun of St Cecilia's Abbey, Ryde. Born in Philadelphia, Pennsylvania, in 1957 of Palestinian parents, she was educated at Loyola University (New Orleans), the University of Virginia, and Christ Church, Oxford. After teaching English for two years at the College of William and Mary (Williamsburg, Virginia), she entered St Cecilia's Abbey, belonging to the Solesmes Congregation, where she made her Solemn Profession in 1991.

THE SPIRIT OF SOLESMES

Dom Prosper Guéranger (1805-75)
Abbess Cécile Bruyère (1845-1909)
Dom Paul Delatte (1848-1937)

Selected, edited and introduced by
SISTER MARY DAVID TOTAH, O.S.B.

Burns & Oates

Saint Bede's Publications

First published in Great Britain 1997 by
BURNS & OATES
Wellwood, North Farm Road,
Tunbridge Wells, Kent TN2 3DR

First published in the U.S.A. 1997 by
St Bede's Publications
P. O. Box 545, 271 N. Main Street,
Petersham, MA 01366-0545

ISBN (U.K.) 0 86012 269 7
ISBN (U.S.A.) 1 879007 22 3

Library of Congress Cataloging-in-Publication Data

Guéranger, Prosper, 1806–1875.
    The spirit of Solesmes / Prosper Guéranger, Cécile Bruyère. Paul Delatte :
selected, edited and introduced by Mary David Totah.
      p. cm.
    Includes bibliographical references.
    ISBN 1–879007–22–3 (alk. paper)
    1. Benedictines—Spiritual life. 2. Spiritual life—Catholic Church. 3. Guéranger,
Prosper, 1806–1875—Correspondence. 4. Bruyère, Cécile, 1845–1909—
Correspondence. 5. Delatte, Paul, 1848–1937—Correspondence. 6. Benedictines—
France—Solesmes—Correspondence. I. Guéranger, Prosper, 1806–1875. II.
Bruyère, Cécile, 1845–1909. III. Delatte, Paul, 1848–1937. IV. Totah, Mary
David, 1957– . V. Title.
BX3003.G84 1997
271'.104417—dc21
                                                     96–50990
                                                         CIP

Typeset by Search Press Limited
Printed and bound in Great Britain by
Biddles Ltd, Guildford and King's Lynn

CONTENTS

ILLUSTRATIONS

(Between pages 96 and 97)

Sources: 4. Archives Lambert; 5. Photo Lambert, Sablé; 7, 8. 9. Abbey of Sainte-Cécile de Solesmes; 10. Ministry of Public Building and Works; 12. Aerofilms and Aero Pictorial Ltd. All others Abbey of Saint-Pierre de Solesmes. The diagram of the Congregation of Solesmes (Appendix 2) is based on that in "Dieu est amour" nn. 164-5 (April-May 1995), published by Editions Pierre Téqui, Rennes.

To

The Right Reverend Dom Jean Prou, 1911-
Fifth Abbot (Emeritus) of Saint-Pierre de Solesmes

and

The Right Reverend Dom Aelred Sillem, 1908-94
Second Abbot of Our Lady of Quarr

*". . . studeamus amare quod amaverunt et opere
exercere quod docuerunt."*

FOREWORD

by

Philippe Dupont, Abbot of Solesmes

St Benedict founded monasteries with the disciples who had gathered around him, but he never dreamed of setting up an Order. This explains the special character of the Benedictine Order among the religious institutes of the Church. The vicissitudes of history have led the various monasteries to form separate Congregations, all of which follow the Rule of St Benedict while remaining autonomous. The Congregation of Solesmes is only one among these; it is characterized by its purely contemplative way of life, and in its recent revision of its Declarations and Constitutions following Vatican II, resolutely placed itself among the institutes "totally dedicated to contemplation."

It is to Dom Prosper Guéranger that the Congregation of Solesmes owes this wholly contemplative orientation. Desiring to restore the Benedictine life in France, where it had disappeared at the time of the Revolution, he put himself at the school of the Rule of St Benedict, perceiving, under the inspiration of the Holy Spirit, its character of total separation from the world, with no direct apostolate.

Everyone knows about Dom Guéranger's liturgical work; but his monastic achievement is probably less known. The beginnings of the restoration of Solesmes were difficult, but marked by the evident action of Providence, by the maternal action of Our Lady, for whom Dom Guéranger had a great devotion, and by an unfailing attachment to the Roman Church.

Faithful to the spirit of the Rule, Dom Guéranger made the liturgy, the *Opus Dei*, the centre of the day for monks and nuns. The liturgical life, the prayer of the Church, is their principal work. This is their response, made up of adoration, praise, and

9

supplication, to the choice God made when he called them to serve him in the monastery. But this liturgical work is not limited to a few hours of the day; it informs their whole life of prayer, of reading, and of work. The liturgy, said Abbess Cécile Bruyère, is doctrine put into practice, experienced. The saying *lex orandi lex credendi** is always true. Liturgy is the worship rendered to God; it is also the means par excellence to profess and preserve intact the doctrine of the Church.

Benedictine monastic life as restored at Solesmes by Dom Guéranger is in reality nothing other than the full unfolding of the Christian life received at baptism. This is why the doctrine taught and transmitted through Dom Guéranger and his disciples is a perfectly simple doctrine, yet rich and profound; it is that of the gospel itself. When those living in the world see monks and nuns, they think above all of the sacrifice, the renunciation these have made to enter the monastery; they forget that this is only the negative side of a much more important reality, whose positive side is union with God. These monks and nuns can say, "We know and believe the love God has for us" (1 John 4:16). To believe in God's love sums up perfectly their lives, which consist in contemplating the invisible, of living already "a noviciate for eternity," to recall an expression of Dom Delatte. Faith, hope, and charity are for them, as for all the faithful, the unique driving force of their lives; indeed, it is only through this spirit of faith that they can strive toward the essential.

Dom Guéranger tirelessly taught this doctrine to his disciples. He strove particularly to instil it into the thought and life of Jenny Bruyère, who would later become the first Abbess of Sainte Cécile. In her turn, Abbess Cécile Bruyère would transmit to Dom Delatte, third Abbot of Solesmes, what she had inherited from Dom Guéranger. The sons and daughters of Dom Guéranger endeavour in their turn to preserve, protect, and enrich this family heritage, as they entrust it to new monastic foundations in Europe, the American continent, and more

---

* "The law of prayer is the law of belief."

recently, Africa. We can therefore be grateful to the Benedictines of Ryde for making known to the public the undeniable value of this teaching, thanks to the extracts from the three great representatives of the Solesmian monastic life: Dom Guéranger, Abbess Cécile Bruyère, and Dom Delatte.

Solesmes, 11 July 1996

PREFACE

This volume represents the first attempt in English or French to combine the writings of Dom Prosper Guéranger, Abbess Cécile Bruyère, and Dom Paul Delatte, and includes much material published for the first time. For most of the selections, this is also the first English translation. It is not possible in a single book to do justice to the range of interests of these writers; while the book tries to be comprehensive, it cannot claim to be exhaustive, nor a work of critical scholarship. Its aim is to communicate something of the spirit of Solesmes, and to contribute towards a deeper understanding of a life lived in and for God, of what Dom Delatte calls "the splendour of our supernatural destiny."

This book is not only about a monastery called Solesmes; it is even more about Christ, and the mystery of Christ in us. He is the fourth protagonist of this book, the eternally Living One, embracing all phases of existence. Beginning with baptism and the seed of Christ-life within us and ending with death "when Christ our life appears," the chapters of this book present the unfolding of the gift that is Christian life and work—"until He comes." Each chapter is preceded by an introduction, showing the inner coherence of the texts that follow, grouped under each writer.

My thanks are due in the first place to the Abbot of Solesmes and to the Abbess of Sainte-Cécile, Solesmes, who have kindly given permission for the use of unpublished letters, manuscripts, published material and photographs printed in this book. These include the privately printed and circulated letters of Dom Guéranger, his unpublished retreat of 1874 to the nuns of Sainte-Cécile; Dom Delatte's unpublished life of Abbess Cécile Bruyère, his Scripture commentaries (only part of which were published in his lifetime), numerous unpublished retreats and conferences; a privately published collection of some of Abbess Cécile Bruyère's writings, *In Spiritu et Veritate* (1966), produced by her monastery on the occasion of its centenary. Unless otherwise stated, texts by Abbess Cécile Bruyère are from this source. I am also grateful for the use of several unpublished conferences on Our Lady. Some of the unpublished texts have come to us as monastic *florilegia*, as collections of extracts springing from the practice of *lectio divina*,* compiled either for the monk's or nun's own use or for reading in chapter or refectory, and widely disseminated among other houses of the Congregation: hence the lack of critical information from time to time. I am grateful to the Abbey of Notre Dame, Wisques for two such florilegia, "Via Clarescente" and "Domus Orationis."

It is perhaps worth noting, too, that the bulk of this material was written to be read in a community and never by a wider public. It represents a monastic form of preaching and thus has all the limitations—and immediacy and vigour—of the spoken word.

Other selections have been drawn from the recently published selected letters of Dom Delatte (Solesmes, 1993). Other published works by Dom Delatte represented here are: *Retraite avec Dom Delatte* (1961), *Demeurez dans mon amour* (1963—conferences on John 15, given in 1902); *Contempler l'Invisible* (1965—retreat preached in 1889 to the nuns of Sainte-Cecile); *Vivre à Dieu* (1973—*Notes on the Spiritual Life*, 1899).

I also wish to thank Dame Eanswyth Evans for permission to use material drawn from Stanbrook's archives; "Dieu est Amour" (Librairie Pierre Téqui), nn 164-165, avril-mai 1995, for permission to reproduce the diagram in Appendix 2; the Department of the Environment for photograph 10, and Aerofilms and Aero Pictorial Ltd for photograph 12; and finally, Mr Paul Burns for invaluable help in preparing this manuscript for publication.

Dom Delatte has said that "all natural and supernatural things are carried out on the level of the family, the form of life of

---

* See Note 3 to Chapter 2.

society both in time and in eternity." I acknowledge with deep gratitude the contribution of both my families: my parents and sister, for teaching me things not found in books; and the monastic community that formed me, and made this life and book possible.

INTRODUCTION

We are nine hundred years old this year. Yes, we have lasted nine centuries, just about half the time that the Church has lasted. Nine centuries of prayer and of homage to God. A little thing like us, tiny, insignificant, threatened, put to death, rising on the third day, and alive since the twelfth of October 1010. Don't you think that is delightful?
(Dom Paul Delatte, Letter to Marie Le Blan,[1] *3 January 1910)*

Solesmes is a monastery on the banks of the river Sarthe in western France. Its critical study of Gregorian chant and work of restoring original melodies have made it internationally famous. Its founder, Dom Prosper Guéranger, is well-known as the restorer of the monastic life in France, who initiated the liturgical revival in his own country, and, through a network of influences, in other parts of Europe as well, so that he is rightly called the father of the present liturgical rebirth. Perhaps less well-known is the monastery's rich spiritual tradition, moulded by the meditative reading of Scripture and the Fathers, by liturgical prayer in choir, and by the teaching of a trinity of remarkable personalities: Dom Guéranger, Dom Paul Delatte, his second successor, and Madame Cécile Bruyère, first Abbess of Sainte-Cécile de Solesmes.

Dom Prosper Guéranger

The great lines of the spirit of Solesmes may be traced in the life and work of its first abbot, a key figure in what has been called the nineteenth-century monastic revival. Why was revival necessary? With the French Revolution and the extension of its principles by Napoleon's conquests, the monastic life in Europe had come close to total extinction. Weakened already by the atmosphere of the Enlightenment, which regarded religious life

15

as legitimate only in proportion to its immediate social useful-
ness, the monasteries suffered severely from the French inva-
sions, and from the subsequent liberal and anti-religious movements. It is not possible to be precise, but it is reckoned that
while in the middle of the eighteenth century there were still
some 1500 Benedictine abbeys in Europe, by the middle of the
nineteenth there were only about thirty. The remaining houses
were few in number, reduced in size, and relaxed in observance.
In February 1790 monastic vows—which seemed an outrage
against Liberty—were declared null, and by a decree of 4 August 1792 all monasteries in France were suppressed. This legis-
lation was applied wherever French armies were victorious—in
the Low Countries in 1796, Switzerland in 1798, Italy between
1807 and 1811, Spain in 1808, the Papal States in 1809.

Revival was slow in coming. In France, after two unsuccessful
attempts from former monks of the Congregations of St Maur
and St Vanne, there was an entirely new beginning due to a
young secular priest of the diocese of Le Mans, named Prosper
Guéranger. He was not a founder in the strict sense of the word:
he did not desire to create a new form of religious life. For him
the return to Benedictine tradition could only be accomplished
by the adoption and observance of the Rule of Saint Benedict:
"It is by the Rule of Saint Benedict," he wrote, "that we will be
Benedictines." In one sense he changed nothing. But in another
respect he did everything: as the homilist at his profession
would note in recalling Ezekiel's vision of the dry bones, Dom
Guéranger called the dead to life.

It was to one of those "bare ruin'd choirs" that he made his
way, on the very day of ordination, 7 October 1827:

> I soon found myself on the site where Marmoutiers had once
> been. There was nothing but rubble everywhere, but the situation
> of a large cloister was still distinguishable, the walls of which had
> been razed almost to the ground.... I found the expression of
> what I was feeling in these words of Isaiah: "Your holy cities have
> become a desert, Jerusalem is a waste, our holy and glorious
> temple in which our fathers praised you." ... I besought God to
> raise up zealous men to rebuild all the ruins, to release Holy

Church from the yoke of captivity that had weighed upon her since she had been deprived of the holy institutions that were her glory and liberty.

Dom Guéranger was a native of Sablé and grew up, a schoolmaster's son, in the shadow of another abandoned priory at Solesmes [2]. As a seminarian and priest, he developed a deep love and knowledge of the Fathers, and he saw the monastic life as a life centred on the liturgy. In 1833, at the age of twenty-eight, he acquired the ancient priory of Solesmes and resumed monastic life there with a few companions. A contemporary of the Romantics, he had a taste for poetry and art, especially architecture; yet his return to the first principles of monastic life had little in common with the medieval revival frequently attached to the Romantic period. He possessed, rather, to a marked degree that "historical sense," which T. S. Eliot defined as involving "a perception not only of the pastness of the past but of its presence." More than a mere antiquarian, he sensed the need of reawakening the deep consciousness—and this long before Vatican II—that the life of the Church is the life of Christ, and that its prayer is the prayer of Christ. The Church was his "ruling passion," in the words of Dom Laurence Shepherd, and monks and nuns of the Solesmes Congregation are above all men and women of the Church who contemplate Christ in the mystery of the Church.

In 1837 he departed for Rome to have his Constitutions approved by the Camaldolese Pope Gregory XVI. On the journey from Marseilles, he met his first Benedictine, William Bernard Ullathorne, monk of Downside and later bishop of Birmingham, on his way to Rome to report on his work in Australia. Gregory XVI gave his approval to Dom Guéranger, and even gave him the right to launch a Congregation from Solesmes. After a fortnight's retreat at St Paul's-without-the-Walls, his first stay in a Benedictine house, he made his solemn profession and was appointed abbot of Solesmes—without ever having made a novitiate or been a simple monk. Like Saint Benedict himself, Dom Guéranger did not put himself at the school of any existing institution; he knew monastic life only from his wide and deep reading. It seems that the Holy Spirit alone prepared him for a work that was to be at once deeply traditional and a new beginning. In what amounted to a real charism, he acquired a sureness of touch for things Benedictine, a clear-sightedness and a precision that he was able to pass on to others.

To many of his contemporaries, Dom Guéranger seemed solemn and imposing; in his age of diatribe, he is remembered more as an apologist, a polemicist who defended the unity of the Roman liturgy against the local liturgies of the French, and denounced naturalism in all its forms.[3] Mgr Fayet, bishop of Orleans, with whom Dom Guéranger had often crossed swords, spoke of his impressions of the Abbot of Solesmes to a Jesuit acquainted with the monastery:

"I picture the Abbot of Solesmes as tall, thin, gaunt."

"I'm sorry, my Lord, he is quite small, and plump rather than thin."

"But at least he is dark, with jet-black hair, and looks stern and humourless?"

"I regret to have to tell your Lordship that Dom Guéranger is very fair, with blue eyes, a smile always on his lips, and that he is full of life and extremely amiable."

His literary output was prolific, his most widely-known books being *Les Institutions liturgiques* and *L'Année liturgique* (The Liturgical Year). Neither was completed in his lifetime, but they taught Christians to find the life-giving source of their personal prayer in the prayer of the Church and so paved the way for the present liturgical renewal. In a tribute to Dom Guéranger on the occasion of the 100th anniversary of his death, Pope Paul VI called him the "author of the liturgical movement." This understanding of the liturgy as the highest expression of the Church's life and the source of contemplation and holiness gave rise to Solesmes' critical study of Gregorian chant and the work of restoring original melodies. Dom Guéranger also contributed significantly to the formulation of the two great dogmas of the nineteenth century: the dogma of the Immaculate Conception, the absolute purity of the "*Sedes sapientiae*"; and the dogma of the infallibility of the Holy See, the absolute integrity of the "*Cathedra sapientiae*".[4]

It was his unshakeable supernatural confidence, his ardent love of God, his tremendous resilience, that enabled Dom Guéranger to maintain the pace of his many occupations while in the utmost material want or physical discomfort. He was nearly deposed by his young, inexperienced community in 1836; he wrote his voluminous works under financial constraints that would have worn down anyone of lesser faith and vitality; he endured calumnies directed against himself and his monastery. Despite the success of foundations at Ligugé and Marseilles, one at Paris failed and nearly caused the ruin of his work. Possessing what Madame Cécile Bruyère called "the least meticulous and the least suspicious mind in the world," he had not by nature the gifts of an able administrator or a talent for financial affairs. It was she who, in 1874, delicately succeeded in restoring order to the labyrinth of the accounts. He was more an inspirer, a creative genius, who had a simplicity of outlook that directs all its energies to the furthering of a kingdom not of this world.

Dom Guéranger's work of monastic revival radiated far beyond the confines of Solesmes. The founders of the influential Beuron Congregation,[5] the Wolter brothers, took their first novice to Solesmes to be trained, and Dom Maurus Wolter himself made a long stay there, both before and after the Franco-Prussian war. Although Dom Guéranger cautioned Dom Maurus against the temptation of turning Beuron into a German Solesmes, and insisted on seeing local conditions as an expression of God's will, the Wolter brothers would settle questions raised at Beuron or its foundation at Maredsous by the declaration: "At Solesmes it was always done in this way." Dom Bastide of Solesmes (later abbot of the ancient monastery of St Martin at Ligugé) was lent to Beuron to become its first novice-master. The Beuronese Constitutions were modelled after the Declarations Dom Guéranger wrote for Sainte Cécile. It was to the young prior of Beuron that Dom Guéranger wrote this testament that reveals so much of his mind and character:

Take care of your health; you need it, and it doesn't belong to you. Encourage in every way you can a holy liberty of spirit among your monks and do everything you can to make them love their state of life more deeply than anything in the world. Make yourself lovable always and in all circumstances. Be a mother rather than a father to your children. Imitate the patience of God, and don't demand that spring bear the fruits of autumn. Be always accessible to everyone; avoid formality and ceremony. Adapt yourself to everyone, and don't try to adapt others to yourself; for God has created us all different, and you are the servant of all, like Our Lord Jesus Christ. Take a scrupulous care of the health of each one, and don't wait for a serious illness before giving a dispensation. Establish the observance progressively, and don't be afraid to retrace your steps if you have gone too far. Inspire the love of the Sacred Liturgy, which is the centre of all Christianity.

His ideas entered the English Benedictine Congregation via another enthusiastic disciple, Dom Laurence Shepherd, monk of Ampleforth and chaplain at Stanbrook for twenty-two years, who translated his work into English. The expulsion of the monks of Solesmes, along with other religious orders, from France in 1880, 1882 and 1901[6] led to the founding of monasteries of refuge in England, Spain, Holland and Luxembourg. When these exiled monks eventually returned to France, these houses lived on in their native soil, while still belonging to the French Congregation. Through the Benedictine community of nuns which he founded at Solesmes, Sainte-Cécile, Dom Guéranger's ideals were transmitted to the nuns of Jouarre, Stanbrook, and Sainte Croix, Poitiers, among many others.

Madame Cécile Bruyère

Dom Guéranger's life and work lived on in his successors, Dom Couturier and Dom Delatte, and perhaps most especially in the young Abbess of Sainte-Cécile, who, he said, knew his mind better than anyone. Jenny Bruyère was born in Paris on the anniversary of the dedication of Solesmes' abbey church, 12 October 1845. Dom Guéranger was forty years Jenny's senior, an almost mythical figure in the wider ecclesiastical arena, when he agreed to prepare the eleven-year-old girl for her First Communion. This was in the spring of 1857. The deep harmony, at once so complete and unequivocal, that existed between them from the beginning, lasted until Dom Guéranger's death. "I have never raised a question with this child without realizing that the Holy Spirit had been there before me. It is like playing the piano; when one strikes, she resonates."

It is difficult to say which of the two was guiding or preceding the other, for in the following year she revealed to the Abbot of Solesmes her precocious and powerful instinct for the things of God, a determined will to tend directly to God alone. He made her wait until her sixteenth birthday, however, before allowing her to make a private, temporary vow of virginity at Solesmes. The following year saw her promise made permanent. Strong-minded and bold, Jenny Bruyère became, under Dom Guéranger's wise and discreet direction, more open, supple, engaging and generous, giving herself to all that was demanded of her. Years later, the Abbess of Stanbrook, Dame Gertrude d'Aurillac Dubois, was to admire "the wisdom and simplicity (which) seemed to play within and around her, strength and sweetness, activity and unshakeable peace, extraordinary intuition and childlike grace."

Dom Guéranger had no desire to found a monastery of nuns. But there were a number of independent forces at work, developing with a co-ordination that he realized later could only have come from God. It was Jenny's mother who, knowing her daughter's aspirations, first suggested the idea to the Abbot of Solesmes, who dismissed it as "a castle in the air." The infirm and tireless abbot, who snatched time between the Office and the visits of those who sought his help to add a few sentences to his latest work, had little energy and strength to undertake such a project. He was surprised, however, that his prior and future successor, a man of caution and prudence, seconded the proposal. Finally, the foundation of the monastery of monks at Marseilles led Dom Guéranger to a number of young women, a veritable "nursery of vocations," who desired the Benedictine life. Near Solesmes, too, other vocations were shaping. But it was Jenny Bruyère who was the cornerstone of the foundation:

"Without Mère Cécile, I should never have undertaken any-thing, and I should never have been able to achieve anything."

The fruit of his monastic maturity, Sainte-Cécile sprang forth, "an adult from birth," as Dom Delatte remarks. Although the foundation was to experience material difficulties, it was spared many of the pains and mistakes that are the price of pioneerdom. Jenny had taken the name of Cécile at the time of her confirma-tion, placing herself under the patronage of Saint Cecilia, the great Roman martyr for whom Dom Guéranger had such ven-eration. The future monastery, too, was placed under the saint's patronage: "He recognized in her," wrote Madame Cécile Bruyère, "an embodiment of the Roman Church of the first centuries, strong, serene, majestic, invincible."

It was characteristic of Dom Guéranger, who did not allow matters of detail to disturb the great lines of his projects, to move the young community of seven into the new monastery while it was still a building site. This was in August 1867; on the 15th they received the habit. The following year saw the first professions, for which Dom Guéranger composed a new cer-emonial. The day after, Mère Cécile was elected prioress, and Dom Guéranger ceded the government of the monastery into her hands. Four years later, Mgr Fillon, bishop of Le Mans, acting independently and without Dom Guéranger's knowl-edge, asked of Pius IX the favour of the abbatial blessing for the twenty-seven-year-old prioress, in recognition of the abbot's service to the Church. Granting the request, the Pope remarked that this was to put the cart before the horse, since the monas-tery had not yet been raised to the rank of an abbey. The monastery itself would be given abbatial status only nineteen years later.

Writing to a member of her family fifteen years after the event, Madame Cécile described her feelings at being raised to the highest dignity the Church can confer on a woman:

> I dreaded the irrevocability of the Blessing. I dreaded the honours attached to the title; I was very aware that the obscurity for which I so much longed would be impossible.... It pleased Our Lord that the Blessing should change my whole being. And he has

allowed my soul to see, with intense clarity, the total detachment to which it was called. Until then I had felt that the love of God would make me undertake anything; but from then onwards I saw that the second commandment was like the first, and that I must be to my neighbour—through Our Lord and for his sake—what I was to him. I felt that I must give my time, my thoughts, my whole life to souls, and that the Blessing would put the seal on that complete holocaust to the honour of God.

She was, as Dom Germain Cozien, fourth abbot of Solesmes, would call her, "the inheritor of Dom Guéranger's spirit and the mother of the whole French Congregation," proving herself a vitalizing and spiritual force in the lives of both monks and nuns, and playing an important role when the monks were dragged unceremoniously from their stalls by armed force in November 1880.[7] She made practical provisions for the welfare of the monks scattered among the village houses, in countless ways showing a truly motherly solicitude.

In 1885, just as her monastery was "enlarging the space for its tent" to accommodate the increasing numbers, she published *The Spiritual Life and Prayer*. Based on the Scriptures and the teaching of the Fathers, it was more than a synthesis of all that was best and highest in spiritual doctrine; it was her spiritual autobiography, and stands between Dom Guéranger's living monastic culture and Dom Delatte's contemplative theology, containing something of both. There is a vein of moderation, of proportion, of good sense running through it, that shrinks from rigid systems and extremes in outlook or behaviour. What characterizes the spiritual life for Madame Cécile Bruyère is a spirit of order, of the forming of nature to receive grace by a slow, steady, gentle growth, "the tranquil and spontaneous development of a living seed that grows, flowers, reaches perfection, by the working of its own innate energy," as Dom Delatte described it. At the same time as she describes the essence of the perfect life and its interior qualities, she also indicated practical, external steps: be perfectly simple, banish all anxiety, be prompt and resolute in overcoming self.

The agent of this spiritual growth is prayer, both liturgical and private: "It is meaningless to set up a contrast between liturgical prayer, determined by the Church, and individual prayer, free both in its direction and in its method. The first does not exist fully without the second; and the second takes its strength from the first, and finds in it a reliable support." The last chapter, "There is but one Liturgy," shows the importance of the liturgy for the Christian life in the context of God's merciful design for humankind; the Incarnation involves all creatures in a liturgical act, the one liturgy of heaven. Being a Christian does not only mean accepting Christ's teaching and receiving the graces won by him; it also means becoming a worshipper in spirit and in truth, reliving his mysteries, ascending to God in the liturgy in the way Christ descended to us and returned to the Father. Here is realized the unity of our human life, the participation of whole persons in their highest act, which is worship. Here is realized too what will be one of Dom Delatte's great themes: the opening out of time on to the eternal.

Sainte-Cécile prospered; by 1888 the numbers had reached seventy-five. Two foundations were made: Notre Dame de Wisques (1888) in the diocese of Arras, and St Michel de Kergonan in Brittany, ten years later. The Abbess' luminous, penetrating, but eminently practical intellect exerted an influence over a large and varied circle: princes and dignitaries of the Church, priests, religious, and layfolk. And not only individuals but whole communities sought her experience, wisdom, and guidance: Maredret, Dourgne, the Servants of the Poor, the Franciscan Missionaries. The Prioress of Bonlieu made a stay at Sainte-Cécile in September 1887 and has left an account of her daily interview with Madame Cécile Bruyère:

4 October. I have had a long discussion with Lady Abbess about the examination of postulants and the consecration of virgins. I noticed that, during the whole of this interview, Lady Abbess spoke as one perfectly sure of what she was saying, with great authority not so much in her voice and manner as in the force of the reasons she brought forward. And she expresses herself with a great liberty of spirit, with simplicity and humility, and there is nothing so striking as that contrast, which one always notices in her, between the perfect understanding of her subject, the preci-

sion of the terms she employs, and the simplicity of manner in which she explains the most exalted truths as if they were the simplest thing in the world, and such as anyone would be able to grasp. One does not feel in her either effort, or labour, or research.

She gave willingly and unstintingly, but not without effort; by nature self-effacing, wholly immersed in the divine life, she was not especially drawn to what has been called "the apostolate of the parlour." She was a deeply contemplative soul who described herself as "like a coin with one side facing toward eternity and the reverse towards time. That is the origin of a suffering caused by a contrast which God sometimes makes very keen, so keen that remaining here below seems against nature."

The gap between the two extremes was to close in exile. She was not surprised by the definitive vote for the Law of Association in 1901 directed against religious Congregations of men and women; but she was somewhat disconcerted, Dom Delatte tells us in his biography of her, when the General Chapter of Solesmes decided unanimously to go into exile rather that to submit to a servile authorization. Did her valiant, determined heart feel that it was her duty to face the onslaught, prepared either to win or perish? Her hesitation did not last long, however, and by mid-August her community had found a refuge on the Isle of Wight.

The last eight years of her life saw her subject to frequent and prolonged bouts of weakness, a trial not only to herself but also to her community, as she realized:

> As you can see, my children, my health is not outstanding; but we must accept what God gives us and bow our heads. The times are evil; it is up to us to redeem them. Let us observe our Rule with fidelity. I ask you to forgive me for speaking in this way, since I no longer observe it myself; but I did follow it for as long as I was able to do so; and today, if I can no longer follow it, I still love it.

The *Acta* of the martyrdom of St Cecilia relate that just before her death she asked the Lord for three days that she might consecrate her house as a church, "*ut domus meam ecclesiam consecrarem*," a line that has found its way into the liturgy for her feast. It was fitting, then, that the last phase of Madame Cécile Bruyère's illness took place just after the dedication of the church in exile, at St Cecilia's Abbey, Ryde, on 12 October 1907. Her whole life had unfolded within the framework of the liturgy for the dedication, and this was to be the last joy of her life. As the days passed and her physical infirmities increased, she lapsed into greater silence, her solitude and dependence growing more complete as the paralysis spread, her prayer becoming a habitual state, that state of waiting, trusting, adoring, that belongs to a worshipper in spirit and in truth. She died on 18 March 1909.

Dom Paul Delatte

Born at Jeumont on 27 March 1848, Dom Paul Delatte came to monastic life comparatively late, with a character and mind already formed and exercised. He was twenty-six when he visited Solesmes for the first time, but he felt even then that he was too old, "too ossified," as he put it, to embark upon monastic life. This was in October 1874. Dom Guéranger, who had only a few months to live, met the young priest from Lille. "We have in the Abbey just now," he wrote to Madame Cécile Bruyère, "a young priest from the north, quite exceptional. If you could see his great height, his jet-black hair—what an impression of strength and life!" Perceiving his desire for a life of study, Dom Guéranger reminded him that "a monk is not a man of study but a man of the social prayer of the Church." He was thirty-five when, at the onset of a brilliant career in theology, he finally entered the Solesmes noviciate: "The Lord literally seized me by the hair." By this time, he had occupied the chair of scholastic philosophy at the Catholic University of Lille, and was a doctor of theology. Madame Cécile Bruyère recognized that this was "a vocation of major importance" for the future of Solesmes: "I have never seen greater breadth of thought, of the kind we love, a deeper understanding and love of Holy Church, a more complete understanding of the miseries and needs of our times, combined with the suppleness and simplicity of a child." From his decision to enter until her death in 1909, the role of Madame Cécile Bruyère was preponderant. Writing to her in 1906, he said: "I have received so much from you in the past quarter of a century that it seems to me that it is your hands that have made and modelled me. I would not be a monk if it were not for you; and it is certainly against my will, and thanks to you, that I am an abbot." He entered Solesmes on 7 September 1883, and was professed two years later on 21 March; in 1888 he was named prior, and on 9 November 1890, five years after profession, became abbot of his monastery. His abbatial motto, *Donec veniat* ("Until he comes," cf 1 Cor. 11:26), expressed his devotion to St Paul, to the eucharistic mystery, to the things of eternity and, as he himself explained, "to the works and words promised until he comes."

Although they were one in their understanding of the monastic life, Dom Guéranger and Dom Delatte differed much in mind and character, the one small, expansive, kindly, ingenuous; the other powerfully-built, intransigent, meticulous, excelling in speculation, remaining his calm, consistent self in the rough chaos of events that saw first the expulsion of his monks from the monastery, then the exile of his community, and even opposition and enmity among those of his own household. Dom Delatte was elected abbot without ever having lived in a cloister; twenty-five of his thirty years as abbot were spent either outside the walls of his abbey or in exile. The new abbot had to borrow the church of Sainte-Cécile to receive his abbatial blessing. "If I had been shown," he wrote in 1918, "at the threshold, the future that awaited me, I think I would have turned back. And I would have been wrong. Nothing is so precious as being in God's hand."

Strength and tenderness were the qualities he admired most in his patron, St Paul, and they were the very ones that set him apart in the eyes of his contemporaries. By strength, they understood not only the physical strength that demanded periods of hard manual work, the ability to administer and organize firmly, to act courageously and clearsightedly in times of change and crisis; but also a robust faith, a strength of mind and will, a nobility of soul that enabled him to transmit supernatural truths with great power and clarity. His monks recalled leaving Chapter feeling like the disciples on the road to Emmaus, their hearts burning within them.

In 1894, Dom Delatte regained his abbey in the face of gendarmes, only to choose exile in 1901 rather than compromise "the freedom to exercise our profession and to live our life in its entirety." In the interval, he saw to the material growth and reconstruction of Solesmes, but his enduring work was effected in the building up of the family of the house. He was, like Dom Guéranger, a real father to his monks and nuns. St Gregory the Great in his Life of St Benedict shows the Rule as most important for understanding St Benedict, "for his life and his teaching were one and the same thing." In his classic commentary on the Rule, we find a true portrait of Dom Delatte. The abbot's contacts with his monks, he writes, resemble "a sacrament," "an anticipated vision of God." "Until the day when he shall contemplate God face to face, he will nowhere see him more clearly than in souls, in the living crystal of their purity." During the exile on the Isle of Wight, he played an outstanding part in keeping together the scattered houses of the Congregation, by his numerous visits and letters, always striving to safeguard the essential conditions of monastic life. Along with these external activities went a steady output of writing; apart from conferences to the monks and nuns, he preached retreats, wrote the lives of Dom Guéranger and Madame Bruyère, and still found time to devote to manual labour and tennis.

His firm rule and lofty conception of authority, endorsed by the Rule, gave Dom Delatte the reputation for being something of an autocrat. J.-K.Huysmans, who desired to try his vocation at Solesmes and eventually became a secular oblate of Ligugé, admired Dom Delatte's "great heart" but called him "the colonel ... with his barracks on the Sarthe." To those who knew him well, however, he possessed a childlike simplicity and humility. He loved to say "one must know how to inherit," and he saw himself above all as a son: "Our Lady is what she has always been.... I do not feel that I am really in my vocation unless I am standing before her and before God the Father. I know myself

to be—I was going to say I feel myself to be—essentially a son."
Madame Bruyère saw this idea of sonship as the key to Dom
Delatte's vocation and his mission:

> It was right that St Benedict should preside over your monastic
> profession, because you, more than any other, needed to receive
> that spirit of adoption, which is part of the mechanism of our
> lives. To be a son, for you, is not so much a quality you possess, as
> your very essence. You are a son in order to acquire a special and
> particular resemblance to Our Lord Jesus Christ. You are a son
> because you are the legitimate heir of your two "abbas"; the roles
> of those two fathers are one single paternity. You will be a son by
> the very nature of your vocation, of your mission, by the mode of
> your activity.

This dimension of sonship, the full realization of the spirit of
adoption inaugurated at baptism, was central to his teaching.

Dom Delatte's resignation in 1921 coincided with the return
of the Solesmes monks and nuns to France. He lived on at
Solesmes for another sixteen years, enjoying the life of a simple
monk and radiating peace and joy: "I believe that it is only
toward the end of his life that a monk can really appreciate his
vocation in all its charm. Every day it all seems to him so alive,
so new, so astonishing in its peaceful grandeur and simplicity.
Yes indeed: if this life did not exist, one would have to invent
it."

Solesmes and England

Solesmes' contacts with England began long before the exile to
the Isle of Wight in 1901. Through his remarkable friendship
with Dom Laurence Shepherd, Dom Guéranger contributed
significantly to the English monastic revival of the late nineteenth century. In later years the abbot liked to claim that it was
he who had sent Fr Laurence to Stanbrook, and indeed had it
not been for his reiterated recommendation and encouragement
Fr Laurence probably would never have accepted the post.

It was Dom Laurence who translated *L'Année liturgique*.
Through his mediation the nuns of Stanbrook adopted constitutions framed on those that Dom Guéranger had written for

Sainte-Cécile. Dom Laurence had also preached Dom Guéranger's ideals at a retreat he gave to the Downside community. The influence of Solesmes was to affect the constitutions of the monks of the English Benedictine Congregation at a later date via Beuron. Fr Laurence's visit to Solesmes in 1855 was the first of very nearly annual visits, the last being in 1884, four months before his death.

The consecration of the Belmont priory church in September 1860 provided the occasion for Dom Guéranger's first visit to England. We are well informed about the visit, for we have both Fr Laurence's account of it and also the abbot's own description and impressions from a journal he kept. Fr Laurence went to Gloucester to meet the abbot but he could scarcely recognize him. Dom Guéranger had been assured by the community of English Benedictines at Douai in France that he could not possibly wear the habit in England, where religious dress was proscribed by law. A secular suit and "chimney pot" hat had been rapidly purchased for him, but the coat was so tight that he could lower his arms only with difficulty. As they travelled by train to Hereford, Dom Guéranger discoursed on the significance of the dedication which was to take place the next day, shouting all the louder when the train entered a tunnel. On their arrival at Belmont they found that First Vespers of the Dedication was about to begin. "There can be no First Vespers for what does not yet exist," said Dom Guéranger with a smile, and the arrangement was changed.

From Belmont, Dom Guéranger and Fr Laurence embarked on a tour of England, beginning with Gloucester, Bath, Prior Park, and Downside. During his first few days at Bath, the abbot was urged to have his photograph taken ("It was hard work," noted Fr Laurence). The photographer suggested that he fix his eyes on a rose. He began to enlarge on the symbolism of the rose with such enthusiasm that Fr Laurence had to remind him that the photographers were waiting.

From Downside they proceeded to Stanbrook, where the abbot said Mass. From Worcester they travelled to Birmingham, where after an excursion to Oscott, they called on John Henry

Newman. Dom Guéranger greeted him warmly, but Newman was in Fr Laurence's words "unresponsive," answering only in monosyllables and declining to give extended answers to the abbot's overtures. Both men, however, were more at ease in the Oratory's library. After visiting the Benedictine nuns at Colwich, the two went on via Derby to York (whose cathedral Dom Guéranger greatly admired) and Ampleforth, where they met Bishop Ullathorne, who had missed them in Birmingham. Bishop Ullathorne regaled Dom Guéranger with Irish anecdotes in French. The abbot laughed heartily, recalled Fr Laurence, "not at the Irish wit but at the good bishop's French."

After York there followed visits to Peterborough (where the abbot chided his young disciple for not knowing that Catherine of Aragon was buried there: "a monk should be an historian") and Oxford. The tour ended in London where they were the guests of Mgr Manning.[8] Their visit to Fr Faber at the Oratory was a happy one. Dom Guéranger found him "frank, open and full of life, having the spirit of St Philip Neri." Faber has recorded his meeting with Dom Guéranger:

> I shall remember the face, the voice, and the manner which betokened the tranquil yet fervent, the deep yet gay spirit of the excellent monk. . . . So humble, so modest, so kindly and yet with an odour of prayer about him, he seemed the very spirit of the Benedictine beauty of holiness. (Letter to Miss Nugent, 17 September 1860.)[9]

Faber's name often appears in the conferences of Dom Guéranger and Dom Delatte; in one of his letters, Dom Delatte recommends *All For Jesus*, and admits to having read it twenty times.

Their conducted tour around Westminster Abbey caused some anxiety to Fr Laurence, as Dom Guéranger expressed his feelings by kicking the tomb of Elizabeth I, and praying at Mary Stuart's and that of Edward the Confessor. Fr Laurence had to interpret the guide's angry remarks that he should keep with the party, and that since this was a public place of worship, no one was allowed to pray in the way he was doing. Having abandoned his clerical suit after York, it was in his habit that he visited Westminster Abbey, the Houses of Parliament, and the

Tower, claiming proudly that it was "the first time that a monk in his habit has been in these places since the Reformation." Neither he nor England guessed at that moment how much they were to receive from each other in the future.

After Dom Guéranger's death, the monks of Solesmes were led to make a fifth foundation, this time in England. The exiled Napoleon III had died there on 9 January 1873; his son, Louis, the prince imperial, had been killed by Zulus in South Africa in 1879 during a British military expedition. A couple of years later, in 1881, while living at Chislehurst, Empress Eugénie had bought a property at Farnborough in Hampshire for the purpose of establishing a *chapelle mortuaire* for the Imperial family. Designed by the architect Gabriel Destailleur in the flamboyant French style of the late middle ages, it is considered one of the masterpieces of French neo-Gothic. The crypt containing the tombs of the Imperial family is under the apse. It was completed in 1888.

At first the empress called on the French Premonstratensians to serve the sanctuary; when this community withdrew after eight years, she approached Solesmes in 1895. In view of the uncertain political situation in France, Dom Delatte accepted. The monks moved in on 10-11 December 1895. The abbot of Solesmes accompanied the group on their departure, and wrote to his prior from Farnborough:

> It seems that the Empress was momentarily put out when she learned I was coming: she takes me for a grand person who never goes anywhere without mitre and crozier, and she did not want me in the house until all the repairs were finished. She is doing these with great care and excessive splendour; although we are not paying for it, it is nevertheless annoying as it takes time.... Tomorrow we shall sing the votive Mass of St Michael after the Little Hours, and the regular life of the priory will then begin. Everyone seems in grand spirits.... I have never seen anything begin with such enthusiastic joy. Nothing anywhere but perfect joy.... I commend this little child whom I love to the prayers of all.

In 1903 the monastery was granted abbatial status, with Dom Fernand Cabrol at its head. By 1909 there were forty monks.

From the beginning the monastery was devoted to intense intellectual efforts, the breadth and quality of which is perhaps best represented by the thirty-volume *Dictionnaire d'archéologie chrétienne et de liturgie* by Dom Cabrol and Dom Henri Leclercq. There were also Dom Marius Férotin's excursions into the ancient Hispanic liturgy; Dom André Wilmart's work on the spirituality of the Middle Ages; Dom Louis Gougard's work on the Celtic world of Ireland, Great Britain, and Brittany; and Dom Augustine Gatard's study of Gregorian chant.

The Solesmes monks were to withdraw from Farnborough in 1947, after offering the monastery to English Benedictines of the Subiaco Congregation under Prinknash Abbey.

More remarkable still was Cardinal Vaughan's plan to restore the life of the ancient cathedral monastery at his newly-built Westminster Cathedral—with monks from Solesmes. Cardinal Vaughan desired Solesmes to provide a monastic foundation that would perform all the liturgical functions in his cathedral. Monastic chapters were, of course, as old as the English monastic order, and were something of an English speciality. His desire to introduce foreign monks, however, was something novel. Dom Cabrol wrote of the plan to Madame Bruyère in the early months of 1899:

> I leave Cardinal Vaughan in order to write a few words to you. I haven't said anything yet to you about this important business, because everything has moved too fast. I shall leave Solesmes as soon as the Cardinal has left us. He is offering us his cathedral under conditions which seem to me to be to our advantage. However one looks at it, it is a great honour for Solesmes that the Prelate should have thought of our Congregation and made us this offer. Pray hard that our Father Abbot will be granted the necessary light, because this affair is important for the future of our Congregation. The Cardinal is a man of the Church, a man of God, and at the same time a perfect gentleman. His outlook corresponds with ours.

After submitting his proposal to Pope Leo XIII, Cardinal Vaughan visited Solesmes and discussed the matter at length with Dom Delatte, who was deeply impressed by the cardinal's ardour and quiet resolution. The cardinal presided at the office of Corpus Christi, carried the Blessed Sacrament in procession, and conferred the sub-diaconate on three monks. Dom Delatte, however, did not think a foreign body of monks in a national cathedral, at the heart of the political and social life of the Empire, would further the English Catholic cause. All his efforts were directed toward preparing the way for English monks to succeed those of Solesmes. Moreover, he dismissed the idea of a solemn charter fixing the organization of the cathedral:

> No, Your Eminence, no Charter, none of those papers that shape the future in advance, that keep people attached to each other by an exterior constraint, guarantees that are unnecessary while one gets on well, and from which one disengages oneself with great difficulty when one ceases to get on well. After the spontaneous offer which Your Eminence has made, coming to us of your own accord, it is better that we should be at Westminster merely in order to render service for a certain time, and that the archbishop of Westminster should be absolutely free to dismiss us as soon as we are no longer necessary or of service to him.

Cardinal Vaughan returned to England to face still more objections and, in the end, decided to entrust the cathedral's liturgy to secular clergy. The Westminster Cathedral Choir, under Sir Richard Runciman Terry, was to be directly influenced by Solesmes at a later date, especially through Dom Gatard of Farnborough.

Meanwhile in France the anti-religious campaigns were mounting. The storm broke on 1 July 1901, when the French Parliament passed the Law of Association to be applicable from October. The law provided that no religious Congregation, whether of men or women, could be formed without a legislative authorizing act, and that this act would determine the functions of its members; but this status imposed obligations and kept the *congréganistes*, as they were called, under a perpetual threat. On the one hand, they had each year to draw up a list of their members, an inventory of their possessions, and a statement of their receipts, and to present these documents to the prefectorial authority on demand. On the other hand, to deprive any congregation of its authorization, nothing more was required than an ordinary decree of the Council of Ministers. Finally, these authorized Congregations could found "new establishments" such as schools or hospitals, only in virtue of a decree of the Council of the State. Government authorization had to be requested within three months. Those Congregations not authorized were to be dissolved.

The General Chapter of Solesmes was unanimous in preferring exile to a precarious and demeaning authorization. Dom Delatte wrote to one of the other abbots of the congregation:

> To ask permission to exist from people who hate us seems to me to be a base thing to do; and, as things stand, we are too well authorized by God, the Church, by natural law and by the services we render, to go and ask for the authorization of Satanism. We have no need of it; and I am firmly resolved not to commit such a blunder. The government, which has been left free to do whatever it likes by the cowardice of the whole people, also has no need for that right to be acknowledged. I cannot refuse an authorization if it is imposed upon me; however, I will not ask for it, I will not ask anyone to make the request for me, and I will never lay claim to it.

For the fourth time in the twenty-five years since Dom Guéranger's death, Solesmes was on the move. By September the monks and nuns had arrived on the Isle of Wight and settled down unostentatiously to their regular life. The monks were first installed at Appuldurcombe House, not far from Ventnor, where there was a priory of Benedictine nuns founded by the Abbey of Paix Notre Dame, Liège. They would one day become part of the Solesmes Congregation. Of Appuldurcombe, Dom Delatte wrote: "We have found a house, or rather, a large manor, with fairly large grounds, and we are living there, if not in perfect comfort, at least all together. We were about ninety when we left Saint Pierre. As you can well imagine, when the English lords or baronets built their stately homes, they didn't have in mind the French monks who were to come and live there one day."

The nuns of Sainte-Cécile found refuge first at Northwood, which belonged to the Ward family, then, five years later, at

Appley House, Ryde. The nuns of St Michel de Kergonan (Brittany) stayed for a time in the suburbs of London, before moving into the house vacated by nuns of Sainte-Cécile in Cowes. Other houses of the Congregation found havens in Belgium, Holland, Italy and Luxembourg, giving a new impulse to the monastic life in those lands.

This period of exile bore abundant fruit: persecution and exile seemed to stimulate the influx of aspirants to the monastic life. In a little over a decade, the Congregation saw the birth of four new abbeys: those of Farnborough, St Paul de Wisques exiled at Oosterhout, and the two abbeys of Kergonan. When the exiles returned to France in 1921, they left behind them the nucleus of some five new communities. "I am happy," wrote Dom Delatte, "I do not stop to ask myself, like the Jews, mournfully, how one can sing the songs of God in a foreign land; our Homeland is everywhere. It doesn't worry me in the least if such statements scandalize fervent patriots; I will say what I think all the same. We say Mass, we sing the Office, we study and pray in complete liberty. As long as we live, God is also with us; the Blessed Sacrament does not seem to find it disagreeable to be on English soil; and when we die, we will not have to travel any further in order to go to God."

There were visits from Bishop Cahill of Portsmouth, who every year on Maundy Thursday blessed the holy oils not at the Cathedral but at Appuldurcombe, and from Princess Beatrice, governor of the Island. In the course of July 1902 the royal yacht was moored in the Solent, within easy sight of Northwood. One evening, just as the nuns were sitting down to their supper, Queen Alexandra dropped in unexpectedly and asked to see King Edward VII's cousin, Mère Adelaide of Braganza, formerly queen of Portugal and a member of the community.[10] A few days later, the king himself appeared. On the occasion of the coronation of Edward VII later that summer, the abbot of Solesmes presented to the king, through the duke of Norfolk, an address, hand-lettered and illuminated by the nuns, which was favoured with a response. The address read:

Sire, in the midst of the immense acclamation which, from one end of the British Empire to the other, greets the accession of Your Majesty, and makes the glorious ceremony of your coronation into a festivity for a whole people, the religious of the Congregation of France, who have taken refuge in England, request Your Majesty to receive the homage of their gratitude and of their loyal devotion. It has been granted to us to find, in this land of liberty and justice, a welcome characterized by such perfect courtesy, such warm hospitality, such absolute respect for the convictions of the individual that, since we are not able to thank each one of the members of this great nation, we have felt that sheer justice obliges us to bring to its august Head the heartfelt expression of our gratitude. Whatever may be the designs of God in our regard in the future, it will never be possible for us to forget this signal kindness; it will be a perpetual motive for us to pray for the glory of this English nation which has consented to protect our liberty with its own; and, on this day on which the close union of England with its King is confirmed, a reason to implore from God the blessings which make nations prosper, which make reigns peaceful; and the graces which make great kings. In the name of the monks and nuns of the Benedictine Congregation of France who have taken refuge in England. Your Majesty's most humble and respectful servant.

But the fabric of the monastic life is woven of more prosaic things than royal visits. Dom Delatte paints a more homely picture in a letter to one of the exiled communities in Holland:

I don't believe there is any melancholy at all in Holland this month. It must have taken refuge here where the rain is coming down in floods. Fortunately Fr Paul Blanchon has found a most effective way of distracting ourselves from the tedium of long, motionless recreations: we shell peas conventually, at the price of choking ourselves conventually on the strings which we absentmindedly leave on the old pods. And it has never stopped raining! As if the heavens had remained shut up since the Flood, or as if the sea wanted to reconquer its old domain. Even in Holland they have no idea of the calm power, the implacable continuity, of English rain.

It was this same Dom Paul Blanchon who, armed with equipment that was *avant-garde* for those days, travelled through

Italy, Germany and Austria, photographing thousands of plainsong manuscripts for the scientific comparisons and collations of the research team under Dom André Mocquereau, which enabled Solesmes to discover the authentic shape of Gregorian chant melodies. The years at Appuldurcombe also coincided with the rise of the great Gregorian revival at the turn of the century. In 1901 Pope Leo XIII sent the Brief "*Nos Quidem*" to the abbot of Solesmes expressing his full approval of the Benedictine editions of the chant, while continuing, nevertheless, to uphold the official, distorted Ratisbon version of the chant "for the sake of unity." It was his successor, however, Pope Pius X, who set the seal on the reform of Church music in his famous *Motu Proprio* of 22 November 1903 and officially adopted Gregorian chant in its traditional form. A second *Motu Proprio* announced a new Vatican edition of the Roman chant books. This edition was to follow the earliest manuscript tradition, and the work on it was entrusted to the Benedictines of Solesmes. The Vatican Commission for the revision of the chant, headed by Dom Joseph Pothier, met at Appuldurcombe in the summer of 1904. The two succeeding summers saw the arrival at Appuldurcombe of choirmasters, scholars, and liturgists from England and elsewhere for Gregorian "summer schools."

The rich spiritual tradition of the English medieval mystics, with their simplicity of vision and reality of expression, their homely and practical analysis of the spiritual life, attracted the Solesmes monks, who translated their writings into French. Dom Maurice Noetinger, the community's cellarer, and Dom Émile Bouvet, later Quarr's first superior, prepared a French critical edition of Walter Hilton's *Scale of Perfection*. Dom Noetinger went on to translate *The Cloud of Unknowing* and Richard Rolle's *The Fire of Divine Love*. The *Revelations of Julian of Norwich* were translated by Dom Gabriel Meunier of Farnborough.

Toward the end of their seven-year lease at Appuldurcombe, the monks began to look for a more permanent site. The auxiliary bishop of Portsmouth, Timothy Cotter, then in residence at St Mary's, Ryde, drew their attention to Quarr Abbey House, and the purchase was completed by the beginning of 1907. A small group of monks was sent to make the necessary arrangements, and from 26 May 1907 onward Mass was once more offered daily on the spot where liturgical prayer had been silenced 370 years before. In less than a year, Dom Paul Bellot, a monk of the community, had designed and built the principal monastic buildings—cloisters, cells, chapter house, refectory, library. By early June 1908, the entire community had moved from Appuldurcombe to Quarr. The Abbey church was built later, between 1910 and 1912, and was consecrated on 12 October 1912. Like the rest of the monastery, it is built of Dutch brick. Called "a poet in brick" for his bold use of that material, Dom Paul Bellot translated the spirit of Solesmes into buildings at once traditional and profoundly original. "Works of art," he wrote, "do not originate in self-sufficiency and pride, but in knowledge of reality. True art builds on a foundation of good sense and simplicity; it grows up in silence and humility; it is the fruit of the whole spirit and heart of man. The Gospel tells us that Paradise is for those who are like children; and art is like a door opened upon the achievements and harmonies of blessed eternity, but which can only grow from pure hands. It is clear that I am here speaking of Christian art, which is perfectly human art, just as a man is perfect only in proportion to his sanctity."

* * * * *

The foregoing pages will have sufficed to show that the writers of these texts were not recluses writing in oaklined studies, untroubled by the harsh realities of life. Christ promised the hundredfold to those who followed him—and persecution besides, as Mark's account adds. St Benedict, too, told his disciples to expect harsh treatment, humiliations, hardship and trial. All this, but especially their daily contact with the timeless mystery of Christ as revealed in Scripture and contemplated by the Church's liturgy, forged the spiritual "temper" of Solesmes. This spiritual temper is compounded of the vivid sense of the transcendence and presence of God, the confident abandonment of "one who sees the invisible and holds fast" (Heb. 11:27), and the acceptance of human nature as it really is, with all its limitations, without any diminishment of what Dom Delatte calls "the splendour" of its supernatural destiny. With this deeply balanced and wholly supernatural outlook goes a spiritual teaching that is suited to all Christians, no matter what their state in life. It possesses a touch that is firm yet delicate, a sanctified common sense, a wise understanding of human weakness, a constant appeal to the deep truths of the faith. "It is precisely these fundamental truths that should be the most attentively studied, because they are the most rich in practical consequences," wrote Dom Delatte. In the spiritual teaching of Solesmes, Christian faith and Christian life are two sides of the same coin.

The monastic ideal represented by Solesmes is essentially a contemplative one; worship and prayer are the *raison d'être* of its life. Yet its story contains a message for all who are striving to live the gospel, for it bears witness to the way the Church grows from within, not vice versa. Madame Cécile Bruyère has called the Church "the type and model of the contemplative soul. She is first Rachel before she is Leah; she shows herself to be Mary before she becomes active like Martha; she gives to the exterior only from her own interior fullness." Contemplatives mirror this mysterious inner reality of the Church, and remind us that the Church is something interior, something that lives within our very selves. It is not a question of making the Church but of being the Church, of allowing faith to shape our lives. The Church's external mission, her building up of the City of God on earth, does not exhaust the fullness of the Church's mystery, that mystery which transcends all who belong to her.[11] Only to the extent that we serve God in worship and prayer can the work we do for God become meaningful.

A monastery, like the Church herself, is more than an institution; it is a life that is passed on and received, and thus made present. It is, in the words of St Benedict, a craft to be learned: one must know how to inherit. Being a monk or a nun, being a Christian, means learning a craft. More than acquiring information, it is a way of living. This is the ultimate meaning not only of the Benedictine tradition, but also of the universal traditions of humanity and those of the Church. This understanding of tradition is summed up in the prayer:

> Raise up in your Church, O Lord, the spirit wherewith our Holy Father Benedict, Abbot, was animated; that filled with the same spirit, we may strive to love what he loved, and to practise what he taught.

"To love what he loved, and to practise what he taught": it is not a matter of servility, but of fidelity; not blind conformism, but receiving in knowledge, gratitude and love. This truth has been illustrated by the sketches of Dom Guéranger, Madame Bruyère and Dom Delatte, covering the early history of Solesmes. But the spirit of Solesmes lives on in their successors, in the monks and nuns who have come into their inheritance.

Notes

1. Marie Le Blan, a pupil at the small boarding school run by the Benedictines at Ventnor, now at St Cecilia's Abbey, Ryde. Dom Delatte took a keen interest in the school and community, founded in 1882 from Liège, Belgium, and later to become part of the Solesmes Congregation.

2. The priory of Solesmes was founded in 1010 by Geoffrey, Lord of Sablé. It was made a dependency of the Abbey of Saint-Pierre de la Couture in Le Mans, which had been restored by Abbot Gauzbert of Saint-Julien de Tours, who introduced the Cluniac observance there. An important rallying point in the region for the Crusades, the monastery still treasures the Holy Thorn brought back by one of the Crusaders. The monastery's subsequent history typifies the fortunes of French religious and secular history: in 1375 it found itself at the centre of the battling provinces in the Hundred Year's War; in 1452 it was destroyed by the English. Yet the monks, never very numerous, succeeded in keeping their life and discipline intact. In the centuries that followed, however, the Huguenots, the Wars of Religion and the practice of *Commendam* (whereby an outsider, not himself a monk, was appointed abbot of a monastery, so that he could collect its revenues) did their work, and by the end of the Revolution, the priory was a ruin.

3. Dom Guéranger called naturalism "the master error of all those of our time" and considered it responsible for "the secularization of society." By naturalism, he meant the tendency to veil or diminish what is difficult or amazing in Christianity in order to bring non-believers to the faith. In some

forty articles published in *l'Univers* from 1856 to 1860, Dom Guéranger described the danger of substituting a true, living, demanding Christianity with a respectable religiosity.

4. I am indebted to Père Henri de Lubac's *The Splendour of the Church* (London, 1956) for bringing out the connection between these two ideas so dear to Dom Guéranger. *Sedes sapientiae*: seat or throne of wisdom, title from Our Lady's Litany. Mary is given this title because she is the human throne of Christ, the Wisdom of God. *Cathedra sapientiae: cathedra* is the bishop's chair or throne in his cathedral church, and is used figuratively, e. g. in the phrase *ex cathedra*, to denote those declarations uttered by the pope when defining the faith of the Church, the truth by which she lives. There is a correspondence, an analogy, between Our Lady's preservation from original sin and the pope's preservation from error when defining the faith of the Church. It is clear that both privileges are free gifts of God and express another aspect of faith's certitude that Mary is figured in the Church and the Church in Mary.

5. This German Congregation, founded in 1862 by two brothers, Maurus and Placid Wolter, received great material help and encouragement from Princess Katharina von Hohenzollern. Beuron distinguished itself from the Austrian, Bavarian and Swiss Congregations by representing a more contemplative form of monastic life. Although the influence of Solesmes and Dom Guéranger was very strong, it rapidly developed an accent of its own while explicitly renoucing pastoral and educational commitments. Beuron was nevertheless more open to other forms of pastoral work than Solesmes had been: preaching retreats, giving parish missions, especially of a liturgical nature, and encouraging pilgrims at their centuries-old Marian shrine.

6. From 1880 to 1920 the history of religious Orders in France was a turbulent one. Despite the Constituent Assembly's suppression of religious orders and congregations whose members took solemn vows (1790), the officials of the Empire, the Restoration, the July Monarchy, the Second Empire and the Third Republic all nevertheless provided that civil authority could by decree formally authorize such associations after examining their rules and statutes. Application of that principle varied with changes of government. The abbots of Solesmes always refused to request such authorization, considering that "We are too well authorized by God, by the Church, by natural law and by the sevices we render," as Dom Delatte would later sum up their position.

Nevertheless, during this forty-year period of expulsion, special taxes, exile, and appropriation and sale of its monasteries, the Congregation of Solesmes saw a rapid growth, with the birth of some fifteen new monasteries.

7. The drama has been recorded by a contemporary eyewitness, Etienne Cartier, writer, translator, and a permanent guest of Solesmes. In order to prevent a demonstration, two hundred soldiers arrived in the village to

protect the administrative authorities and gendarmes responsible for the operation. In addition, a special team of police had to be brought in from Paris to break down the doors, since the local locksmiths refused to cooperate. The large number of Catholics who had gathered in the abbey church in support of the monks was evacuated by the authorities, while the monks themselves were forcibly removed from their choir stalls as they were chanting the Divine Office. Since the monastery legally belonged not to the community but to some of the monks, these were re-admitted after the expulsion, provided they did not use the church. The rest of the community was scattered among the châteaux of the region or in the village houses. After several months, the monks gradually returned and took up monastic life once more.

A second expulsion, more discreet but more radical, took place on 22 March 1882. This time all the monks were expelled, seals were fixed on all the doors, and a special detachment of police had the duty, for more than ten years, of remaining permanently at the porter's lodge of the monastery to prevent access. Dom Couturier, second abbot of Solesmes (1875-90) avoided having his monks too dispersed by grouping them among twelve houses in the village. The monks came together from their various locations to celebrate the office in the parish church, and on Sundays and feastdays at Sainte-Cécile. Despite his motto, *Consortia tecta*, Dom Couturier spent only five years of his abbacy with his monks under one roof.

The protest of Catholics and general criticism at the archaic nature of these laws were such that, after the brutal application of these decrees to Congregations of men, the Government dared not apply them to unauthorized Congregations of women, and hence Sainte-Cécile escaped the worst in 1880 and 1882.

8. At the time of Dom Guéranger's visit Henry Edward Manning (1808-92) was provost of the Westminster Cathedral Chapter; in 1865 he succeeded Cardinal Wiseman as archbishop of Westminster and in 1875 was created a cardinal.

9. Letter to Miss Nugent, cited in *Faber, Poet and Priest: Selected Letters 1833-63*, edited by Raleigh Addington (Glamorgan, 1974), p. 319.

10. Adelheid von Lowenstein Wetheim Rosenberg, born in 1831, married Dom Miguel I of Portugal in 1851, some years after he was exiled. Widowed in 1866, she devoted herself to the education of her children and grandchildren. At the age of sixty-four, she became a Benedictine nun at Sainte-Cécile de Solesmes in 1895. She died on 16 December 1909, at St Cecilia's Abbey, Ryde. In 1967, the remains of Mère Adelaide were exhumed and flown to Portugal by military aircraft. Arrangements had also been made for the exhumation of the body of Dom Miguel in Bavaria, so that the royal consorts entered Lisbon together for a state funeral at the Royal Pantheon.

11. For the sake of consistency with the three writers, and for the deeper truth that is pointed out in note 1 of Chapter eleven, "she/her" has been used when referring to the Church.

BIBLIOGRAPHY

Bruyère, Madame Cécile. In *Spiritu et Veritate* (Solesmes, 1966)

"Madame Cécile Bruyère," in *l'Univers* (22, 30 Mars 1909)

Charlier, Henri. "Dom Paul Bellot," in *l'Artisan et les arts liturgiques 4* (1946)

Cozien, Dom G. *L'oeuvre de Dom Guéranger* (Paris, 1933)

Delatte, Dom P. *Lettres* (Solesmes, 1991)

Delatte, Dom P. "La vie inédite de Mme Cécile Bruyère," typescript

Delatte, Dom P. *Dom Guéranger, Abbé de Solesmes,* (Paris, 1909)

Evans, Dame Eanswyth. "Dom Guéranger as seen by an English disciple," (mss., Stanbrook, 1975)

Johnson, Dom C. "Prosper Guéranger: A Liturgical Theologian," *Studia Anselmiana* 89, (*Analecta Liturgica* 9) Rome, Pontificio Ateneo S. Anselmo, 1984.

Oury, Dom G. "Introduction to the History of the Solesmes Congregation," unpublished conferences.

Regnault, Dom L. "Portrait de Dom Delatte," in *Lettre aux amis de Solesmes 1987*, No. 3, pp. 7-28

Savaton, Dom A. *Dom Paul Delatte, Abbé de Solesmes* (Solesmes, 1975; first published: Éditions d'Histoire et d'Art, Librairie Plon, Paris, 1954)

Soltner, Dom L. *Solesmes et Dom Guéranger* (Solesmes, 1974)

Soltner, Dom L. "Portrait spirituel de Dom Guéranger," in *Lettre aux amis de Solesmes 1976*, No. 1, pp. 10-25

Soltner, Dom L. "Beuron and Abbot Guéranger, " (mss., 1975)

Soltner, Dom L. "L'Expulsion des moines du 22 mars 1882," *Lettre aux amis de Solesmes* 1982, No. 4, pp. 9-27.

Tissot, Dom G. "Solesmes en Angleterre," Conference given on 2 August 1959 to the Association "Les Amis de Solesmes"

Tissot, Dom G. "Le Rayonnement de Ste Cécile," Conference given on 6 August 1967 to the Association "Les Amis de Solesmes"

CHAPTER ONE

"If you knew the gift of God" (John 4:10):

Eternal Life is Here and Now

The spirituality of Dom Delatte is dominated by the fact of our baptism. "All our dignity," he wrote in a letter, "springs from the fact of our baptism. On that day, without any merit at all, we were drawn into the society of the Father, the Son and the Holy Spirit. All that is worth anything in our life goes back, in point of time, to a moment of which we were unaware, and in point of purpose, to a moment that is eternity and the beginning of God's life. All that happens in time is only a lesser work, a pale reflection of a splendour that is above time, words, or symbols. It seems to me that this should be received with gratitude and childlike simplicity."

Dom Delatte loved to remind people that Christians are not merely creatures of God but children of God, sharing in the divine nature, immersed in the superabundance of God through Christ. By virtue of their baptism Christians are rich beyond measure. They do not have to live and act as if God and eternal life were something that they had to elicit by their own efforts. It is more a question of receiving the experience as gift than of reaching for it, still less manufacturing it, or making it happen: God dwells here and now within each of us. "It isn't a matter of making toward something," he writes, "but rather of making use of what we already bear within us. We are not in the state of those who are moving toward their perfection. Why? Simply because we possess our end, our perfection, in our heart; for if the supernatural life is not the indwelling of God within us, it is nothing."

Yet Christians dwell in time, and God wills them to cooperate at each succeeding moment to bring about the full flowering of the initial gift. On the one hand, baptism is the starting point of the supernatural and the moral life; and on the other, in this starting point, everything is already present, like the seed that already carries within itself the structure of the plant, the flower and the fruit that will one day appear. The fact that it contains its whole being within itself does not mean a narcissistic turning inward. On the contrary, the fullness of its being is the very cause of its fruitfulness. What Dom Delatte admired in Sister Elizabeth of the Trinity[1] was the full unfolding of the supernatural life we all receive at baptism: "Somehow, I never really manage to see as extraordinary, but only as too rare those cases in which the supernatural riches of a baptized soul are completely developed. What *is* extraordinary is the goodness of God, the Incarnation, the Redemption, the Eucharist, the Church; from these flow quite naturally and normally, the manifestations of doctrine and virtue in souls."

This gratuitous gift of God does not preclude labours on our part; for, having received this "germ of God," this "sap" of God within us, it is necessary to purify our hearts, accept and deepen our union, put into practice what we carry in us, grow in insight into God's life flowing in us, cooperate by prayer, faith, hope and love to form, feed, and sustain the essential source of that life. Nor is this a contradiction: it is quite possible, in Christian terms, for something that is perfect to develop over time. Our Lord himself, always totally obedient to the Father, "learned obedience" (Heb. 5:8); Our Lady's *fiat* was deepened in a human way throughout her life.

Dom Paul Delatte

What is the essence of Christianity? When that question is posed outside the Church, it is only a pretext for reducing religion and Christianity to instinct, to some interior emotion, to a blind sentiment; it is an opportunity to expand a new theory on a subject that has never ceased to be of interest; it is the entirely literary pleasure of currying favour with some new philosophy that will benefit from its supposed affinity with religion; Christianity is a stage in evolution; Christianity is a phenomenon slotted into its exact place in a preconceived system created in us by our studies, upbringing, or prejudices.

All these diverse conceptions are undoubtedly vitiated by the arbitrary element they invariably contain. But above all, Christianity is not an abstraction we can enclose within the rigid terms of a definition, nor even a coordinated ensemble whose key point will be revealed to us by attentive study. Christianity will never be definable by a fragment taken from its structure, from the truths it teaches, from the effects it has produced. That isn't Christianity; that is the fruit or the conditions of Christianity. At the end of his Gospel, St John declares: "… these [signs] are written that you may believe that Jesus is the Christ, the Son of God, and that believing you may have life in his name" (John 20:31). Nothing more rigorously correct has ever been said. One can see how in the thought of the evangelist all these things—revelation, Scripture, faith—are ordered toward life. Christianity, if it is its essence that is being sought, is essentially reality of an interior and living order. Christianity is a thing of the soul, an interior reality; in a word, life.

(Notes on the Spiritual Life, 1899)

Baptism is the act whereby the Lord, forgetful, in a sense, of his dignity, has presented himself at the first opportunity to a human heart that has not yet sought him. He anticipates the awakening of the reason, the free choice of our will; and even before we have had the chance to choose, he establishes himself as sovereign at the centre of our heart. However, that is only "the beginning of his substance" (Heb. 3:14; Douay), a vital link. Baptized infants have in themselves the seed of God, the sap of God, the beginnings of God; but our effort, blessed by God, is necessary for the development, the cultivation of that life we have received.

(Commmentary on Colossians 1:9)

The "adoption as sons" that makes us become children of God and brothers of our Lord Jesus Christ is not an exterior denomination or fiction with no deep reality. Baptism is not simply a ceremony. Our adoption is real, interior; it corresponds to a transformation of the very being and to an infusion of new life; if it were not so, St John would not have the right to tell us that we bear the name and the reality of children of God, and St Paul could not mark out with such firmness the distance separating one who is baptized from one who is not: "And such were some of you. But you were washed, you were sanctified, you were justified in the name of the Lord Jesus Christ and in the Spirit of our God" (1 Cor. 6:11). Such indeed, in the eyes of the Apostle, is the real, intimate and profound nature of that supernatural transformation, that as from now, and as from baptism, we become an entirely new being that has no further need to disengage itself from the former one: "If anyone is in Christ, he is a new creation: the old has passed away; behold, the new has come" (2 Cor. 5:17). And so indeed it must be, in order that the baptized baby, if it were to die before the age of reason, should spontaneously—I was about to say automatically—by the mere fact of its baptism, without having itself performed a single act of virtue, find itself at the level of the angels, in the midst of the joys of eternity, and should enter the house of God as if it were its own. In very truth, there is in us, by the mere fact of being inserted into Christ, a new state, and our adoption as sons, far from being fictional, is something infinitely real.

(Notes on the Spiritual Life, 1899)

Ever since baptism the Lord is present, active at the centre of our life as the hidden principle of all our actions; this principle comes from him, from that uncreated source; it is the conscience, the true "I" of each one of us, to such a point that we cannot say we "are" without including the Lord in the definition we give to it.

(Commentary on Romans 14:10)

We are "the Lord." Each one of us must be a new edition of the life of the Lord, and not only in the sense that our actions must be conformed to those of the Lord himself, but in the sense that the life of our Lord must be active within us. There must come to pass in us what was in the Lord, whose whole nature was in the grip of the Word. Everything in us must be brought into unity in Our Lord Jesus Christ; for what is the living and active principle, the unique agent, that sets everything in motion and applies it to the task? It is he.

But, you will say to me, you say that quite simply, "We must be the Lord," ... but that's too much, we can't even attempt it! God never gives himself the lie. God's desire is of great breadth; what is demanded of me is out of proportion—yes, quite true! "God has sent the Spirit of his Son into our hearts, crying, 'Abba! Father!'" Our hearts have been given everything we need to carry out God's programme, and the gift of God is amply sufficient for you. We don't bear God within us simply as a guest, but as a real influence in our life, and that Spirit is the very Spirit of the Lord. We have within us someone who makes us pronounce the words which belong by right to Our Lord; he puts what the Lord said to his Father on our lips, in our heart. We say it to him ourselves under the inspiration of the Spirit; we present ourselves in very truth with the title, the rights, the life and the words of the Lord himself. His voice is ours, his Spirit is within us to inspire our prayer, to direct, to guide our life; here again is the influence of the Lord, spreading through our existence and governing it.

(Commentary on Galatians 4:6)

Through baptism I am enclosed within the Saviour; his supernatural beauty is mine, his grace is mine.

(Commentary on John 15)

It is God himself who has established in the centre of our heart, in the silence of our baptism, the pillar of our Christian life.

(Commentary on 2 Corinthians)

By baptism you have been "plunged" (that is the force of the Greek term) into our Lord Jesus Christ, as into an ocean of life and perfection. "You ... have put on Christ" (Gal. 3:27). We have been plunged into him like a crystal plunged into the light;

the light is not a garment for the crystal, it surrounds it and penetrates it; similarly in the case of souls. One must understand the "putting on" in that sense of transformation into our Lord. We have entered into the Lord like the crystal into the light and, in the same way as it allows itself to be penetrated and invaded by the light, just so our souls are transformed into our Lord. There is only one life, only one Lord Jesus Christ. "You are all sons of God through faith" (Gal. 3:26). Faith, here, means the vital belonging to the Lord who communicates to us his life, his beauty, his purity. God pours into our souls not just any beauty, but that of his only Son, so that in eternity there should be no other splendour, no other brilliance but that of the Lord Jesus. So much so, that when we enter into eternity, we who are children of God shall enter not only as into the home of the Father, but—God forgive me—we shall enter into our own home. If our divine sonship is a reality, if we are truly one with the Lord, if his life is our life, I don't think we can escape that conclusion.

(Commentary on Galatians 3:27)

We must take our baptism, our supernatural life, seriously: live by the life that has been established in us, behave like people who have truly received divine adoption. Once we have been given such a stature, is it not demanded of us, as an absolute obligation, to live according to what has been created in us by God himself? If baptism is what we know it to be, there is only one thing to be done: to belong entirely to that sovereign and blessed influence which is within us.

(Commentary on 2 Corinthians)

Our whole supernatural life stems from an interior reality and beauty which we carry within, in the very sanctuary of our heart. That is where that beauty lies. It is active. It influences our whole life, orders all our activity, regulates and defines all we do, and it keeps us attentive to itself while we are doing all this. The only examination of conscience you should make is: "Have I lived in the presence of God? Have I been attentive to

him? Have my heart and my life always rested in him?"
(Letter to a mother, 1 February 1914)

I think the life of Sr Elizabeth of the Trinity is extraordinarily faithful and strong, and supple in God's hands. I also think that everything that has taken place in her is no more than the complete blossoming of the supernatural life that our baptism has created in us. I can never really manage to see as extraordinary, but only as too rare, the cases of full development of the supernatural riches of the baptized soul. What *is* extraordinary, my child, is the goodness of God, the Incarnation, the Redemption, the Eucharist, the Church; the manifestations of doctrine and virtue within souls flow naturally, normally, from that. And when we encounter supernatural perfection in souls, we must take care to avoid copying anything at all. We must not ape anyone; we must not try to reproduce a character. No; we must stick to the grace that is ours, and allow the Lord to develop within us. "Earnestly desire the higher gifts" (1 Cor. 12:31). The only thing that we should imitate in these souls is their liberation from created things, their incomparable docility to God, their charity, their eyes always turned to him; a profound disposition to be always in perfect harmony with God's whole will for us…. Continue, my child, to live with the beautiful realities of the supernatural world before your eyes. Close your eyes to all that is not simply God: "We look not to the things that are seen" (2 Cor. 4:18).

*(Letter to Mère Ida Sellerier, a Benedictine nun
of Notre Dame, Wisques, 31 May 1912)*

I attach supreme importance to this statement: Union is not something toward which we are moving; union is not an ideal condition toward which our life is proceeding; union is not something we must bear away as a prize. Union with God, total union with God, is the real condition in which God himself has established us…. Union is the primary thing: the union of baptism comes before our moral life.

(Conference, January 1916)

Eternal life is not only life in eternity, life after death. Eternal life is what we have carried within us ever since our baptism, in the sanctuary of our heart. Eternal life is a revelation of God as he is, of God in three Persons; it is union by entering into the life of God through living communion with our Lord Jesus Christ who is himself of the Trinity, and who carries us with him and brings us into it with him. And the essential act of our present life is almost exclusively to become conscious, in ever-greater faith and love, of the society in which we live, of the uncreated realm, of the living homeland in which we find ourselves. That is eternal life: to know the Lord to whom we belong, from whose life we draw our life; to know the Father to whom the Son leads us. Read the sixth chapter of St John. It is in this awareness, this conviction of the uncreated region in which the Lord has placed us, that we exercise a faith that is daily more luminous, a charity ever more fervent; that is already eternal life, and it begins here and now. The likeness is already begun, since we are already in our Lord Jesus Christ: "for those whom he foreknew he also predestined to be conformed to the image of his Son, in order that he might be the first-born among many brethren" (Rom. 8:29). The likeness will be perfected in eternity: "We shall be like him, for we shall see him as he is" (1 John 3:2). But everything that is in the ripe ear of corn is virtually contained in the seed; and the same God is the object of our faith and of our vision. One equals the other: the God who conceals himself and the God who manifests himself.

(Letter to a Bernardine at Esquermes, 14 August 1906)

We are in possession of eternity.... Not only election and predestination but the actual work of our salvation is a work that is accomplished, something already carried out, completed. It isn't a matter of making toward something, but rather of making use of what we already bear within us. We are not in the state of those who are moving toward their perfection. Why? Simply because we possess our end, our perfection, in our heart; for if the supernatural life is not the indwelling of God within us, it is nothing.

(Commentary on Colossians 1:14)

"You are not your own; you were bought with a price. So glorify God in your body" (1 Cor. 6:19-20). Now it can only be in the name of some reality that the Apostle can claim our whole lives for God. One doesn't devote oneself entirely to a metaphor. Oh yes, I know it only too well, we are not brave. We are afraid of our greatness, and heights make us dizzy. We should like to escape, so much do our responsibilities terrify us; it is almost annoying to have been loved in such a way and, through the love of God, to have been raised so high. But these timidities and terrors do not seem to me a sufficient motive to diminish the work of God or to belittle his love; things must be measured by their own essence and not by our pusillanimity. We musn't minimize the Christian life. If the life that was in the Father has manifested itself to us, says St John, and if the Apostles have announced it to the world, it is in order that we may enter into fellowship with God (cf 1 John 1:3).

(Notes on the Spiritual Life, 1899)

Do you seek God? But you already have him! Go down into yourself, or rather, let him make himself at home in you. Allow the kingdom of God, which rests in the mysterious sanctuary of your soul, to extend itself there, to install itself there. Let God be free and sovereign within you. You have eternal life, let it take you over. You have nothing other to do than to allow that life that is in you to penetrate all things.[2]

Notes

1. A Discalced Carmelite of Dijon, Sr Elizabeth of the Trinity was beatified by Pope John Paul II on 25 November 1984.

2. From an unpublished monastic florilegia compiled at the Abbey of Wisques called *Via Clarescente* (see Preface).

CHAPTER TWO

"Do all in the name of the Lord Jesus Christ" (Col. 3:17):

Contemplation in a World of Action

For these writers, as for St Paul, the formula "in Christ" is not a mere pious phrase but the expression of the deepest reality of our faith. For Dom Delatte, the entire ethic of Christian activity lies hidden—and manifest—in the depths of baptism. The indwelling brought about by baptism not only objectively permeates body and soul, but it can also govern thought, faith, willing, loving, feeling, acting, so that it almost obliterates the distinction between Christ and us: "The Lord is considered as a reality so fluid, so supple, so penetrating, that it envelops everything in our life, every part of our activity." This chapter, then, is about making the gift of baptism our own, "taking our stand honourably in the Mystery of Christ that is in us," demonstrating its reality, by "lending ourselves to the influence of the Lord within us," so that our activity is "a continuous expression of the life of the Lord," making our action contemplation and our contemplation action.

God dwells in all of his creatures, as St Augustine says, more profoundly than the creatures themselves. Without destroying the difference between God and us, or infringing our nature as creatures and persons, there comes about a reciprocal presence. This is the Christ of St Paul, divine, omnipotent, but also living and acting in Christian hearts, so that it is not longer they who live but Christ who lives in them. Christians, in whatever they do, in prayer, in suffering, in external works carried out in the service of their fellows, are acting, collaborating with God "in a glorious communion of wills," as Dom Delatte describes it. Or perhaps it is more true to say that Christians are themselves the object of God's working: "It is certain that we are the Lord, that

56

he lives on in us, that the law of our moral life is not so much to act as to allow him to act in us. That, my child, is obedience; it is adoration; it is charity ... the accomplishment of all perfection." Christians work primarily through being; their activity lies not so much in what they do as in what they allow to be done, God acting in and through them in both their effort and their prayer.

These writers, then, set no boundaries between everyday life and the supernatural life, the life of prayer, theology, Scripture. "God is not greater at this minute than at another," notes Dom Guéranger. "And he has, in the strict sense, a right over every instant of our lives. There is only one thing that matters in the service of God: *Age quod agis*. Do what you are doing, and you will get there." They regret the dichotomy, "the airtight partition," that can arise between devotion and action: "You belong to God," insists Dom Delatte. "You have no right to split your life into two parts, one trying hard to be supernatural, the other developing itself freely, at random, separated from God." The spiritual and the secular, contemplation and action, interpenetrate and mutually influence one another. For the Christian these are two sides of a single, living reality. This mode of existence, this unified life, is one that Our Lord himself inaugurated: while living fully on earth, he did not leave his Father's heaven. The Church, too, though she looks heavenward, is not dispensed from fulfilling her mission on earth. Dom Delatte most often refers to the angels, however, who with their exterior tasks "habitually combine a ceaseless gazing at him." The Christian life, then, is a life of looking and working, of "remaining very recollected within and very flexible without" (Dom Guéranger), one that transfuses the life of action and service with the spirit of contemplation. Perfection, then, is not a matter of choosing between obligations, of accepting one and rejecting the other, but of harmonizing the two so that the whole of our life reflects and radiates our union with God. There is no risk here of losing contemplation in an excess of action or of seeing action from only a human point of view.

For these writers, following the ancient understanding of the relationship between contemplation and action, contemplation consists in drawing out and realizing the supernatural dimension and truth of the Christian life; while action is the application of that truth in all the demands of the present life. They do not designate two states of life, two parallel lines that never converge, but two complementary elements of every Christian life; they are more like concentric circles, rippling outward from a single source, "the life of the Lord within us." It means that the eternal life in which we already participate informs our life on earth and gives it meaning.

Dom Paul Delatte

"Do all in the name of the Lord Jesus Christ" (Col: 3:17). It is the Christian law of our whole activity that is formulated here, a universal law that embraces everything: prayer, study, words, food and drink, recreation, sleep, everything. There are no exceptions. The Lord is considered as a reality so fluid, so supple, so penetrating, that it envelops everything in our life, every part of our activity. And so, when we are given the command to do everything in the name of our Lord Jesus Christ, we are simply being invited to take our stand honourably in the Mystery of Christ that is in us.

(Retreat, 1908; Commentary on Colossians 3:17)

The imitation of our Lord consists not so much of basing our lives on an external model, but of lending ourselves with flexiblity to the living influence of the Lord who is within us, in such a way that our activity is a continuous translation or expression of the life of the Lord within us. That is simply taking our part in what God has done for us and with us.

If this were simply words, a concept, a manner of speech, you would be absolutely right to feel annoyed. Let the old man continue to live in you. Be yourself. It wasn't serious: just a formula, a system, a theory.

But if this is true, if it is no longer I who live but Christ who lives in me, don't you see the nature of this imitation, don't you see the rigour of the concept?

Don't distress yourself, don't try to escape from the words of the Lord: "Today if you will hear his voice, harden not your hearts" (Ps. 94[95]:8). Voluntary inattention doesn't do away with reality, nor with our duty, nor with our responsibility before God. You belong to God. You do not belong to yourself. You have no right to split your life into two parts, one trying hard to be supernatural, and the other developing itself freely, at random, separated from God.

(Retreat, 1909)

It is a question of maturity. You must grasp that in our life, nothing is achieved by fits and starts and by violent efforts. Life in its entirety, the moral life, the supernatural life, consists of continuous sincerity, continuous honesty, continuous flexibility and docility. We are not to believe that a fruit attains to perfect maturity by a sudden violent growth, but simply when it has received all its succulence from its root, which is faith, and all its savour from the sun. For that, it has to turn its face to the sun.

Above all, love the Lord and have the firm assurance that nothing in us will resist the almighty power of his love. Take up every day, gently and courageously, the work begun the day before. Nothing hot-headed. A continuous and gentle strength. Never speak shrilly.

(Letter to a young girl, 20 March 1905)

If there are things that God has granted to us to understand and grasp definitively, it is certain that we are the Lord, that he lives on in us, that the law of our moral life is not so much to act as to allow him to act in us. That, my child, is obedience; it is adoration; it is charity; it is at the same time, in one and the same disposition, the accomplishment of all perfection.

(Letter, 10 May 1908)

There is really no incompatibility whatever between the life of union with God and the duties of your charge. It is not as if you had to abandon some part of those duties in order to devote more time to God. You can do better than that. The Angels of

God take care of us—and we give them plenty of work some-times—and with that charge they have received from God, they habitually combine a ceaseless gazing at him. Never yield to the temptation of neglecting part of your work in order to have the pleasure of free time for contemplation; souls will lose thereby, and God will require you to give an account for it. "What am I to do in that case?" you ask me. This: say to the Lord, "Let us go together to the work I must do." The two of you will go together; you won't work feverishly, hastily, or in a rush to finish. You will have time for everything, and will not for an instant let go of the hand of God. The Bride should at all times be leaning on the arm of the Bridegroom.

(Letter)[1]

This ceaseless cleaving should be present in all our actions. We walk, we talk, we act, we look at something: none of these movements in which our interior activity is involved should be outside the sphere of God's action. There must not be a single parenthesis in our life that escapes it. It is upon the whole extension of our soul that God's action must work. "For the earth shall be full of the knowledge of the Lord as the waters cover the sea" (Isa. 11:9).

I leave the rest to your judgement. All people need is to be alerted. When people are honest, when people are straight, when people belong to God, one only has to provide them with the opportunities.

(Conference on John 15, 1902)

I like to recall to contemplative souls, as well as the phrase of St Paul, "all who are led by the Spirit of God are sons of God" (Rom. 8:14), the prayer we address to the Lord who is present in our midst, an instant before Communion: ". . . Keep me faithful to your teaching and never let me be parted from you."[2] We thus implore of him not only that we may not be separated from him in eternity—may his mercy preserve us from that—but, in addition, the grace never to be separated from him in any instant or action of our present life. There is no one but him in the world. We need look at nothing here below but him. Don't let us become distracted or diverted by anything at all in the world. That is possible. God is spirit; he is so subtle, so pure, so fluid, that he can spread over all the moments of our life, like a perfume. Why should we not be ceaselessly attentive to him who is never absent from us?

(Letter to Mère Marie de Saint-Jean, Ursuline, mistress of novices, later superior general of her Congregation, 29 May 1917)

The Lord did not come only to be a spectator. And what is God, if not pure Act? Since God came to be not simply active but Act, Act in himself and Act also in us, there is only one way for us: a living docility to this uncreated Act, at every hour and at every instant in our interior life; in what we think, in what we seek, in what we desire, in what we love; a persevering contact with the intimate Act of God; docility, joyful suppleness like a sort of joyful elasticity, as if God had passed into us fully, as if we were nothing but acquiescence, living docility. Lord, how lovely that would be! What glory it would give to the Lord.

(Conference on John 15, 1902)

Do your work well; avoid feverishness and excessive effort: success and progress come from God. We must do as much as in us lies, calmly, as if our activity were decisive; and then enter ever more deeply into the calm and confidence, as if everything were to come to us from God. One can never go too far in a spirit of self-abandonment to the Lord. Calm any over-violent emotions; gently push aside those you recognize to be without foundation or cause: they are a moral poison that must be instantly expelled.

(Letter to a mother, 4 December 1905)

It isn't a question of renouncing anything, but of living attached to today's duty. I don't think about tomorrow; God will think about it for me, and will put me, by the exercise of his lovable Providence, exactly where he knows I will be of use.

(Letter to a young girl, 6 April 1906)

To do all things in the name of the Lord, to act in the name of the Lord, means that whenever we act, we never act superficially, moved by our temperament or our capabilities, but base all our actions, our activity itself, on God. Since our life in its entirety is before God as the region from which all our activity proceeds, we must base all the thoughts, all the loves, all the affections of our life on the Lord.

Nothing in us must escape from the action of the Lord and the comprehensive universality of the practical corollary of his mystery in us. And in order that this mystery may triumph, may shine forth, may take possession of everything, we must base all the regions of our life on the Lord. Do all the things we do really have that starting point? The formal plan of God is that our life in its entirety should be an assiduous collaboration with the accomplishment on earth of the Lord's programme. And so, every time in our life that there is a deduction—even in a small detail—from the fidelity of this collaboration of our will with that of God, every time we withdraw ourselves from this glorious communion of wills, there is a denial to God of some thing that belongs to him by right.

(Commentary on Colossians 3:17)

Be very attentive to God, without saying anything. We do not talk all the time when we are together. One can say a good deal more by a simple glance than by all the words and acts in the world. Acts are goods, especially in that they create and maintain this attitude of peaceful recollection before the Eternal Beauty. No one can make us leave it; no one can expel us. This very day St Augustine said to us, "It is enough that you know it: for you do not love and forsake."[3] And so I will not tell you that it makes no difference where we are, my dear child; your heart and mine would protest too loudly. There is only one house, our Father's house, because it is there that everything is ordered toward keeping our soul close to God; but that being the case, at least we can have the courage to face everything and the patience to wait: "I waited patiently for the Lord, and he heard my cry" (Ps. 39[40]:1). "No one who waits for you shall be put to shame" (Ps. 24[25]:3). A Dieu,[4] my child.

(Letter to a young monk doing military service,
13 March 1891)

All Saints sheds light on many things. Don't forget that you are "undergoing treatment" and that you must bless the Lord, even through your troubles, if the procedure he employs with us forces us to get rid of ourselves, to work in the sweat of our brow, to take refuge in him. We shall have to go out of ourselves and enter into him once we realize that every other region is uninhabitable for us. "Yes, but if only I could find him!" True. And that is the present condition of your soul: you have, today, neither the distractions of yesterday nor the joys of tomorrow. For the moment you are under a cloche, where one hasn't enough air to breathe. That is intentional; we have enough air to die to ourselves.

Accomplish your present duties with generosity, calmly, under the interior direction and influence of the Lord. Twenty times a day, return to him in your thoughts and say: "What do you want of me?" God does not let us down. You will obtain from him light, strength, and rest for your soul.

Take an hour or two for serious reading each day. Don't neglect the reading of the New Testament, especially the Gospels. But as for that, I don't simply ask you to take it into your mind as to enter into it yourself; pass your eyes over it slowly, at length, with the sustained attention due to God's Word addressed to each one of us.[5]

Be brave. We must never forget that we have our happiness within us. When we have renounced our attachment to a thousand exterior things that bring with them only worries, regrets, and sufferings, then we will have the profound and serene joy of feeling our spirit, our life, our thoughts, to be in perfect harmony with God and his will. Thenceforth nothing can touch us any more.

(Letter to a mother, 2 November 1911)

"You are the salt of the earth.... You are the light of the world" (Matt. 5:13-14). The temptation here is a certain liberalism, the hidden weakness which makes us reduce the truth to puny propositions so that it will cease to be a scandal for the world and threatening to us. Now the doctrine and office of the apostles are not personal goods, over which they are qualified to make concessions. That would leave the world to conclude that a doctrine is not divine, since it seems that individuals have the option to reduce it, to diminish it to their liking. Apostles and Christians, you are the salt of the earth: beware of becoming insipid! From the moment you no longer act on the world to limit its corruption, the world will begin to act on you.

"You are the light of the world." It is the Lord who is life and light; but the Lord causes those who belong to him to become life and light through communion with him. Note the nature of the metaphor used to delineate the mission of apostles and Christians. He does not say to them: You are thunder and lightning! He tells them: You are salt, an active substance, which does its work without violence; you are light, a radiatory power, but gentle, kindly, acting in silence.

(L'Évangile de Notre Seigneur Jésus Christ I, pp.189-90)

Abbess Cécile Bruyère

When an action in the soul finds itself combined with perfect calm, deep peace, and this peace grows in proportion to the intensity of the act, the soul has attained—as far as one can judge—to union with him who is pure Act and essential Peace. And then nothing can express its activity, just as nothing can disturb its peace. For the more deeply it penetrates into the peace the more active it is—because it is more free—and the more it gives itself over to action the deeper becomes its peace.[6]

Dom Guéranger's varied letters, his multiple occupations, his diverse preoccupations, which nevertheless leave him in a state of perfect equilibrium, seem to us to be a gauge of that state of his soul. He never leaves the supernatural element: on this point he gives himself away on thousands of occasions. And he, so delicate and so serious in all that concerns one's relations with God, does not feel the need to get back into the flow and to gather together the treasures that have been dissipated. However encumbered his life is, he does not seem anxious, or feverish, or over-excited. One always feels the deep bond that keeps his soul united to God in its depths, in the midst of a multiplicity that to us would seem enough to drive one out of one's mind. This solidity, this fixedness can only be effected in a man by immediate contact with the divine light.

(Unpublished Life of Dom Guéranger, 1867)

You say that both time and strength are limited. Yes, certainly, when one calculates. But if we let the Lord act, if we take everything he sends, if we abandon ourselves in pure faith, if we bow our heads and say, "Behold the handmaid of the Lord," I believe that he solves all the problems himself. It was hard for me to believe that. Common sense told me that there are only sixty minutes in an hour, but he for whom a thousand years are as one day has proved to me hundreds of times that he is the Lord of time as of everything else.

* * * * *

I am pleased that you have a great deal of work and that you are very busy. That is an excellent way to become holy. Life is so short, and heaven will be so wonderful that we shall desire to have laboured and suffered!

(24 July 1876)

As I see it, our feelings of repugnance or of revulsion cannot regulate our actions. In order to see things as they are, we must not look in ourselves but in God. If we look in ourselves, there is hardly a single one of our duties that will not appear burdensome. It is incredible how that way of looking at things constantly misleads us. By a just law, when we seek after ourselves, we always harm ourselves, as regards our real interest; while if we seek God, all works out well for us.

Your feelings of repugnance, then, cannot be considered a

determining motive or insight. When our Lord redeemed us, he felt great repugnance, but he overcame it, because it was the will of his Father that he should do it.

And do not say that you will succumb to the suffering. I truly believe that one never succumbs to suffering except through imperfection. I am quite aware that my words have left the beaten paths and the realm of commonplaces, but I believe you to be capable of understanding them. Our Lord did not die during his agony at Gethsemane; Our Lady did not expire on Calvary; one does not die from suffering unless one ceases to look at God, unless one seeks joy in something other than God, and allows oneself to be hypnotized by one's affliction.

(Letter to a nun in the face of accepting a heavy responsibility, 16 September 1889)

How good God is to grant us, in the prism of events, *inter mundanas varietates,* [7] a glimpse of something of his unchangeably radiant Beauty!

(Letter, November 1893)

The customs of the King's dwelling are altogether special. One never rejoices in anything there until one has renounced all enjoyment; one never sees anything until one has renounced all knowledge; one never possesses anything until one has renounced all possession. It is truly the place of God, "the dwelling of God with men" (Rev. 21:3), where everything is known and is done in God. The soul feels that it is placed there at the centre of everything; its knowledge and its action are far more extensive than when it was limited to the riches of its faculties and senses alone. It doesn't waste time by passing from one object to another, nor even in leaving these objects to go to God. It is always borne to wherever it ought to go, always present to whatever it ought to attend to, always praying for whatever it ought to ask for.

That is the most accurate picture I can give of that state in which the soul becomes so simple, so flexible, so absolutely docile. The divine Spouse does with it what he will. He employs it for what he will. That creature belongs to him. Sometimes he takes pleasure in sharing himself as belonging to it. It is a mysterious exchange in which God fills with himself everything which, in that soul, has been given over to him in perfect self-abnegation.

* * * * *

The state of perfect, consummated charity is a veritable Sabbath where God rests in the human soul, and the human soul in God, even before eternity. But what does it mean to rest from one's labours before eternity? It is when, by perfect self-abnegation, the soul never considers itself in anything. For we shall never find rest in turning in upon ourselves, since we are not our own end; for the true goal of our rest is in God who made us and toward whom we tend.... In this mysterious, sanctified Sabbath, the soul no longer labours, but she does "work," and her working is living, powerful, efficacious, as it is silent, peaceful, calm. Moses "worked" on the mountain when he raised his hands to heaven (cf. Exod. 17:8-13). He experienced nothing of the heat of battle nor of the dangers of the struggle; he did not deliver or receive blows, but high above all, the only one admitted to the divine repose, he "worked" the deliverance of his people and carried the day. One might say that the whole life of Moses shows this working without exterior action. Our Lord Jesus Christ, our model, imitated the rest of the seventh day after his immense labours. Having trodden the wine-press alone and considered all that he desired to accomplish, he said: "*Consummatum est*," and he entered into his Father's rest, without ceasing to work those works entrusted to his holy humanity. This repose of Christ ought to be incorporated by us, like the other phases of his holy life.

(Conference)

Dom Prosper Guéranger

One single Communion is more than you need to sustain yourself; keep that in mind and guard with greater care the fruits of those you make. Our Lord says to us in the Gospel: the

Kingdom of God is within you. Since that is so, what have you to fear from without? Keep yourself within, applying yourself externally to whatever is not wrong; let yourself be thwarted with good grace, and be assured that Jesus who is within you will make it up to you. Leading an interior life is painful to nature; we should like rest and liberty, but our Lord considers that the soul advances better under this constraint, becoming detached from sweetness in its devotion; and so we must will what he wills, remaining recollected within and very flexible without.

(Letter, 27 March 1860)

We can't always be on retreat; so we must be sure that our entire life consists in seeking the Kingdom of God in itself, using all the means given us for that end. It is not necessary to check what time it is for that, because it is for every time, for every moment; there are so many good opportunities that it is surely the fault of the soul if it doesn't take advantage of them. God is not greater at this minute than at another. And he has, in the strict sense, a right over every instant of our lives. There is only one thing that matters in the service of God: *Age quod agis*. Do what you are doing, and you will get there; don't look for anything else. Then all is well, and there isn't even an effort to be made; rather, it would be an effort to do the opposite; the faculties of the soul are dissipated; it is a real upset, a terrible upheaval to go in another direction when the magnet is drawing us. That is a sort of senseless bravado from which it is essential to distance ourselves with energy. *Age quod agis*.

(Retreat, 1874)

Notes

1. Letter cited in *Dom Paul Delatte: Abbé de Solesmes* by Dom Augustin Savaton (Paris, 1954), p. 315.

2. *Roman Missal*, prayer of priest before Communion.

3. "Sufficit ut noveris; non enim amas, et deseris." St Augustine on the words of Martha to Jesus, John 11:3. "Well, what was the message the sisters sent?—'Lord, he whom you love is ill.' They did not say, 'Come' but only,

'Lord, he whom you love is ill.' It is enough that you know; for you do not love, and forsake" (*In Ioannem* 49:5).

4. Dom Delatte habitually concluded his letters with *A Dieu* instead of *Adieu*. The expression sums up his favourite teaching: to live and act under the interior direction and influence of God, to possess ourselves and all things in God and from God, to go beyond all things in order to go to him in whom they have their true being.

5. Dom Delatte is alluding here to the monastic practice of *lectio divina* (literally, "divine reading" or "holy reading"), a slow, meditative reading, a "chewing over" the text, an activity never very far from prayer. See his commentary on the *Rule of St Benedict*, chapter 48: "The hours which St Benedict would have us devote to this reading every day are essentially hours of prayer."

6. Abbess Cécile Bruyère is expressing the paradox that the more we are receptive to God, abide in God, the more we participate in God's activity, so that as the power of contemplation increases so does that of action. Contemplation is not passive looking and receiving; it is an act in which action and receiving are combined; indeed it is the highest activity of the human spirit.

7. Collect, 21st Sunday of the year: "... among the sundry and manifold changes of this world ..."

CHAPTER THREE

"That we should be holy and blameless before him" (Eph. 1:4):

In the Communion of Saints

When speaking of holiness and perfection, Solesmes instinctively turns to words like abandonment, simplicity, docility, trust, availability. Theirs is not the language of high spirituality, of rigid divisions of spiritual progress, but that of everyday life. Theirs is a spirit alien both to a merely material austerity and to extraordinary mystical phenomena; it is a spirit, like that of the Benedictine Rule itself, of the forming of nature to receive grace by a slow, steady, imperceptible growth. "Our supernatural life," wrote Dom Delatte to an eighteen-year-old girl, "develops just as spontaneously as our natural life. It is enough to carry out its works, to make use of our baptism and Communions. We were born without knowing it, and we grew up without desiring it." For these writers, perfection is nothing but the natural unfolding of the Christian life we have received at baptism. It is the life of the saints. There is not another mystical perfection beyond; this is mystical perfection. "What is extraordinary, what is desirable," noted Dom Delatte, "is not some personal state of ours, a thrill, a transport, or any delight, however pure it may be. No: the extraordinary that is given universally and that may be possessed by all is God, the Incarnation, the Eucharist, the life of the Lord within us, the Church, eternity.... People turn their backs on true mysticism by allowing themselves to be preoccupied with mystical phenomena." These writers are preoccupied with mysticism in its widest sense: the contact with those eternal realities that are the very subject matter of our faith. "We must be realists," insists Dom Delatte, which for him is almost synonymous with being saints.

Yet while they insist that for holiness there is no need for states, works, or favours that theologians describe as "extraordinary," they are equally aware that the way of grace and union with God is attained by all too few "not because God has become niggardly with souls," says Abbess Cécile Bruyère; "the grace of the unitive life would be far more common among Christians if it were better understood, more highly prized, and if it became the object of a more ardent desire."

By abandonment, docility, simplicity, they mean, first of all, an acceptance of God's will as expressed and confirmed in everyday acts. "Cleaving with all one's heart and under all circumstances to God's will, this is what will bring holiness," affirms Abbess Cécile. The life of holiness is an everyday life: we "enter into the genuinely supernatural by the common, simple, ordinary way the Lord has chosen for us" (Conference, 1 January 1896). This is to affirm that the search for holiness takes as its fundamental raw material the everyday components of a life of faith and receptivity to God's initiative.

But this abandonment, in Solesmes' vocabulary, means something more, the real effective gift of all the powers of the soul. It is what Dom Delatte calls "the perfect act," the state, the attitude, the habit of a soul caught up into God's world, for whom the supernatural life is more real than the natural. Dom Delatte makes holiness an aspect of realism in the deepest sense of that word: "The difference between people lies in the difference in the contact they make with supernatural realities; and what is most lacking in everyone is the sense of reality." Theirs is a spirituality that puts the whole emphasis on developing a sense of the reality of God, perpetually turning to God, losing oneself in God, refusing to allow life's most pressing demands and problems, even sin and failure, to distract from God.

No more than with baptism does this abandonment preclude labours on our part, which Abbess Cécile Bruyère describes as "the conscientious fidelity in overcoming self, constant seeking after virtue, persevering imitation of Our Lord, unfailing obedience to God's commands." Far from being a passive programme, this abandonment and confidence in divine generosity are most exacting because they can and must be applied to every incident of everyday life. They demand selfless patience, attentiveness, flexibility, and spiritual firmness. And there is a deeper sense in which this act of abandonment and docility is not passive, but, on the contrary, imparts a powerful impetus: "God within us does not remain inactive. He is Act," as Dom Delatte reminds us. "How I wish these cold formulas were understood in their full and wonderful truth!" For these writers, authentic spiritual life is nothing other than dogma-in-action, the realization—the becoming real within us—of what we believe.

What the Church celebrates in the lives of the saints, then, is not so much their activity and merits but the working and beauty of God in them. It is God's beauty and grace that are refracted, multiplied, as it were, through the multiplicity of creatures, split into many colours, "the beauty of the Lord ceaselessly reproducing itself, fragmented, diversified, but always One," as Dom Delatte puts it. God is always the unique One, and all he gives to and does in his creatures bears his stamp.

Dom Prosper Guéranger

When will you understand completely that the irrecoverable abandon that we make to God of all that we are and all that we have been is the only thing he asks for? Ah! When will we learn that he is not generous by halves, and that if he has wanted us, it is not that he did not see in us all those weaknesses, and so many others we are not even aware of. We must have faith in God's goodness, as well as in his truth. At the same time as you say: "My God, I believe what you have said because you could not deceive me," you should also say: "My God, I believe that you love me, although I do not merit it, although I am covered with faults." And since it is the essence of faith in God's truth to be surrounded with shadows and darkness, since it is necessary for us to seek this truth through impenetrable veils during this life, so also divine charity has its mysteries. We need courage to raise ourselves up to God, from the depths of the abyss of our imperfections.... But it is love that crosses that abyss, that throws itself body and soul into the arms of the One whom it loves even more than it fears him. Once it is united to God the soul should not look behind any more. What does it matter now to know how it has arrived there, and whether it deserved to arrive? It loves its God, it feels that it loves him and it knows very well that as long as it loves him, he will not send it away.

(Letter to Euphrasie Cosnard, 23 January 1832)[1]

Make every effort to have peace of soul. This meets with two great obstacles in you: 1) a head that darts this way and that, and pays attention to everything, which gets lost in tiny details, as if virtue were no more than a holy hassle; 2) the total lack of detachment, which you should nevertheless practise in all things.

(Letter to the same, 2 March 1832)

Become steady, even-tempered, firm, without ceasing to be agreeable; on the contrary, by doing these things, you will become all the more so. Guard against that exaggeration which makes us unduly distressed and merry. Abide so much with God that everything else seems to you next to nothing. You complain about many troubles; so much the better, it is proof that you are coming to know yourself. God demands much of you, but he doesn't ask for reckless acts. Frequently receive Holy Communion with a heartfelt desire based on your many afflictions for which you are seeking a remedy. When you have received Our Lord, pray to him very simply that it should be his will to give you the strength to detach yourself from yourself and from creatures as much as necessary for your perfection; make this request sincerely, without violent effort and also without looking back.... Offer your will to God purely and simply; let him act in you; do not disturb his work, either by taking back your request, or by desiring to analyze too curiously your condition.

(Letter to the same, 7 March 1832)

It would give me great pleasure to hear that you are becoming more confident toward God, because that is how you will make progress.

(Letter to the same, 1 April 1832)

73

Go to God by every way, for all ways lead to him.... His love never troubles our heart; on the contrary, it establishes it in peace. The soul thus gives forth a full sound and never the false and discordant note it would give out if it remained empty.... Do all that you know is pleasing to him, and do not do what you know is not pleasing to him. In all that, above all, do not rely on yourself; do not be surprised at your imperfections but be wholly simple, wholly unaffected, very compassionate toward yourself and others. Don't get it into your head that you are holy just because you want to be; and yet that is what we think when we are surprised at our faults. You are not a saint, indeed, but love God, and that will help you to become one. Through love, you could even become one all of a sudden! Work this miracle, go fifty-fifty with Our Lord.

(Letter to the same, 25 November 1832)

It is so striking when one reads the lives of the saints to realize how, as long as they are in the world, God always finds something to purify in them, while to us it seems, when we follow their actions, that they are already perfect and entirely transformed. Nothing makes us understand better how profoundly fallen human nature is, or leads us more effectively to humility. If he treats saints in this way, constantly testing them and ceaselessly making them purge their personality, as if he needed some sort of surety against them, how ceaselessly do we sinners need to watch ourselves and to be vigilant on every point, if we are to become worthy to be looked upon by him!

(Cited in "Portrait of Dom Guéranger"
by Abbess Cécile Bruyère, 10-12 October 1867)

To fast, to mortify one's body, and then to pay attention to one's own will—that is the height of absurdity! It would be extremely inconsistent, and an essential point in the supernatural life is never to tolerate inconsistencies in oneself. Only on that condition is one a rational creature. To have ups and downs and whims in the service of the Great King—what is that? Foolishness and inconsistency. If some inconvenience blocks our path, our action is mapped out for us; we take a good stride and jump over it. Both duty and good sense demand that we should act in that way.

(Cited in "Portrait," 10-12 October 1867)

Between the absolute good toward which one should always tend and the relative good that one realizes, there is always a chasm. Nevertheless, God is content with this relative good that one attains and he draws glory from it. Supernatural wisdom consists then in aiming always higher without flinching and to suffer failure with serenity, without allowing the energy of effort to be diminished by the certainty that it will not have its full effect.

(Quoted by Abbess Cécile Bruyère)

Do I possess the desire to advance? Am I resolved to go out of myself in order to belong entirely to God? These are the questions you should be asking yourself all the time. This desire not only excludes all attachment to whatever displeases God, but it supposes as well the search for all that pleases him. The two things are intimately bound up with one another. The separation from all that displeases God, yes: but that is not enough. The desire for perfection is the fruit of love. And when one loves someone, it isn't enough to avoid what might displease him; one looks more for what might give him pleasure. It is in devotion that one recognizes true affection. We must, then, seek to do what is pleasing to God. The religious life is based on this double foundation. The saints were saints only because God was their principal preoccupation, because they sought him and advanced toward him by making progress in perfection. Now perfection consists principally in love, the theologians tell us. This love must enter into all the practices of our life, otherwise we will be outside the essential idea of our state of life.

(Conference, 15 July 1874)

Humility, detachment, penance—all that with consistency and unity. That is what will not only subdue you but will unite you, with time, very closely to our Lord.

(Letter to Reverend Mother Elisabeth de la Croix,
Prioress of the Carmel at Meaux, 3 December 1861)

Abbess Cécile Bruyère

It is so easy for us to make out a little programme of the spiritual life for ourselves, quite nicely constructed according to our capabilities, our aptitudes, the means we have to hand, etc., and so, pleasantly, happily, we would end up living a nice honest little life. But the Lord passes, and with a single gesture brushes aside this construction, which was harmless, but which would have led us only to mediocrity; and, instead of allowing us to be an expounder of beautiful theories on the spiritual life, detachment, self-denial, he arranges things in such a way as to make us practise them. That is how saints are made. No one ever arrived at sanctity except by that complete and absolute overturning of their projects, their plans, their arrangements. The remarkable thing about the religious life is that, unless we actually break our vows, we become saints either willingly or by force.

(11 January 1891)

To hold fast, from the bottom of your heart uninterruptedly and through all the circumstances to whatever God wills: there is no work that leads to salvation more surely than that. That is what brings us to holiness, and we have the true Bread from heaven to give us that continuing strength.

(Conference, 25 March 1884)

All that God wishes, and all that God is, is infinitely holy. When one plunges oneself entirely into that holy will, the result will inevitably be holiness.

* * * * *

To tell you the truth, I am not surprised, if our Lord wants you to achieve not merely goodness but holiness, that he puts you in conditions where the horizons expand somewhat. Holiness cannot grow simply in precise fidelity to the duties of our state: that is only the preparation we must provide. If God does us the favour of desiring to lead us further, he brings about circumstances that oblige us to be more generous in our fidelity. "It is circumstances that make saints," was the profound way our great Father Abbot used to put it, "it is not saints that make circumstances." A sensible nature like yours always runs the risk of stopping at good sense, unless the Lord breaks up that rather narrow little boat in order to fling us into that boundless and bottomless ocean that is himself; to swim and fly belongs to that world, while walking seems safer and more in harmony with our nature.

So, has God decided to make you achieve sanctity in that way? That is the real point of the question. As for X, God can always make another saviour appear if you refuse, and it is you, not X, who will lose thereby.

(Letter, 16 September 1889)

Give yourself totally, and do not merely lend yourself, to the intentions of God.

* * * * *

A man does not become great enough to become worthy of the confidence of God until he has lost his soul. To lose one's soul means to take God as one's only moving force, and not to make any decisions except in accordance with his wishes.

* * * * *

The greatness of an act does not lie in itself, but in its perfect consonance with the will of God.

* * * * *

Let us believe that the Lord knows the paths to his paradise; let us leave it all to him.

* * * * *

Yes, everything should serve you as a ladder to go toward the divine Spouse; after my own experience and that of others, I no longer believe in obstacles coming from without. On the contrary, I believe that our Lord gives us everything that will best lead us to the attainment of our goal and to the fulfilment of his plan, and that we are deceiving ourselves when we imagine that something other than what he has given us would be for our good. I believe that we have made great progress when we are thoroughly convinced that we must adapt ourselves to our surroundings, and not adapt our surroundings to ourselves.

(Letter, 28 November 1882)

The true perfection of any creature is to fill completely the place God has marked out for it from all eternity.... The good, the true, and the beautiful cannot be embraced in an absolute and total fashion; what God demands is that each creature should embrace it in a fashion relative to what he desires for that creature.

* * * * *

Conscientious fidelity in overcoming oneself, constant seeking after virtue, persevering imitation of our Lord Jesus Christ, unfailing obedience to all that God demands, are effective in calling down upon us the grace of union with God; nevertheless, it is only from God that we can obtain it. The Lord, in any case, frequently demonstrates to us that this is the sphere of his free generosity. At times he unites himself almost without warning to a soul that has done nothing to prepare itself for this high favour; at times he refuses it for a long time to another, who seems to be giving him conscientious and faithful service.

This observation, far from turning us away from the desire for union with God, far from making us slow down in our efforts, should, on the contrary, stimulate us to multiply the acts that might attract the attention of the Lord to us. Why should we be surprised, after all, if the most excellent gifts that may fall to us from God's liberality should often require of us a great deal of desire, effort and prayer? And if there are few who attain to this goal, that is not because God has become niggardly with us; the grace of the unitive life would be far more common among Christians if it were better understood, more highly prized, and if it became the object of a more ardent desire.

(The Spiritual Life and Prayer, 1885)

Dom Paul Delatte

It seems to me that one of the greatest dangers threatening the life of perfection is to hang on to one's own temperament and character. That does not manifest itself in the first stage, but later a real dualism grows up. The supernatural life exists, but it is hindered by our temperament. We haven't been redeemed by halves, and yet we think we can live as if only part of ourselves had been redeemed. Now if that is only a passing mistake, a slip—which is always possible—then one picks oneself up and often starts again with increased generosity. But there is also a dualism that is reasoned, resolved, consented to, a condition we have constructed for ourselves, a state that has been intentionally created. Life is made up of two compartments, separated by a screen—no, an airtight partition. On one side, there are the religious duties, carried out with regularity and correctness; on the other, the infinite multitude of thoughts, words, actions, decisions carried out by our temperament; and the supernatural life can't penetrate. The supernatural life is encased in a shell; a whole vast region escapes it, a region that is precisely the region to which our efforts toward perfection should extend. "Well, what can you do?" you say. "That's how I am; you can't change me." Myself, I should have thought that the supernatural life could indeed attain to, correct, transform all that; that just like the perfume poured over the head of the High Priest, which flowed down his beard and spread as far as the fringe of his robe, the supernatural life could envelop and transfigure your entire life, your character, your temperament, the very tenor of your life. Yes, all that. That is the fruit of humility, abnegation, mortification. That is charity. You're not willing? Then you will live a petty, joyless life, with no great dignity; you will die prosaically; and on the first day of your eternity, the Lord will show you the contrast between what he has done for you and what you have consented to do for him.

(Commentary on Job)

There is no measure for the good, and we should never be satisfied with ourselves. We must not sit down and tell ourselves that we have arrived at Jerusalem and at perfection, and that the Crusade is over. But there must be discretion in the balancing of virtues, and there must be no violence or feverishness or tension in our search for the good and the better. Our supernatural life, as long as we are in good moral health and well-established, develops just as spontaneously as our natural life. It is enough to carry out its works, to make use of our baptism and communions. We were born without knowing it, and we grew up without desiring it. Supernatural works take place in us in the atmosphere of delicacy, discretion, and peace.

(Letter to a young girl, 5 October 1904)

My children, it is a question of evangelization, but evangelization of ourselves first of all; a question of being missionaries, but in ourselves first of all. You don't look as if you believe me.... The characteristic fruit of our supernatural life is to become disciples to a greater and greater extent, to belong more and more to all the directions of the Lord. We are all too willing to be missionaries to others, all too willing to reform, correct, elevate others. How easily we are moved to correct the souls around us. I'm just like that myself....

(Conference on John 15, 1902)

There is a phase from the Gospel which, it seems to me, people have a slight tendency to forget: "If you then, who are evil, know how to give good gifts to your children, how much more will the heavenly Father give the Holy Spirit to those who ask him!" (Luke 11:13). And so, as far as I can, I advise souls to employ the practice of the outstretched hand, the hand stretched out to God to receive. It's not that I want to rule out the effort of our own will, or the perseverance and vigilance that are required to provide for it. But I believe that everything in us is done by the hand of God, and that he desires us to know it. All virtue, all purity, all fidelity come to us from him. And perhaps the fact that there remain within us certain traces of impatience or of overspontaneous reactions is only permitted by our God in order that we may be reduced to turning to him and asking of him humbly, in a filial spirit, the victory he has not granted to us.

(Letter, 29 May 1917)

This act of abandonment we have spoken of is a perfect act; it seems to me that it contains and sums up within itself all the supernatural beauty of the various acts we may accomplish in isolation. When one looks closely there is, in an act of abandonment, the simultaneous exercise of faith, hope, charity, adoration; that is to say that that act by itself is a complete act, a perfect act, which contains in itself all the specific and particular beauty of all acts of religion, of all the theological virtues.... Even if it may appear passive at first sight (how odd to say "passive"), even if it may appear an act without energy—since it is a question of letting oneself go, of abandoning oneself into the hands of God—I am firmly convinced that when one looks at it more closely (just try it!), and especially when one strives to carry out that act of abandonment, one can see very well that it is the most energetic and most active of all acts; it is the act that leaves everything to the infinite activity of God, that activity in virtue of which the work of our sancification is accomplished; it is the act that leaves to the divine activity all the fullness of its energy and its efficacity.

(Retreat, 1894)

We aren't like watches we open to count the jewels and to study the springs. That would be a troublesome diversion, a real distraction, to look at anything but God. There is nothing in the world but his totally unique beauty. And, what is more, all that collection of interior conditions normally catalogued under the heading of "extraordinary grace" doesn't seem to me to deserve that name. What is extraordinary, what is desirable, is not some personal state of ours, a thrill, a transport, or any delight, however pure it may be. No: the extraordinary that is given universally and may be possessed by all is God, the Incarnation, the Eucharist, the life of the Lord within us, the Church, eternity, the indwelling, veiled today, tomorrow without veil, God in his totality within us. And I'm always afraid that psychological investigations of a certain type might distract us from this great theological fact, which is the only one worth considering. People turn their backs on true mysticism by allowing themselves to be preoccupied with mystical phenomena.[2]

* * * * *

My little child, to adore God means to belong to him with one's will. It means to be his, and in his hand, at every moment, by the accomplishment of our duty, which is his will, and by the acceptance of events, which are also his will. When I tell you that, I am also telling you what it means to "live with sincerity as a child of God." Sincerity means adherence to and conformity with the law. "His delight is in the law of the Lord, and on his law he meditates day and night" (Ps. 1:2). Isn't that essentially what our attitude should be before God? Isn't that the attitude of all creation? "By thy appointment they stand this day; for all things are thy servants" (Ps. 119:91). And it is particularly, under the interior influence of the Spirit of God, the attitude of baptized creation: "All who are led by the Spirit of God are sons of God" (Rom. 8:14).

That attitude belongs to everything, to everyone, to me, to you, my child. All the special forms of vocation that might be added to it, do no more than respect and give precision to that primary attitude for each person: monks, nuns, priests, bishops, the faithful—they are all what they are in order to adore in spirit and truth, and each person's interior vocation is never anything but a modality of adoration....

You have been told many times that the truth of Christianity, and the fruit of baptism, consist in three things:

(a) The life, the beauty, the likeness of our Lord Jesus Christ in us, through sanctifying grace;

(b) A new understanding, a new will, a new heart, through faith, hope and charity;

(c) The real presence of God in us, as our beloved, as our good, as our possession. "If a man loves me, he will keep my word, and my Father will love him, and we will come to him and make our home with him" (John 14:23).

(Letter to a young girl, 15 December 1904)

Have the courage to judge your life, and your soul, and your conscience according to another's light, which as regards the species, is the light of God. Disown rapidly, simply by pronouncing the name "Jesus," any bizarre thoughts. But above all, resolutely avoid any melancholy and minute investigation, examinations, analyses. That last point is of sovereign importance for your health and your moral education.

(Letter to a mother, 2 October 1908)

We must make God at home with us.

(Conference, 1916)

Allow me to suggest to you a strange idea: why has the Lord not left us a portrait of himself? Tradition, I know, has passed down to us an adequate general picture of the features of the Lord; but why, after all, did he not come in the era of photography? Quite simple: everyone would have believed naively that this portrait of the Lord was the Lord himself. No; where is the likeness of the Lord to be found? In souls. What is the true portrait of the Lord? It is yourselves. Another question: why is Holy Scripture, which is a continuous story from the "*in principio*" of Genesis to the "*Veni, Domine Jesu*" which ends the Apocalypse, why is Scripture interrupted from the time of the Apostles until the last days? The reason is the same: it is up to the saints to write that story of our Lord Jesus Christ.

(Retreat, 1899)

83

It must be said that one sometimes feels surprised to see, in the course of the liturgical year, this multitude of saints who succeed one another without a break. At times it seems that this varied multitude distracts us from the beauty of the Lord and turns us away from God. Why don't we keep the ferial office every day? Why isn't every day the feast of the Lord? The truth is that, in fact, there's no question of anyone but him in the Church. St John says it explicitly: "And from his fullness have we all received, grace upon grace" (John 1:16). The Lord has come, and we draw everything from him. All these varieties of sanctity we study in the course of the year, and which we combine in one feast of All Saints because of our incapacity to give each the attention it would deserve—all these varieties of sanctity spring from that Source; all these varieties of supernatural beauty originate from that Beauty; all these rivers from that Ocean; and the Church, in proposing to our admiration and goodwill these supernatural splendours of the saints,[3] is doing no more than showing us at all times the beauty of the Lord ceaselessly reproducing itself, fragmented, diversified, but always One.

You know that theory, dear to me, according to which all supernatural beauty is a beauty that has already been used. All the splendours to be found in the holy souls who appeared successively at their own time in the course of the ages have already existed in the soul of our Lord Jesus Christ, capable of giving to all, without ever becoming impoverished.

(Retreat, 1899)

Purgatory is enough to demonstrate that every Christian is called to perfection, that is to say to the perfect degree of charity, which is to love God, to love as God loves, to love nothing except according to God. If at the gates of eternity, the Lord chastises the souls he loves, isn't that because they had a real duty to attain to that degree, and they only suffer because they did not attain to it? Would there be punishment if there had been no transgression, and would there have been transgression if there had been no duty? God is jealous; he has the right to be. There is a law, even while we use the things of the world, that we are not to be attached to the world, but to keep our strength and our self for God.

Once again, let no one misunderstand the sense of such an affirmation. From the fact that perfection is a universal duty it does not at all follow that everyone must enter the religious life and that everyone is obliged to live "the life of perfection," to complete renunciation of all that is not God, and to the indiscreet exercise of the counsels. However, the fact remains that everyone is obliged to essential perfection, that is, charity according to their condition and their state. The law of God is not a revolutionary one. Charity, and the interior degree of charity that makes for perfection, are compatible with the variety of human situations. Neither wealth, nor marriage, nor politics, nor action, nor kingship, nor military life are incompatible with charity. It is simply the duty of all of us to defend our life at the points at which we feel that it is vulnerable. Bossuet wrote to Louis XIV to teach him what charity and Christian perfection consist in for a king. It is a fact of experience that a certain delicacy is necessary to the exercise of charity; perhaps we cannot accomplish our whole duty unless we do a little more than our duty? Perhaps the inertia of our nature dictates the law that we must always surpass ourselves?

(Notes on the Spiritual Life, 1899)

God has no other interest but having saints. Everything exists for that. We should take care that God is not frustrated in his one desire.

(Letter, 1895)

The difference between people lies in the difference in the contact they make with supernatural realities; and what is most lacking in everyone is "the sense of reality." Our whole life hangs on that. Satan makes a continuous effort to cause the diminishing, the disappearance within us of all sense of reality....

My children, we must be "realists"; we must recognize reality, affirm reality, above all, bear it within us in the assiduous contemplation of the mystery of Christ. The perfection of our life hangs on that and is largely subordinated to it.[4]

* * * * *

"Whoever wishes to be my follower must deny his very self, take up his cross each day, and follow in my steps" (Luke 9:23). Since the passion, the allusion is clear, and we see how far the resemblance of the disciple to his Master is meant to go. But when those first hearers of the Lord's pondered this saying, they no doubt saw only a symbolic, perhaps even proverbial meaning. The cross of which he speaks is not a simple suffering nor even a sorrowful burden, according to the metaphorical sense which we often attribute to him today; the cross is a real instrument of death, for in the following verses the Lord puts us on guard against a false love of life. The one who takes up his cross on his shoulders, like the condemned of ancient times, concurs in some way in being offered up and dying; he collaborates with the process. And for a Christian, to take up one's cross is to resolve to go to the end of renunciation, to consent willingly to this putting-to-death, that is to say, to the complete destruction of everything in us that is out of harmony with God. St Luke adds "each day"; it is, in effect, a continuous work, requiring time and effort.

"And follow in my steps." This clause is not a third condition imposed on the one who would belong to the Lord. It means that after leaving ourselves behind, even to death, we come to realize what we have desired: nothing is able to hold us back any longer, we can follow the Lord as true and faithful disciples.... Indeed, when perceived more closely, all that is called denial, mortification, is also called charity. Charity transfigures the cross. What we are thus leaving behind is always a false "me," a personality weighed down, an inferior way of living which makes us slaves.

The Lord is saying: don't defend that kind of life before God, before his fatherly demands and his sovereign dispositions, for the danger is great. Stubbornly to lay claim to and defend one's own will, one's own soul, one's own life, one loses everything and for ever. On the other hand, the one who loses his life for my sake and for the gospel's sake, for the sake of remaining faithful to my teaching and my person, will find it in the truest sense and will be saved. The way to life is thus to die.

(L'Évangile de Notre Seigneur Jésus Christ, I, pp. 475-6)

Notes

1. Euphrasie Cosnard (1809-79), daughter of a notary who had retired to Sablé, was a lifelong friend of Dom Guéranger and one of the great benefactresses of the monastery.

2. Cited in Dom Savaton, pp. 328-329.

3. There is a reminiscence here of the Latin Vulgate of Psalm 109 (110):3: "In splendoribus sanctorum, ex utero ante luciferum genui te" (translated in the Douay version as "in the brightness of the saints, from the womb before the day-star I begot thee").

4. Both these texts are cited in *Via Clarescente*.

Chapter Four

"He endured, as seeing him who is invisible" (Heb 11:27):

The Pattern of the Cross

In the year 1893, the Solesmes communities passed through one of the sharpest ordeals in the whole course of their history. If the state of expulsion and dispersal that was the lot of the monks of Solesmes for fifteen years (1880-95) saw an increase in vocations and new foundations, it also altered the rhythm of their life. Despite the strenuous efforts of both Abbess Cécile Bruyère and Dom Paul Delatte—first as prior to the ageing Dom Couturier, then as abbot—to maintain the common life and regular observance, a few monks inevitably enjoyed a good degree of independence and relaxation. Two in particular looked askance at the prior's efforts to maintain discipline, and determined to undermine his influence. Despite their efforts to block his election as abbot, Dom Delatte was chosen by his monks on the first scrutiny, on 9 November 1890. Undeterred, they endeavoured to get the election declared invalid. Forestalled by Dom Cabrol, Dom Delatte's prior and future abbot of St Michael's, Farnborough, who was sent to Rome to obtain confirmation of the election, they soon began "to weave a dark web"[1] of hostility and criticism, which culminated in the sending of a memorandum, in early 1893, to the Holy Office, denouncing the relationship between Dom Delatte and Abbess Cécile, their teaching and their government. Dom Delatte was suspended from his office and spent eight months of "enforced stay," as he put it, first in Rome, then at Subiaco. Dom Guéranger's achievement hung in the balance until an apostolic visitor reversed the sentence, and Dom Delatte was reinstated on 25 November 1893, by direct action of the Roman authorities.

Extracts from letters describing their cross enable us to glimpse the heroic abandonment it occasioned. When she first learned of the attacks made against her in 1892, Abbess Cécile wrote:

All Saints, 1892

By a happy coincidence I was just explaining in a conference the *laudabiliter vivat, laudarique non appetat....* *Tu ei sis honor*[2] of our Preface. At that moment, I was thinking that my honour, like my life, had been given to God, and that I was no longer attached to it. I even glimpsed that there could be a certain joy in offering that to the Lord, more than offering my life.

In April 1893, Dom Delatte was in Rome, together with Benedictine abbots from all over the world, for the foundation of the College of Sant' Anselmo and the appointment of the first Abbot-Primate, when he received notice from the Holy Office that he had been suspended from his charge—"a shattering blow," as he wrote to Abbess Cécile:

Rome: 27 April 1893

Calvary can take on different forms; but since on that road we are walking toward God in the footsteps of our Lord Jesus Christ, all is well. I want you to be strong and brave.... And say this quite clearly to each of the souls that are yours and mine—to each of those children whom I love a thousand times more than myself and everything, and only less than God. Say only this to them, that I will not allow that any one of them should see anything else in this than the hand of God. If any one of them were to weaken on this point, she would be neither God's, nor yours, nor mine....

"All things work together for the good of those who love him." What a grand thing obedience is, and rarely have I felt as I do today. Do pray for Saint Pierre that they don't suffer from this: I will have few occasions in my life when it will be given me, as it is given me today, to show the Lord how much I value him.

On learning the full gravity of the situation, Abbess Cécile wrote: "Judging by the look of things now, there can be no room for anxiety, sorrow or joy: we can only adore all the ways of God in quiet and profound simplicity.... I humbly bow my head. At the same time, there is within me a conviction, based on no human principle, that God will achieve his own ends, that Sunday will come to crown and fulfil the Friday."

In the following month, Dom Delatte wrote to the Abbess of Stanbrook, Dame Gertrude d'Aurillac-Dubois:

Subiaco: 18 May 1893

I was about to send you my address, but if you call me "Most Reverend Father" again, I will have to denounce you to the Holy Office! All this is for the good. I always believed that I was more meant to be a child than a Father. You know that well. In any case, all this is still to the good, because in the most painful ordeal that could have befallen them, struck down by Rome and in the person of their Abbot, all the monks and nuns of Solesmes have adopted an attitude which quite simply compels admiration.... I am proud of this; I am happy. I bless the Lord for having considered me as truly his own, and I thank him for having taken something from me to seal forever the union among those of my house: for that, Mother, will be the only result of all this.... Pray for those who make others suffer. Ask the Lord that I may not make any blunders and that I may be in all things worthy of him. I tell you again, I am happy.... You yourself know what it is like: to my knowledge, you yourself have already drunk several times from this chalice.[3]

Later that same month, we find Abbess Cécile writing to a monk who was very devoted to Solesmes: "Pray that we may not lose one atom of this trial by our weakness or by mingling our human feelings with it" (25 May 1893). And again, on 25 July 1893: "If he wants Dom Guéranger's work, it is for him to preserve it. If he does not want it, may we have the merit of bowing our heads in full and entire surrender; such deaths as these bring forth new life."

By November the storm was over, and Dom Delatte could write on the first day of the New Year, 1894: "Let us not heap reproaches on the year 1893. It has been what God willed it to be, what he has made it. All is well. I would not change anything. 1894 will also be arranged by God; let everything come from his hand. It is only tenderness."

Like so many beginnings, the early life of Solesmes unfolded under the sign of the cross. The cross stands as the central symbol for faith in Jesus Christ; yet Christianity did not bring the cross into the world but found it there. "Suffering is the law of life," wrote Abbess Cécile, "since sin came into the world." Christians do not love suffering for its own sake, and they try to alleviate it. But their religion goes further to show them that suffering is a precious gift. As these texts show, suffering that is unavoidable, and even death itself, have a positive meaning.

The mystery at its heart is the suffering of Jesus on the cross. Christianity does not transfigure the world by denying suffering and death but by making suffering and death the death of Christ, a death through which death itself dies in the triumph of the resurrection. The source of these writers' confidence and joy is to be found in a life lived in union with Christ, in the mystery of life and death by which the passion and resurrection of Christ are continued in his Body which is the Church; a life found through the death of baptism and renewed in that of the Eucharist.

Suffering constitutes the true nature of Christian witness, the manifestation of that cross and resurrection that is its permanent witness to the world, its "martyrdom" in the etymological sense of the word. Witnessing is not about giving an account of an internal or external experience: it consists in the imitation of and identification with Christ, and this is realized by shaping our destiny to the pattern of the cross, since it is on the cross that Christ completed his mission. "What are all these things that afflict us," wrote Abbess Cécile in a letter, "if not simply the testing of our love and our faith? How good it is to bear witness to our love! The martyrs witnessed by their blood; we witness by divine fire" (1873).

Dom Paul Delatte

We still need to repent frequently, to be converted frequently. We have succumbed to evil; or perhaps we have made a mistake in our calculations, and we become discouraged when we come up against unexpected obstacles; we get surprises, we meet with failures. But the intelligence of God already has the measure of it all; it includes the unexpected in its calculations. His will infallibly hits the mark; and, finally, the Lord does not become discouraged; he loves with perseverance, his tenderness is incapable of turning back. When he makes as if to turn away, it is only to provoke our regret by the intolerable loneliness that is felt when he is no longer there. Even when our delays and our thoughtless actions have been innumerable, on the day when our soul turns back to him, he welcomes it and seems to remember nothing. "His going forth is as sure as the dawn ..." (Hosea 6:3). Even when many go away, he remains, as if chained by the invincible fidelity of his love. An attentive soul will pause before this characteristic of God: the patience of his eternal love, his peaceful waiting, the way he waits despite everything, waits without discouragement, as if, for him, to wait cost him nothing, as if his love made him forget his infinite dignity, as if, in the invincible patience of his love, he no longer remembered that he is God.

(Retreat)

Have confidence. Be a true Christian. The Lord has given abundantly to you. He has thought fit—and we belong to him, we are at his disposal—he has seen fit to mix a great suffering into your life; do not weaken. I would like you to be enough of a Christian to bless the Lord, to bless him for everything and to say to him, even through your anxieties and your tears: I have confidence in you. There is a sort of provocation and compulsion that, under the appearance of this sorrow, comes to you from God. Don't try to escape from God; you will grow; maybe the Lord is only waiting for that act of confidence, and heroic self-abandonment, to solve all the problems. It is by means of the Christian heroism of the mothers that God blesses the children.

(Letter to a young mother, 12 January 1913)

We must respect the sorrow that is sent by God, and not mingle anything human with it. You understand very well what I mean, I know. I am no Stoic; and it is saints and elect I want to prepare for God, not Stoics. But I'm afraid of that painful desire that makes us put our hands to a wound in the soul, irritate it, re-open it, poison its edges, and prevent God from healing it with the balm that comes from faith and from his hand.

(Letter to the same, 26 June 1919)

I feel that there are thousands of things and thousands of events in our life—which I won't discuss—that God allows only to make us overcome them, to make us pay no attention to them, to raise us above them. What is all this business and all this trouble for?—to make us despise them. To make us pass through them. It is a perpetual "*egredere*"[4] that the Lord makes us carry out throughout our sojourn here below in order that, at last, freed from all things, we may belong fully and exclusively to him.

(Letter to a nun, 10 May 1908)

Worldly people generally demand a life without troubles; true Christians courageously take their portion of the dose of hidden bitterness God mixes into their life in order to put them in a position where they must lean on him. You will never have perfect peace; there will always be hard rubs and tribulation. It is certainly not by eliminating these annoying details that we will find peace; on the contrary, it is by accepting them in tranquillity and making a gentle effort to lean upon God. You are simply serving your apprenticeship as a creature.

(Letter to a mother, 3 March 1904)

To give pleasure to God, to give joy to God: that is best done on the cross.

(Letter to a nun, 23 May 1920)

When we are suffering from the incapacity you describe, it is not helpful to investigate whether the cause is to be found in ourselves, in our health, in our infidelity, or whether it is God who wants to try us. Such psychological labours only lead to uncertainty and sadness. When recollection becomes difficult for us at the time when it is most essential, there is only one cure: to strive to be recollected at all times. Constantly to bring one's soul back to God, at every moment of the day, and to keep it there. To return ceaselessly to the centre. To work and live in his presence. To take up before him the attitude we know to be pleasing to him. Constantly to recollect and to take hold of our soul in order to place it before God is an act of perfect charity.

This sounds like a paradox, because that is precisely where your difficulty lies. But our intelligence, our will, and our soul are always in our hands. Let us ask God, even—especially—when he conceals himself, for the generosity necessary to seek, in the sweat of our brow, the hidden pearl. We may struggle all night in darkness, but without wearying. And when God sees that even by his delays he cannot discourage us from seeking without ceasing, he breaks something in our temperament and blesses us because we have said, "I will not let you go, unless you bless me" (Gen. 32:26). For there is only one blessing, there is only one grace: Uncreated Grace, God.

(Letter to a young nun, 26 October 1904)

Don't spend your life moaning. Being miserable depresses us, diminishes us, discourages us; and expressing it makes it worse. The more we say, "It's hard," the more miserable we become. No, nothing is hard, if we look at life from the point of view of him who gives it to us. We musn't think about tomorrow. Almost the whole of our suffering comes from our imagination and from looking ahead pointlessly. We should live in the present moment. Wherever I am, God is with me, even on a chaise longue. I believe, I hope, I love. I am and I do what I am supposed to be and do. Well then? I think all our suffering is a mirage, unless it is the fruit of our passions. Suffering can find no hold on a soul that has submitted itself to God. It may even happen that in the case of certain imaginative and literary people suffering may become a pose, an attitude, and a verbal expression, which rekindles their misery. We must keep the head of our horse high—that is the law of riding. It is also the law of our whole life. It is our loss—and God's—if we see life as contrary, against the grain, and moan about it. That is true of all of us—how much more true of those who are eighteen years old! We will never carry out our duty unless we have enthusiasm, and what sort of enthusiasm, what sort of perseverance are possible if we are sad, if we drag life along like a ball and chain, and if at every step, we repeat, "It's hard!" ? Are things more pleasant for us once we have allowed that discouraging phrase to escape us?

(Letter to an eighteen-year-old girl, 6 April 1906)

Avoid completely that absorption, that contemplation of the difficulties that may come up tomorrow! This tendency to be miserable about what will happen, what could happen, what might happen, seems to me equally contrary to reason and to faith. We will reach eternity by living from day to day. It is always possible to live; there is always a way to breathe, to eat, and to have trust in God. I have known some of those obstinate seekers of problems or of ingenious solutions, those eternally discouraged people, who were never convinced by the calm with which the Lord untied, throughout their lives, their perpetual Gordian knots. Heavens! When a difficulty does come, an urgent one, we will see it! Above all, don't change your temperament; let's remain sober among those who are drunk on heady wine!

(Letter to a superior)

From a natural and human point of view, the Holy Virgin was the one person in the world who, it would seem, should have been spared the spectacle of Calvary. A woman, a virgin, a saint, a mother: should not all these titles have joined arms to keep her apart? Yet God desired that she take her place at the foot of the Cross. He had obtained her consent for the preparation of the victim; now he desires to obtain her acquiescence to the consummation of the sacrifice. On the Lord's part her presence brought about the occasion for a supreme despoilment and allowed him to enter into an absolute solitude. Distanced from his Father because of human sin, he now gives over his Mother to the humanity reborn in his blood and establishes her as

95

Mother of his Church.... He is now completely alone, "without father or mother" like Melchizedek; even his clothing is in the hands of soldiers, as if he were already no longer of this world. Alone, suspended between an earth which scorned him and a heaven which seemed to be closed to him.

(L'Évangile de Notre Seigneur Jésus Christ, II, p. 370)

Abbess Cécile Bruyère

Isn't suffering the law of life since the first sin? Have you ever seen anyone escape it? So the happy ones are not those who do not suffer, for then there would be none in this world, but those who know how to suffer.... You must take your courage in both hands and turn to our Lord, from whom will come your help. I assure you that I have experienced this very forcefully since the death of our great abbot. One must bear everything, and be no longer borne up by anyone; and I can state firmly to you that with that burden I am perfectly content, as long as I do not look at things from the point of view of self-love and as long as, in the depths of my heart, I throw myself upon Jesus, who alone possesses within himself beauty, goodness, truth, and all that could ever captivate us.... Believe me: do not be afraid to suffer in this world.

(Letter, 11 August 1877)

I can see that our Lord does, and will do, his work, as long as we become holy. Suffering is an excellent cement. Oh! We have to be well crushed before we can be used to make joints! To become liquid is not a comfortable business.

(17 February 1885)

Don't be surprised at being constantly and strangely buffeted. You will be tossed back and forth between God and the devil, but it is this action of the winnowing-fan that will purify your nature and free it from the chaff. Note that the grain that is being winnowed does not move of itself but is being shaken by another. Let yourself be thrown about, but do not, yourself,

1. *Dom Prosper Guéranger (1805-75) at the age of fifty-five. This photograph was taken at Bath at the urging of Dom Laurence Shepherd during the abbot's trip to England in September 1860. "It was hard work to induce him to consent," he noted in his journal. Dom Guéranger considered it to be the best of his portraits.*

2. *Dom Guéranger, by Ferdinand Gaillard (1834-87). This celebrated Parisian painter-engraver made a retreat at Solesmes in 1874, the year before Dom Guéranger's death. He was greatly struck by the richness of the abbot's expression, and made a crayon sketch from which he later produced this engraving.*

3. *Dom Laurence Shepherd (1825-85). Monk of the English Benedictine Congregation, chaplain to the nuns of Stanbrook, translator of Dom Guéranger's* Liturgical Year. *It was exactly ten years to the day after Dom Guéranger's death that Father Laurence followed his friend and guide. Dom Charles Couturier, Dom Guéranger's successor as Abbot of Solesmes, attended his funeral.*

4. Solesmes at the time of Dom Guéranger, including the famous tower of 1850.
Springing from the imagination of the cellarer, this romantic guesthouse offered
a view of the whole region.

5. Solesmes today, overlooking the Sarthe. The history of the monastery may be
read in its succession of buildings: the bell-tower, church and court of the
eleventh to fifteenth centuries; the eighteenth-century priory house; then the
imposing romano-gothic façade of 1896, inspired by Avignon and Mont-Saint-
Michel and built by Dom Jules Mellet as part of Dom Delatte's vast building
programme. This century has brought a new second cloister and library by Dom
Paul Bellot (1937), a new wing (1958), and guest-house (1976).

6. *The choir and nave of Solesmes as seen from the altar. The photograph was taken during the exile of the Solesmes monks at Quarr (1908-22).*

7. Abbess Cécile Bruyère (1845-1909), elected prioress at the age of twenty-two, and named abbess four years later. When some wondered whether the abbess was too young, Dom Guéranger replied with a smile: "It's a fault about which I am easily consoled, given that it is the only one that is corrected every day."

8. Abbess Cécile Bruyère: "Give yourself totally, and do not merely lend yourself, to the intentions of God."

9. Sainte-Cécile, Solesmes. "The house of the Lord's field," said its first abbess. The monastery was in fact built in the middle of pastureland and fields. At the dedication of the church in 1871, Dom Guéranger exclaimed, "To think that less than ten years ago, corn grew there!"

10. Appuldurcombe House, Isle of Wight. First refuge of the Solesmes monks and scene of Gregorian "summer schools". "We were about ninety when we left Saint-Pierre," wrote Dom Delatte. "As you can imagine, when the English lords or baronets built their stately homes, they didn't have in mind the French monks who were to come and live there one day."

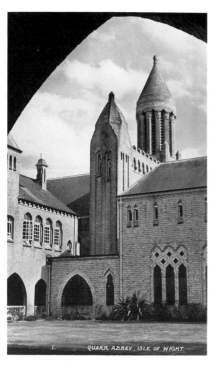

QUARR ABBEY, ISLE OF WIGHT.

Solesmes in exile
(10, 11, 12)

11. Quarr Abbey. By early June 1908, the entire community had moved from Appuldurcombe to Quarr. "The abbey church," wrote Dom Delatte to a friend in France, "may seem to you, as an Englishman said, 'a very strange building.' Père Paul Bellot is of a very original stamp: he has lived in Spain, and I'm sure that the lines of Moorish architecture have lived on in his eyes, even to the point of permeating his spirit. But in the midst of all that, you will breathe an atmosphere of faith and renew your strength..." (Letter, 18 October 1912).

12. St Cecilia's Abbey, Ryde. The community of Sainte-Cécile moved from Northwood House, West Cowes, to Appley House, Ryde, in May 1906, most of the property going by boat. The construction of a church and monastery, modelled on the lines of their own abbey at Solesmes, was built on to the existing manor house.

13. *Dom Paul Delatte (1848-1937). "The vocation of the abbots of Solesmes is very simple. I have understood it to be a question of working, suffering, and dying" (to the nuns of Sainte-Cécile the day after his abbatial blessing).*

move; far from helping the operation, you hinder it. Remain perseveringly calm. You will not always manage to unite yourself with our Lord, but you must always seek after it—without struggling, however.

Do the best you can, work more by prayer and by example than by words; but if you then have failures, do not be too distressed about it; our Lord has plenty himself.

(17 February 1887)

Patience is the remedy for all evils. When one suffers, one must not become agitated, but must accept everything for the sake of the hand from which it comes.

(28 November 1890)

Trials are always accompanied by the grace to bear them. When the Lord engages us in a battle, he makes sure that we shall have the means to be victorious.

(28 November 1890)

I have often thought that the grace of martyrdom is not only a grace of strength but, above all, a grace of extreme meekness. I am surprised that this characteristic is not more strongly emphasized. "Like a sheep before its shearers" (Isa. 53:7).

It is a science to know how to offer a perfect holocaust; that is, an offering that is unadulterated and unmixed, in which one does not take anything back ....

Don't you feel that certain sufferings are like a wedge in God's hands? They allow supernatural realities to penetrate right to the centre of the soul.

(28 November 1890)

Certain very hard trials are exquisite graces that make people saints despite themselves. Deadly suffering is a grace one is not always strong enough to look for oneself. If God loves the soul, he imposes on it, and without being stopped by its groans and tears he leads it straight to the goal.

To give up to God things that are not licit is already a good action; to give him things that are licit and good is better; to give him supernatural things is the most delicate and perfect of all gifts.

When God desires to make someone truly holy, he, who knows the best way to go about it, touches the most sensitive point. First we resist, then we submit, and then we throw ourselves flat on the ground; and joy, peace and pure charity are born in the ruins. It is worthwhile. Nothing gives more cause for hope than seeing a soul felled by an unexpected trial.

(20 April 1891)

Holy Church, wonderful teacher of asceticism as of dogma, makes her children sing the antiphon, full of profound meaning, on the feast of the two great deacons Stephen and Laurence: *Adhaesit anima mea post te* ("My soul clings to thee"; Ps. 63:8), placing these words alongside a description of the torment endured by these two great martyrs,[5] as if to give thereby the reason for the divine strength and almost insensibility which they seemed to manifest. Strength, in fact, results from a strong point that is able to endure. Now the creature can only find this strong point in him who is its principle, centre and end.

(Life of Dom Guéranger)

Oh, how few people are willing to love God and suffer for it! I cannot begin to understand the illogicality of even the best of them. They sing their *Credo*, they believe it with their whole heart, they would seal every last syllable with their blood and then, in practice, they live their lives like pagans.

(16 May 1878)

The first thing Dom Guéranger taught me was that marvellous system whereby we make our faults into so many rungs to climb up to our Lord. There is so much love in the cry of a soul who is truly sorry for having wounded the One whom she loves and from whom she has received everything.

(Letter, 18 July 1883)

If God is to unite himself to a soul, he wants it to be malleable; to know how to make use of the things that are shaping us is better than the most exalted prayer.

In my opinion, you are too concerned about the future God has in store for you; that doesn't lead you anywhere, and has a harmful effect on the present. It is necessary to acquire genuine and solid virtues: humility, patience, strength, love.... The only reason why your health is so easily affected is that you are not sufficiently one with God.

(Letter, 14 May 1890)

Patience, prudence, the skill produced by an ingenious charity, and above all, *silence*, will achieve everything.... Never before have I more fully understood the importance of the *media nocte*. God comes in the dark hours of this present life—and in silence. That is a formula that remains with us like a profound lesson. Really, we talk too much ... and perhaps that is the only evil. We talk for good purposes, we talk in order to detract, we talk for the sake of talking, to direct, to console, to make amends: and the result is an unspeakable din made by the best of instruments, since nobody wants to stop playing their own tune. Oh! I beg you, let us have a little of that Mary who "kept all these things in her heart" (Luke 2:51).

(Letter, 24 August 1890)

In pharetra sua abscondit me (Isa. 49:2: "In his quiver he hid me away").

Etsi ambulavero in medio umbrae mortis non timebo mala, quoniam tu mecum es (Ps. 22[23]:4: "Even though I walk in the valley of the shadow of death, I fear no evil; for you are with me").

There comes a moment in the supernatural life when the reason becomes confused, when one must commit oneself to God with blind confidence: without that one would never cross a certain narrow pass; there are some heights one could never approach. Sometimes God introduces this trial under an exterior form, sometimes partly exterior and partly interior, sometimes wholly interior.

One cannot understand, reason is clouded, broken upon that which is impossible to avoid. We must wait for the Lord to do his work: under these conditions the solution always comes, and it comes from God, by a way we least expect.

This situation must be met, in some degree, by everyone, or they will remain for ever in the shallow waters of the supernatural life. This is the reward of an exact fidelity. The soul closes her eyes. She says to the Lord: "You are the Master. I know you look only to my good. I do not know how these things will turn out, but I consent to be without understanding."

She must be faithful, not give free rein to her imagination, make a genuine sacrifice of her reason to God; thus she crosses that narrow pass. Nothing can replace these moments. One can only close one's eyes and remain in God's hands. The humbling of the human reason is what is essential. The law of every resurrection is that death must come first. The Lord had to die before he rose again. So must we die to rise again to a higher life which is the access to a genuine supernatural life.

There have to be trials which harrow a human being to the depths, a suffering so intense that little things no longer count for anything. We become truly detached from everything because we have cast off all our moorings; we become surrendered to God and supple enough to receive all his graces and do whatever he asks of us.

Those who are truly united to God must go through this. If nothing disrupts the perfect confidence and abandonment we should have toward God, we shall be wholly delivered up to his action in integrity and perfect submission; and the Lord will work miracles, if necessary, to come to the aid of those who surrender thus absolutely to him.

But those who make a fuss and try to escape, as it were, from the jaws of this vice, like Jeremiah's square stones,[6] will do themselves more harm than good.

In this state there is nothing to be done but accept. All that we do to try to get out of it is fearful, for God does not wish us to get out. We must drink the chalice to the dregs, the soul must be torn and then die. Every time she tries to rise up, she suffers even more. Often the blunders that we make have formidable consequences.

The mysteries of God are not confided to those who cannot endure, and who give way when something upsets them.

In the state we are speaking of here, we must consent to remain before God alone, saying to him: "You are enough for me, do as you will."

Anything which does not keep nature at bay is not the trial I mean. The manifestation of Our Lord, his birth, becomes real, is actualized, in generous souls; the true life with God is the fruit of this humbling and confusing of reason.

(Conference, August 1901)

Dom Prosper Guéranger

In your relationship with God, don't expect anything from books, but everything from your will, inspired and sustained by grace. Books come afterwards; often they are a help; often they are a hindrance; but we must understand that in this world, the sky of our relationship with God, like the other sky, has its clouds, large and small, and sometimes its storms. God is vigilant throughout it all, and even when our heart is weak and distracted, that doesn't always mean it has left him. We must live like children, and keep firmly in mind not only that we are obliged to go to God with the amount and type of grace that is given us at the present moment, but that we cannot do otherwise. If God wants more, let us give him more. But try to live in his presence without mental effort but as a friend; for there is no bitterness in conversation with him.

Finally, my dear friend, carry on at your own pace, with your conviction of the great necessity of humility and charity, which, in you, are almost one and the same thing; and don't imagine that you can be perfect in a fortnight. It is a great thing to know oneself, but it is only half the battle. For the rest, one needs two things: love of God—and time.

I feel for you in the vexations you are having to suffer. Rise above it, not through disdain for the persons concerned—on the contrary, pray a good deal for them; but because our Lord has revealed to us a peace against which the persecutions of men are powerless. It is the peace of knowing that he loves us, and that we love him a little.

(Letter to Dom Piolin, one of his monks, 29 May 1843)

In the course of our life, many things will shock us; are we to lose the peace of our soul because of that? Certainly not. Anything that does not remove God from our heart is not an evil for us, and so let us remain calm.

There is a method of making good use of many things that are harmful to others and that we cannot ourselves avoid. That is: never to be disconcerted by them, and to judge them from the point of view we have been given by God. In that way X will acquire experience, her judgement will be formed and extended: she will understand more things; she will be better aware of all that she owes to the gratuitous goodness of God, and she will be the better for it, and more able to do good by her example and her influence, once she is no longer a child.

(1 February 1859)

One must never despair; an evil never goes beyond the limits God has laid down. However, God is jealous, and he crushes men or suspends their activity, so that no one can boast, even in the depths of his heart, that he has achieved something. Humiliation is the most important element of success today....

(Letter to Montalembert, 10 March 1846)[7]

I should like to hope that God will restore your poor husband's health; someone is ill and he recovers: there's nothing more normal, with God's help. But it also happens that the person succumbs, and in both cases, it is always the hand of our good Lord that is guiding all things. So let us desire what he desires, and at the same time, behave as if everything depended on us.

(Letter)

The essential thing, in the midst of trials of the interior life, is to be humble and firm as regards oneself; and then to spend oneself for others, with the intention of pleasing our Lord.

(Letter to Madame Cécile Bruyère)

Anyway, a considerable quantity of prayers are offered for our needs in the course of each year; I rarely miss a good opportunity for asking for them, and, after all, God does help us. Let us fall asleep in his arms. Are your troubles immense? I am coming to join you in order to be with you and share them. As for my difficulties, they are no less; but God is so powerful and he watches over us so well! I am touched in the depths of my heart by these examples of compassion and care, and the past answers for the future, as long as one follows up with confidence the kindness one has received....

(Letter to his cellarer, Dom Fontienne, April 1843)

In France the storm is brewing. We must not be afraid of anything. We are in the hands of God who is more powerful than we are. Fortunately, it is also he who loves us. So let us walk calmly along the way he is opening up before us, however limited the horizon may be. If we suffer some setback in Rome, for example, there is no doubt that our help will come later. All the demons in hell have been let loose; all the more reason to hope in the good angels. It is not within the power of man to kill Truth; but an individual may succumb any day. God is keeping watch over us! We must act according to our duty, and never expect to receive our reward in this world: that is true independence.

(Letter to Léon Landeau, 2 October 1843)[8]

But once again, God is with us. We shall smile at all this, and draw from it even greater confidence in our successes. Just eight days ago at recreation someone reflected that we had been at peace for a long time, and that if this calm continued we should have to fear that we were not pleasing to God. Thanks to him, we are now launched: calumny is exercising itself to the full; we may expect anything henceforth; our history will have something of the history of the ancient monastic foundations, often so much opposed precisely by those who should have supported them. They think they are rendering a service to God, as our good Master said to his disciples, and added that we must not have any fear. God permits so many things that the thoughts of certain hearts should be made known! And so pray, Madame, that our hearts at least may show forth only thoughts of charity, thoughts of sacrifice. At any rate, I am very aware at the moment of the truth of the Apostle's words when he speaks of the ineffable way in which God arranges things for us and for our weakness when he judges it right for us to be tested.

(Letter to Madame Swetchine, 5 August 1833)[9]

Return to the source, become a man like any other again; remember that nothing in this world is entirely made to measure for us; take people as they are, take yourself as you are. Laugh at your foolishness, your miscalculations, your mishaps, your attacks of despair, in a word, at everything, except your happiness, for God desires that happiness, and you would be to blame and not merely out of your mind if you did not desire it.

(Letter to Dom Fontienne, 1831)

Love God independently of everything; love him more than his graces, even those which lead to him. To him it comes to the same thing whether you take this route or that, as long as you arrive, and above all, if you have already arrived at your destination which is him. There is a maxim of practical morality which is very true: to work is to pray. I will parody it for you: to suffer is to love. Suffering takes the place of everything, above all when one loves for the same reasons as one suffers, and that is what you are doing, and that is what Jesus Christ did before you, for you, and because of you. When we say that he suffered, that means that he loved his Father, that he loved us. There is no more profound meaning for that phrase. Only, he was God, and he does all these things in a manner superior to ours; and so, he suffered because he loved; love was in him before suffering; the love in him was the cause of the suffering. In our case—for we are creatures—suffering comes first, and then love comes afterwards. Suffering puts us in our place, brings us detachment, shows us our dependence, and above all the nothingness of our virtues while we were not suffering. In a word, it makes us better. It is then that we truly love; our very position as suffering Christians disposes God in such a way that quite apart from what we do, our passivity alone is a great merit in his eyes, by classing us with those whom he loves most, with his own Son.

And so may God continue to do his will in you, and you continue to love that will and find in it peace, harmony, the tranquillity of order. I commend you to Mary who also suffered greatly, and in proportion to the love which she received and gave.... Think of Abraham; that great patriarch loved too; he believed, and it was reputed to him as justice, as St Paul says, and God desired mercy and not sacrifice. That is what God does. Sometimes when he sees that he has been understood, he stops the raised hand. At other times, too, he does not do that, and that too is for the good. Which are we to choose? Which to ask for? His glory, his will first of all, and then, when our heart is well purified, ask him boldly for our will. There is no harm; there is only good in that. Why shouldn't we allow our heart to speak in all frankness before our heavenly friend? That isn't weakness; it is confidence. When one loves God more than oneself and has given proofs of it by suffering with him, why shouldn't one make use of one's rights? Isn't he there to refuse us if we are indiscreet, to grant our prayer if we have correctly understood his heart, that heart which is never mistaken and which has promised us an addition to his kingdom and his justice, an addition which he himself calls a hundredfold, which is paid only in this world. In any case, I will myself certainly tell him; but above all, tell him yourself. He will see clearly that your heart is not shaken by the fear of refusal, and he will treat it gently and with good will. Oh! men, and the best of them, have such difficultly in believing that God is more tender and more sensitive than they are themselves. But I am letting my pen run away with me....

(Letter to Mme Swetchine, 23 October 1834)

One cannot live the supernatural life to the full without difficulties; isn't that the way the soul is stripped of itself and matures? We must remember that our nature is profoundly vitiated and that even supernatural enjoyment, without the counterbalance of struggle and contradictions, could never transform us as we should be transformed. And so, when God loves a soul, he will provide them.

(Cited in "Portrait of Dom Guéranger"
by Abbess Cécile Bruyère, 10-12 October 1867)

What would you have then? The disciple is not above the Master. It was said of the Master, "He will drink from the brook by the way" (Ps. 110:7); but I also know, and I add it under my breath, that the verse continues "therefore he will lift up his head." The two laws are parallel. And with the patience which God has given me I see very clearly that time finally triumphs over all things and all men.

(Cited in "Portrait")

If a person allows himself to become troubled, he no longer belongs to himself, and ceases to hear the voice of God within him.

(Letter to Abbess Cécile Bruyère)

God calls some to himself by ways in which they have only to glide along, so to speak. For others, on the contrary, he desires that they can do nothing without him; he desires, I say, that they owe their salvation, their crown, to great efforts, to spiritual combats. These last are children of his predilection. Now you are called to walk among these. Lay in a good supply, then, of the love of God. It is the only thing that sustains, and with it what is there to worry about? When we love God, nothing can stop us. If we fall sometimes, it is all the more reason for redoubling our efforts; and we derive this advantage, that we know ourselves better for what we are—this is a capital point. Conserve always a great devotion to the divine Heart of Jesus and a boundless confidence in Mary; these are the things that will sustain you, that will increase that divine charity in you which will make you conquer yourself and your petty passions.

(Letter to Euphrasie Cosnard, 15 November 1828)

Notes

1. The phrase is from Dom Lucien Regnault, to whom I am indebted for the details presented here. See his introduction to *Dom Paul Delatte: Lettres* (Solesmes, 1991), pp 8-9, 41ff.

2. From the solemn prayer of consecration to virginity: "May she live in a manner worthy of praise and without seeking praise.... May you be her honour."

3. Cf *In a Great Tradition*, by the Benedictines of Stanbrook (London, 1956), pp 103-4.

4. "Go forth..." (the Lord to Abraham in Gen. 12:1).

5. *Adhaesit anima mea post te, quia caro lapidata est pro te, Deus meus* (My soul clings to you, O my God, for my flesh has been stoned for you): antiphon for the feast of St Stephen; *Adhaesit anima mea post te, quia caro mea igni cremata est pro te, Deus meus* ("My soul clings to you, O my God, for my flesh has been burnt for you"): antiphon for the feast of St Laurence.

6. The reference is to Lamentations (*Lamentationes Jeremiae*, Latin Vulate) 3:9—*Conclusit vias meas lapidibus quadris, semitas meas subvertit* ("He hath shut up my ways with square stones; he hath turned my paths upside down," as the Douay renders it.)

7. Son of a French ambassador and an Englishwoman, and descended from a noble Burgundian family, Comte Charles-René de Montalembert (1810-70) was one of Dom Guéranger's closest friends and most ardent supporters. Both men were passionate for the Church and the cause of unity around Rome. Montalembert stayed at Solesmes in the very early days of the priory during the autumn of 1835, where he wrote his life of St Elizabeth of Hungary, took part in the Divine Office from his own choir stall, and once brought two kittens into the refectory in his coat pockets and had them make the sign of the cross. Shortly after his stay, Dom Guéranger wrote: "Go about this world as you will, but know that my soul will never lose sight of you for a single instant." These words remained true for him even after 1853, when their differences over the claims of Catholic liberalism in its various manifestations caused an estrangement between the two men.

8. See note 2, Chapter Twelve.

9. Madame Swetchine (1782-1857). Daughter of a Russian nobleman and married at seventeen to a general over forty, she was one of the most celebrated Catholic converts of the nineteenth century. For forty years her drawing room in Paris on the rue S. Dominique was the meeting place where

the Catholic élite—Joseph de Maistre, Montalembert, Lacordaire, Père de Revignan, Alfred de Falloux—rubbed shoulders with Cuvier and De Tocqueville. From her first meeting with Dom Guéranger in the spring of 1833, the renowned convert and counsellor understood the significance of the restoration of Solesmes. Despite the great difference in age—he was twenty-eight and she fifty-one—she submitted her spiritual writings to the young prior and often sought his advice. She also inaugurated a system of annual subscriptions to help support the work.

Chapter Five

"Unless you turn and become like children" (Matt. 18:3):

Becoming a Child

In a series of conferences on the Rule of St Benedict given to the Solesmes novitiate in 1899, Dom Delatte noted that Newman had described the spiritual temper of Benedictines as more "childlike" than that of other religious Orders. "There's no need to blush at this," he continued, "as if this evaluation sanctioned an imperfection or inferiority about us. I see here the attitude of the Lord himself, the effacement of the individual, the priceless fruit of our contemplation, the exterior expression of that innermost fact that a monastery is a system entirely interdependent...." Solesmes' understanding of spiritual childhood derives both from the tradition of what has come to be called Benedictine family life and from its understanding of the Church as *Mater et Magistra*, who has received from Christ the words of eternal life. In these pages, we see these writers humble before the truth the Church transmits to them. Their spirits—so often vigorous and independent with regard to the opinions of men—remain children of the Church, among those little ones to whom the secrets of the kingdom are revealed.

As so many saints have realized, and not only Benedictine ones, it is the Christian religion, the religion communicated by God's Son, that awakens and keeps alive in its believers the life-long awareness of their being children. The Incarnation enables all the children of men to be born of God, to become children of God together with the Son (John 1:17). In what is no mere legal fiction or metaphor, the baptized in Christ become children of the Father. This is a filiation communicated to us by the Son and guaranteed by the Spirit poured into our hearts, enabling us to cry "Abba, Father" (Gal. 4:6). Into this life the

Church, *Ecclesia Mater*, gives us birth. All the expressions of the life of the Church are summed up in the image of the mother who ceaselessly gives birth—through the sacraments, the word, prayer, all her activity—to a new humanity in Christ. The idea that the Church was born for us from the side of Christ on Calvary that we might be born from her, and consequently that the Church is our mother, recurs frequently throughout Dom Guéranger's *Liturgical Year*. Far from being a form of naive piety, the mystery of spiritual childhood is at the very heart of our faith and rooted in the depths of the mystery of the divine birth.

If the Church is mother, each Christian is also a mother. Dom Guéranger develops this theme, the birth and growth of the Word of God in souls, in the context of the liturgical year, especially in the celebration of Christmas. "There is a double mystery that is actualized in this holy season," he writes, "the mystery of the infancy of Christ in the soul of man, and the mystery of the infancy of man's soul in Christ" (*The Liturgical Year*: Christmas I). The Church's tradition, he notes, has seen in the three Masses of Christmas a symbol of the three births of the Word: the eternal birth in the bosom of the Father; the historical birth from the Virgin's womb; and finally, as the fruit of the Incarnation, the spiritual birth in the womb of the Christian soul. Each of these births takes place in silence and hiddenness. All this is not merely a symbol of God's attitude toward the world; it is his very attitude: "All our humiliations will never bring us so low that we could be on a level with his lowliness. No; only God could reach the humility of God" (Christmas I). And this application of spiritual maternity to the soul of every Christian springs from the maternity of the Church herself, which all the faithful living the life of the Church spread and mediate. For it was one of Dom Guéranger's principles that "what the liturgical year works in the Church in general, it repeats in the soul of each member of the faithful who receives attentively the gift of God" (Preface to *The Liturgical Year*).

Christian childlikeness and Christian maturity are not opposed, as these texts make clear. And paradoxically, our condition of dependence and docility toward the Father, this childhood in God, is in fact the highest exercise of responsibility and maturity with regard to our Christian vocation. "Our dependence," writes Dom Delatte, "far from diminishing as we grow, increases in direct ratio to our supernatural life." The more our divine education progresses, the more dependent we become. To put it another way, the more Christians grow to full stature in Christ (Eph. 4:13), become adult in Christ, the more does the spirit of childhood grow within them: "Christ does not attain his perfect age in us unless we return to that spiritual infancy in which there is nothing of ourselves in us; there is only Christ" (Dom Delatte). According to these writers, in the spiritual life "there is no coming of age"; each step toward "his perfect age," all progress, is a step toward greater childlikeness, renewal, vitality.

Such a childhood in God is characterized by the simplicity that lets God's will be done; the docility that offers no resistance to his action; the surrender and obedience that offer ourselves for his purposes; the sense of wonder and gratitude that belongs to the heart entirely given to God; the freedom that comes with abandonment to God. If Christian childlikeness brings us to the kingdom, it is also an expression, here and now, of the kingdom: "We can never come to this perfection of simplicity, unity, and strength without beginning to take on, here below, a little of the ways of heaven" (Abbess Cécile Bruyère). In all this, as in so much else, Mary is our model, as perfect child of God and perfect Mother of the eternal Child.

Abbess Cécile Bruyère

It is for you that the Lord said: "Truly I say to you, unless you turn and become like children, you will never enter the Kingdom of Heaven." And again: "I thank thee, Father, Lord of heaven and earth, that thou hast hidden these things from the wise and understanding and revealed them to babes; yea, Father, for such was thy gracious will" (Luke 10:21). The Lord desires for you not the puerility but the simplicity of a child, for he rejected the first and embraced the second; and it is humble and sincere love that will give it to you and will bring about in you the full flowering of grace.

(Letter, 4 October 1882)

You are still too grown up, too wise, too much given to reasoning. Take away that obstacle, and the Lord will bow down toward you with his infinite gentleness. You will find him; he will fill you with his joy, his love, and his ineffable peace. He may do this at once, or tomorrow, but it will certainly not happen before you are humbled in the depths of your being, and so much so, that you become a child again.

(Letter, 5 November 1886)

Perfection does not consist in being great, but in being little.

* * * * *

In all things, the great secret is to take up as little space as possible.

* * * * *

We must arrive at that childlike simplicity where the soul no longer has any difficulties, and everything is in its place; it is ready to enter into the plan God has for it.

Life is so simple. I am always haunted by the text, "In all these I sought rest, and I shall abide in the inheritance of the Lord" (Sirach 24:11, Douay). This is a whole programme of peace, serenity and stability in God, better to endure whatever he wills.

Calm self-abandonment, serenity, and peace are the last word of virtue, and the truest sign.

* * * * *

We can regard simplicity as the peak of the spirit of faith; because, in a soul that possesses the spirit of faith, all is reduced to a unity.

The soul becomes truly diamond when she grows in such a way as to be perfectly united with God. Invulnerable, resistant to all that is not the divine light, transparent as mountain water, but firm and solid as rock.

(Letter, 9 September 1889)

Let us base our life upon humility, upon simplicity, without ever seeking the extraordinary, even on the pretext of virtue. Our cenobitical life has this characteristic, that it removes us from extremes and makes us enter into the genuinely supernatural by means of the common, simple, and ordinary things the Lord has chosen for us.

(Conference, 1 January 1896)

Whatever is truly divine always appears very simple, very peaceful; and it is only those who love the simple, the peaceful, the hidden, who are in the truth and who are capable of understanding the secrets of God.

(Conference, 2 February 1904)

Make an effort to be resolute and simple. You are holding yourself back with these little worries, like a person who is walking and suddenly stops before a blade of grass. Don't be punctilious; perfection doesn't lie in that, but in love. And love, even the most delicate, always gives breath and freedom.

(15 November 1884)

It is never the Lord who fails us, but our trust and love. It is important to become penetrated by the truth that we are, of ourselves, essentially incapable of any supernatural good. Our attitude, then, must be one of patience, accompanied by humble confidence in the goodness of God, which owes nothing and gives everything. Our beloved Lord does his work in us, but he does it in his own way. After all, you say, with the Holy Church: "Lead us by thy ways toward that which we are striving."[1] If you knew how many people change that prayer into "by my ways"! Of course, they do add the rest of the phrase, but they are less likely to be heard, because they have changed the person. The dependence I am talking about is not sleepiness or dullness; it is the result of a profound humility and a gentleness that come from the Holy Spirit. So don't torment yourself about the state of your prayer, but humble yourself and rest in your poverty in joy and peace.

(Letter, 14 June 1873)

Have a blind confidence in our Lord, who is certainly leading you along the path that is the best and safest for you. That act of confidence in God's guidance is the most sensible and most loving act that a person can make.

(Letter, 17 February 1881)

True wisdom consists in being very simple in the hands of the Lord, without trying to see too far ahead of us. Divine Providence does not tend to tell us its secrets in advance, but rather unfolds them little by little before us, once we are really trustful and really detached.

(Letter, 1890)

Dom Prosper Guéranger

Think of a pair of scales, where one of the sides rises in proportion as the other descends, and rise in the same way. You have become a child again; have a child's simplicity. Forget all that is past in your life, which has made you so personal as it accustomed you to count upon yourself only.... And so, don't say any more that you are sad unto death because of your tasks; that is a great and solemn phrase that has nothing in common with childhood.... So, go simply. God's action is never more effective than when human means have run out....

When will you finally be calm and abandoned to God? Suffer in peace everything he suffers. Why should you be in such turmoil when he is so tranquil? Is his grace not at his disposal? Love naturally and simply. Pray him to do whatever is for his glory, and be in peace....

To do more, and do everything for people who make the least return for your efforts: this is the ABC of all perfection.

(Letter to Reverend Mother Elisabeth de la Croix,
prioress of the Carmel at Meaux, 17 August 1861)

You say that it is a long time since I preached the love of God to you. My sermons can be summed up thus: be simple with God. Serve him with simplicity, love him with simplicity; no violent or extraordinary states, but peace of heart and soul in our Lord. You belong to his court, his house; busy yourself with him more than with yourself. Any mania about becoming "deeper" is dangerous, and apart from the time that it wastes, it leads to nothing. Is it necessary to chew over oneself so much in order to be aware that one is full of wretchedness in the past, of imperfections in the present, of weaknesses in the future? As for the past: love God. As for the present: love God. As for the future: again, love him and that way all will be well. For it isn't the present, or the past, or the future, or yourself that should occupy you, but God: he who gives himself to you and becomes impatient when you amuse yourself by dressing yourself up endlessly in order to go to him, when it is you that he asks for and not all your adornments.

(Letter to Euphrasie Cosnard, before 1840)

The point is to love God a great deal. How is one to love God a great deal? By loving him little by little.[2]

Dom Paul Delatte

Spiritual infancy consists in docility, confidence, self-abandonment, simplicity. It consists in being what we were on the day of our baptism. Life had not yet passed over us; life had not left any trace. There was nothing but our soul, naked, pure; our virgin soul.

There was nothing but God in that soul. God, silent in that soul that was attentive, in ecstasy, ecstatic and so attentive to God that it paid no attention to anything else. The perfection of the supernatural life consists in returning to that state: no temptations, no desires, no sufferings; God is the one treasure in the soul. The little child has no duty at that moment other than to gaze and to rest in that ecstasy in which God has established it.

As for our duty, it is to do what God wants us to do. The perfect age of Christ is the development of the whole Christ within us. It is Christ who has grown so large in us as to have expelled all else. Then there is nothing within us except the Lord; there is nothing of ourselves left. That is how it is with the newly-baptized infant. The infant in its cradle; that is the ideal.

Christ does not attain his perfect age in us unless we return to that spiritual infancy in which there is nothing of ourselves in us. There is only Christ, who occupies our entire soul. He cannot take second place in us—he cannot take first place. He is the Only One, and he works in us and through us.

(Conference)

In the supernatural life there is no coming of age, no emancipation; we remain forever little children, we remain forever beggars.

(Conference on John 15, 1902)

I believe that almost all the work and the effort of the supernatural life comes down to this: to make oneself small in spirit. In the course of our lives we have extended ourselves over a multitude of things; we need sensible emotions, for we are beings of sense, and beings of sense are capable of a variety of activities. I believe that the direction and effort of our life should be, so to speak, to draw our soul back from all this extension, to reduce our affections, to limit our attachments, to allow our soul to return to its deep, intimate centre where God dwells; to reduce our sensibility, which is other than expansion, to reduce our soul until it is no more than a living atom; to lose ourselves in the light of God, to be lost in the tenderness of God. I am only giving you some indications. You will reflect on them.

We cannot bear fruit except on condition that we turn away

from the multitude of things, and understand that only God is interesting, is worthy of attention.

(Conference on John 15, 1902)

In the supernatural life, we are always little children, and when we fail in that essential law, it is to the detriment of our soul and of God. The true law of our supernatural life is childhood: "Unless you become like children, you will never enter the kingdom of heaven" (Matt. 18:3). That is so true that when we are in eternity we shall be in the position of sucking babes, little children who receive from the breast of God the life that never fails.

I was about to say that this dependence is a growing dependence; and it is true. We are the more dependent on God the more we have received; the more we owe him, the more in need we are of being sustained by him. That dependence, far from diminishing as we grow, increases in direct ratio to our supernatural life; since we have more to sustain, we have more to receive.

(Conference on John 15, 1902)

Notes

1. From the hymn *Sacris solemnis* of Corpus Christi: "Per tuas semitas, duc nos quo tendimus."

2. Cited in Soltner, *Solesmes et Dom Guéranger* (Solesmes, 1974), p. 133.

CHAPTER SIX

"Remembering your work of faith, and labour of love, and stead-fastness of hope in our Lord Jesus Christ" (1 Thess. 1:2):

Faith, Hope, and Love

In words that could describe all three writers, Lacordaire wrote to Madame Swetchine in 1837, referring to the young abbot of Solesmes: "It is rare to find a Christian in whom faith dominates everything else." This element in their personalities penetrates all their writing: their sense of faith, in both senses of the word, the holding-as-true, and what-is-held-as-true. And in fact the two sides are inseparable because the act of faith, the act of believing, is the way in which we participate in the content of faith. Faith is not merely a psychological disposition, as Dom Delatte reminds us; it is having the same life as the Lord, a life that implies hope and love; a living faith operating through hope and love to unite the soul to God.

The three supernatural virtues point beyond our existence; they imply God, tend toward God, and only in God have their full meaning. Through baptism we enter the life of God; now we can, to use Dom Delatte's definitions, think with God's thoughts, will with God's will, love as God loves. By faith, these writers mean not only a communion with the truth but a communion with the intellect of God, the lifting up into God of our intelligence, "to see God in all things and all things in God" (Abbess Cécile Bruyère). Even in pain, darkness and confusion, faith transfigures and lifts us up to share in God's creative work of building "on the ruined, the impossible, the paralyzed." It is then that the soul draws nearer to God and discovers that his presence does not depend on vision or feeling, but only on faithfulness.

If faith opens the eyes of the intellect "wide to the light of

God" (Dom Delatte), to see that God alone is fully real, hope is trust in that unchanging reality. By hope, we also possess God without feeling his presence and know by virtue of this "interior guarantee" he gives that he has taken possession of us. This gives that sureness and certitude with which the soul rests in God. By charity, we can love as God loves, consciously enter into the disposition and attitude of the God of love whose self-giving is of his very essence. Thus all three are forms of the human spirit's sharing in the divine life, each penetrating and enhancing the other, merging to form in us a state of loving, active surrender to God. Faith, hope, and love are the graces contained in God's self-revelation to us and our corresponding gift of self to God.

These are not mere words or professions of piety but actions that are assimilated to the action of God himself, a participation in the divine way of looking at things. It is to be caught up into the reciprocity of giving and receiving that is the heart of the Trinity, for faith, hope, and love express something of the inner nature of God. In baptism God gives us himself, his heart, his word, his mind. And he requires a correspondence from us in response, in our faith, hope, and love. The kingdom of God is within us at baptism; it comes through God and from God; and yet our cooperation is required, our adopting of God's approach in a movement that comes from above.

Abbess Cécile Bruyère

You seemed to be reproaching me for never wanting to look at things from the point of view of reason. But how can that rational point of view be of the slightest use to you? It makes thousands and thousands of thoughts flood in on you, thoughts that aggravate your ills without changing anything. As far as I am concerned, I would not be able to keep to the happy medium. If I were to judge according to reason, then, most of the time, I would send everything packing. But only faith can generate peace in the soul; only faith can provide a reason for what seems to have none; a consolation in the midst of unmitigated suffering; strength when one is weak, and hope that God, who sees all things in perfect justice, will also be able to put things to rights at the appropriate moment.

(Letter, 5 April 1891)

We must not be surprised that the greatest graces are the most hidden ones. We must understand that we have to drop everything that is brilliant, obvious from the human point of view, and enter into that region of faith where great things come to pass.

(Notes on the Spiritual Life)

"I will betroth you to me in faithfulness" (Hosea 2:20). Since faith is not in feelings, I have engraved these words in my memory. That was so important to me that I should have liked to have no pleasure in anything, for fear of going against the purity of that faith. That is why aridity did not distress me. Thus abandoned to the One who was feeding me on faith, I considered myself richer in my poverty than if I had had all possible joys. It made me raise up my heart toward this infinite Beauty, and say to him: "I have faith, my great God, I know that you exist and with that I am content." If I had been asked what I was thinking I should have replied: "I am content with the One who is and fills all things." I saw God in all things, and all things in God, and that infinite majesty was to me a vast sea, which, overflowing its bounds, covered me, flooded me, enveloped me from all sides.

* * * * *

Our faith raises us up, as the water, little by little, raised up Noah's ark; it rose above the highest mountains and almost touched the heavens. Our faith also raises us above the earth and makes us reach heavens.

* * * * *

You have always been rather inclined to complain that I never wanted to look at anything except in the light of faith; but I believe that that is the only true and accurate way of seeing things, because that is the one which will be ours before the Sovereign Judge. What use is anything which will not be presentable at that moment? There is no security (especially in the religious life) apart from that element; it is not even perfection and holiness, it is simply security. There are moments in life when, if one stops at reason, one's head spins.

(20 March 1891)

Many times, I have feared that anything might happen; and then our Lord would show me my lack of faith, telling me that I must discuss everything with him, and then leave him the task of genuine action. And whenever I entrusted the matter completely to him, without entering into all the reasonable considerations and legitimate fears, everything sorted itself out in the required time. So much so, that it was not long before I realized that the result depended upon my greater or lesser serene and blind confidence.

In these circumstances, I was often haunted by this memory: "They have no wine." First there is the Lord, who doesn't seem to be in the least concerned, and replies quite unexpectedly; then there is Our Lady, who isn't at all put out, who doesn't argue, who doesn't get upset, and who simply says to the people: "Do whatever he tells you" (John 2:5). Heavens, how vivid it all is! And after all, isn't it the "Have no anxiety about anything, but by prayer and supplication with thanksgiving let your request be made known to God" (Phil 4:6)?

(16 March 1890)

If you knew how clearly I see that God founds and builds only with the ruined, the impossible, the paralyzed. It is like some mysterious game that eternal wisdom plays *in orbe terrarum*. It is true of individuals, it is true of spiritual societies. I am haunted by the thought of the faith of Our Lady on Holy Saturday. If that dear sweet Queen had told the apostles what she hoped for, if she had told even the holy women, before that tomb, in the face of the success of the Lord's enemies, would she have been believed? I dare not affirm it! And yet, it was she who was right.

I beg you to cast all your worries, anxieties, and forebodings upon the heart of God. We, in any case, are not risking anything, since we are not destined to live eternally here. Success and victory are gained for us and cannot escape us. For the Church we love, you must also believe that all will be success.

(17 September 1880)

God clearly entrusts us with a task; obstacles present themselves, they accumulate. Should we leave the struggle, appealing to the name of "impossibility"? But the impossible is the very region of faith. As long as we move in the realm of the possible, we are only half sailing in the supernatural; but when someone leaves the shore and learns how to launch out generously under the watch of God into what he does not believe possible but what is clearly demanded of him, he carries out marvels. Happy are they whom God considers strong enough to track down in this way and compels to spring into the supernatural element of pure faith.... It is this principle which inspired St Benedict's chapter, "If a brother be commanded to do impossible things."

(Notes toward a life of Dom Guéranger)

God, seeing clearly that this soul draws breath only for his glory and for the service of its neighbour, increases ten-fold its powers, its aptitudes, and its means. It is almost impossible to say how much profound compassion, ardent zeal, and boundless devotion is contained in a soul so united to God and transformed into him!

(The Spiritual Life and Prayer)

Give to our Lord whatever he asks of you. Multiply your acts of will—that is where generous love is to be found, faithful love, effective love; that alone sanctifies the soul.

* * * * *

You must ceaselessly pour oil on things around you, appease and calm, pacify and unite. So many people want to be stone, and so few consent to be cement. And yet isn't that the rôle of the Holy Spirit? Isn't he the one who joins with the most admirable joints the members of the Mystical Body of Christ?

(15 August 1877)

Love engenders a supernatural fear of causing the slightest pain to the object of one's love; and to avoid causing that pain, no sacrifice is of any consequence.

* * * * *

During this mortal life, truly divine love does not lie in enjoyment but in devotion.

(24 July 1876)

Dom Paul Delatte

We are not, we cannot be fully in the supernatural life unless we are really firmly established in faith, and faith is quite simple: I think like God, I think what he thinks, I do not think anything he does not think; and indeed, whatever he thinks and does not tell me, I think it all the same. My faith is something more than the objective harmony it establishes between what I think and what God thinks; it is a participation from within in the mode whereby God knows himself. My faith is not only a communion with truth; it is more—a communion with the intellect of God.

(Notes on the spiritual life, 1899)

They say that faith is humiliating for our reason, that it is a trial for our intelligence. What! When our intelligence thinks like God, when it enters into the light of God, when it proceeds in its thinking in the same way that he does, when the things known by God are known by our intelligence, when faith is given to it as a complement to its reason, can it be that, thus enriched and illuminated, it should be undergoing trial and humiliated?

(Commentary on John 15)

True intelligence, in fact, consists of knowing what the true realities that surround us are, in order that we may conform our life in all its entirety to the behaviour and the ways suggested to us by this beauty and this tenderness that never depart from us.

(Commentary on 2 Corinthians)

Our faith, which makes us enter into God through our Lord Jesus Christ, is an act of intelligence. There is no point that needs to be more carefully recalled to people's minds at a time when religion is, in most cases, a matter of practicality, of sentiment, or of good form; while true religion is a matter of supernatural intelligence, and the act of faith is an act of the highest reason. We are not intelligent beings unless our thought enters into contact with the invisible. What is the intelligible world, the world of types, what is the universal, what is the spirit, what is God, what is the soul, what is the body itself, I might say, if not things that are not seen? I have never seen an angel, or God, or my soul, or even a body. I have never seen anything but the coloured surface. I have never touched anything but a resistance.... The sense of the invisible is the condition not merely for faith, but simply for intelligence.

For the human soul, there are only two attitudes before God and the things of God: to enjoy them if one possesses them, and to seek them if one does not possess them. And in this world our possession must always grow, and today's knowledge is never more than partial when compare to the knowledge that tomorrow's fidelity, experience and light will bring us. The rule, then, will be to seek always: "let him examine whether the novice truly seeks God," says St Benedict. Truly to seek God is to seek him without ceasing. It is to make use, for this search, of all that energy of the intellectual curiosity of the soul, which God has intentionally made eternally restless so that it may not be able to rest except in him. "Thou hast made us for thyself and our hearts are restless till they rest in thee."[1] There is no real interest for us except in the knowledge of God, even if we were for its sake to be ignorant of all the rest.

(Letter to a Benedictine nun, written in
a hotel room while on a journey)[2]

Faith cannot remain in us in the state of a Platonic thought or like a buried treasure. We are not safe unless our faith moves from the top strata where it is first sown, down to the centre and the substance of our life. Only then does faith have a real existence. That is why it must be cultivated. A person who does not let it flood his entire life, who does not permit this divine treasure that is in us to flood his whole thought, to envelop it, flood his will to make it entirely subject, flood his love and affections in such a way as to guide them in their entirety, a person who does not make his faith extend its sway over his entire life, that person does not have a sincere faith. For the plenitude of faith is a sincere faith, a vigorous faith, virile, a faith that is unshakeable, an irremediable faith—that shuts its eyes? No!—a faith that opens its eyes wide to the light of God.

(Commentary on Hebrews 10:22)

Faith, in the thought of the Apostle, is not simply an adherence of the intelligence to revealed truth. Obviously, intellectual adherence is the first graft, the vital suture whereby a soul attaches intself to God, but it is also an adherence of the whole being.

If one wanted to define faith as St Paul understands it, one would have to say that it is the repose of the intellect, yes, but also the repose of the will, of the affections, of the whole life, of the being in its entirety, in our Lord Jesus Christ, in whom is the consummation of all supernatural life.

(Commentary on Colossians 1:4)

Faith has not been given to us simply in order that we may bend our will before it, or in order that we may adapt ourselves to the truth that comes from God; but I believe that the final intention of the Lord in giving us faith is to make us live before persons and things of faith; to establish our lives in the regions where we live before God—Father, Son and Holy Spirit; the angels, the saints; among the persons and things of eternity.

(Commentary on 2 Corinthians)

Faith puts us in contact with things hoped for, with things invisible; and not only does it establish in us a conviction and an assurance about these things, it puts us in contact with God. It is in the realm of faith that our union with God takes place, not in that of feelings, or exaltation of the spirit. Faith is the essential condition by means of which we take to ourselves all the supernatural goods gained for us by the Lord. For it is not enough that there should be a treasure amassed by his sufferings; it is necessary that we should manage to take hold of it. Because the supernatural life, which shows itself in me by an act of faith, comes to me from our Lord Jesus Christ, because it is a fragment of his life, a portion of his beauty, something of him in me.

(Notes on the spiritual life, 1899)

If you want to shift within yourself an enormous weight of inertia you have been carrying for a long time, this is how to proceed, there is only one thing you need to do: "He endured as seeing him who is invisible" (Heb. 11:27). In order to bear all his burdens, Moses looked to invisible things, and fixed his eyes upon the beauty and the reality that are invisible.

(Commentary on Hebrews 11:27)

I find within myself, you will say, tendencies that are hostile, antagonistic to the kingship of God within me. Shouldn't I try to liberate my faith, my hope, my charity, which are constrained by inertia and obstacles of various kinds that I find in myself, before I try to use them? After that, I can begin to formulate the acts appropriate to them.

No, no, my children; faith will never come that way. The only effective procedure to get rid of those rebellious lower ranks that are our sensible dispositions is to be found nowhere else but in the exercise of our faith.

Make many acts of faith. Force your interior acts, your emotions, all the voluntary actions of your life to bow before God.

(Commentary on 1 Thessalonians 1:3)

There are realities that are just as certain in faith, just as sure, as those we shall see in eternity. They are the same ones; there will be no more than that in eternity.

A few days ... a few years more, and we shall see face to face what we believe. As we wait for the intuitive vision to show it to us, we have, on earth, faith, which is of as much value as the intuitive vision. I say "is of as much value" because faith shows us as absolutely present those things we do not perceive.

(Commentary on Hebrews 11:1)

St Paul habitually considers hope as an activity belonging to faith; hope is that ardour that is borne toward the goods of eternity; it shows itself by a holy audacity that makes us rely on God with an invincible assurance.

(Commentary on Hebrews 3:6)

In virtue of hope, this interior guarantee the Lord has given us, God is our possession; he belongs to us as he belongs to himself.

(Retreat, 1892)

There is in the theological virtues the indication of the real presence of the three Divine Persons within us. Faith is the ability to see God as he sees himself; charity is to love God as he loves himself; hope is a sort of claim on God, in virtue of which God is duty-bound to us as he is duty-bound to himself. We already carry eternity within us. Having faith, I carry in myself, in this supernatural resource, all that is necessary for seeing God face to face; I carry in my hope all that is required for me to enter into possession of God; I carry in my charity all that is required for enjoying God, for being with him when I enter eternity.

(Commentary on Colossians 1:13)

It is remarkable that the theological virtues are nothing other than divine processes given to us that we might act as God does, act according to a divinized intelligence and a divinized will. We do not sufficiently esteem the theological virtues if we do not think of them as a sort of divine grafting onto our intelligence and our will, so as to make us think, will, and love as God.

(Commentary on John 10)

If creatures are a snare for us, that is precisely because we do not love them enough—even if that seems paradoxical. What a monstrance[3] of God every being would be for us if we could see in them the divine thought which is their true identity! Christian detachment is none other than that divine passion for the greatness of every being, the refusal to value them lower than their origin and destiny warrant.

* * * * *

Souls are beautiful things, and until the day when we see God face to face, we shall never see anything as beautiful as souls. Their contact is so pure, so healthy, so sanctifying, that if we knew how to penetrate the outer shell, if we were to penetrate to the supernaturalized soul, the exercise of charity would always be a continuous exercise of faith in the real presence of the Lord.

(Retreat, 1894)

We love because there is God in our neighbour; just as the Eucharist is an extension of the Incarnation, so our neighbour is an extension of the Eucharist. Faith is a supernatural and clear-sighted understanding, enriched by God, and capable of recognizing God wherever he is. Charity is supernaturalized will; it is a heart enriched and enlarged by God, capable, well-adapted to loving God wherever his beauty is to be found. It is by faith that we recognize the beauty of the Lord in the Eucharist. There is also God and the beauty of God in your brother.... No doubt there are imperfections; but why are you more sensitive to the imperfections of your brother than to all the beauties of the Lord? You are stopping at the shell; be intelligent, be a Christian. Crack the shell; go to the centre. You believe the Lord on his word, but it is the same faith, always and everywhere: in this case, too, he has spoken. He who said, "This is my Body," also said: "Whatever you do to the least of mine, I will consider it as done to me."

(Retreat, 1894)

Even when a person is still occupied with extracting himself from his imperfections. there is no more effective lever for getting him out than charity. And when a person has to a great extent managed to get out of himself, it is still the exercise of charity that increases charity within him. To look is to love; our soul is all in our gaze. And then, to prevent that gaze, which is already all-powerful, from remaining on a Platonic level, one must be docile to him at whom one is gazing. There, it seems to me, is the whole secret of the interior life. That is how a Christian proceeds. All other procedures might have been employed by philosophers and Pelagians. When the object is to form God within us, is there anyone but God who can do it? "My little children," says the Apostle, "with whom I am in again travail until Christ be formed in you!" (Gal. 4:19).

(Letter)

I formulated what I said to you with the definite intention of making you enter into your true vocation, which is this: to do everything as a real witness to charity. God is worth it, my child. His love has no date, no limit, no break, no end. There should be some people on earth who grasp that and respond to it as best they can.

(Letter to a young girl, 16 August 1900)

I beg you: be attentive to the smallest actions of our life. The smallest actions of our life have their importance, their eternal repercussions. All the actions we perform take their place in the shaping of the future; they have an effect by example: each one leaves a good or a bad impression; each of our acts, even the interior ones, is involved in the shaping of the future. The future will be the one that has been merited by an act of faith, hope, or charity; the extent of today's self-denial will determine that of tomorrow, and its persistence in the future. . . . We must be fully convinced that it is an act of charity in our hearts that will finally shape future history. God's victories are not achieved through agitation, bustle, efforts, tensed muscles; but always in secret, through acts of faith and acts of charity.

(Retreat, 1894)

We love only because of beauty; that is what makes me say that the reason for charity is the beauty of God. We do not love God only because he is good: that is the ground for hoping and for being thankful. But the true motive for which we love him is his beauty. Beauty is truly, to my mind, the reason, the cause of charity. This "grace," in other words, this exterior or intellectual beauty, this moral beauty in God, in the Lord, is the motive of charity. Where there is a beauty that arises before the eyes, whether those of the body or those of the soul, there is a spontaneous movement of the heart toward that beauty.

(Commentary on Romans)

If perfection consists in union with God by faith, hope, and especially charity, it doesn't follow that every soul in which these three supernatural virtues are present is, by that fact alone, established in perfection. In fact, it is not the mere presence of faith, nor even the quality of the faith, nor any sort of exercise of faith that makes for the perfection of our Christian thought; it is when nothing is lacking to our faith that it is free and sovereign; when it has eliminated not only exterior obstacles but all inertia and all hesitation; when its exercise, liberated from all impediments, is continual, prompt, easy, joyful, and, when required, heroic. Nor is it the mere presence of hope within us that makes for the perfection of our will, but hope that is sovereign, the triumphant and constant exercise of hope.

The same thing must be said of charity, in that it is the disposition essential for union with God, and that it presides over the exercise of all our activity. It is perfect when it is absolute docility, gentle, calm, and generous aquiescence to all God's guidance and desire. The charity that chooses, that hangs back, that needs to be coaxed, that complains, or allows a slight movement of resistance to show, that charity is not perfection. Charity must be continuous, prompt, easy, joyful; it must give without counting the cost, "for God loves a cheerful giver" (2 Cor. 9:7). It is perfect when it embraces all of life, when it envelops all our actions, and when nothing escapes its sovereignty. It is perfect when it holds our soul very high, above all self-seeking, all emotion, above the apparent and treacherous seductiveness of multiplicity, all that is exterior, created, perceptible to the senses, and all that is personal. Multiplicity dissipates us, things exterior distract us, created things deviate us, things perceptible to the senses disturb us and stain us, things personal separate us from God. Charity holds our soul very high, far from suggestions and reveries, attached to God alone. It is what constitutes our true and spiritual virginity, which is to receive into our soul nothing but God and what comes from him.

(Notes on the spiritual life, 1899)

If you love me today, O my God, it is doubtless because of the beauty of your divine Son, which you have given me and can see in me. At the very moment of your eternity and of your timeless life, when you loved me, chose me, predestined me, and by your thought and will brought me into the life and lineage of your Son, at that moment, O my God, I had no charm, nor even reality of any kind. Nothing in me could have caused, justified, or attracted your love. For that reason, allow me to tell you that I love this nothingness from which you have drawn me, and which remains my only possession. Had there been any charm, any beauty, any kind of being or reality in me, your love would have been less like what you are; it would have been less gracious, less free, less yourself. Now, as the Apostle tells me, your love is your very self. There is only you alone, in the love you have for me, and your love is inexplicable. You are all tenderness; that is why your tenderness has no cause, that is why it is incomprehensible. I love my original nothingness, because I love you.

(Commentary on Ephesians 1:5)

131

We are to love one another as the Lord has loved us. That is possible because we are in the Lord. It is with his heart, his thought, his intention, it is with his seriousness, his forebearance, that we will love. And, like him, we are to love "to the end": the index of perfection in charity will be to give our life for those toward whom it turns, friends or enemies. "No one can love further," Jesus is saying, "than to lay down one's life for those whom one loves" (cf. John 15:13). The Lord is alluding not only to the heroism of the sacrifice he is about to accomplish in a few hours, or to the martyr's devotion, or to the practice of a pure and tender love going as far as death; but he is envisaging as well the constant, gentle cleaving to the law of charity. For this is what it really means to give one's life as well as to consecrate it wholly to one's neighbour.

(L'Évangile de Notre Seigneur Jésus Christ, 2, 306)

Dom Prosper Guéranger

From now on, have faith in the goodness of God. Believe that he belongs to you and you to him.... All faith comes from the heart: "With the heart we believe" (Rom. 10:10), says St Paul. Live then always by faith; charity has its root in faith, that is, in the abandonment of our whole selves and especially of that reasoning faculty, to him who loves us without reason (fortunately for us!) and who desires that we do the same.

(Letter to Euphrasie Cosnard, 23 January 1832)

He delighted fully, and without any mental reservations, in the gift of God, showing how to leave for the morrow the worries which could have devoured him. In Dom Guéranger, there was never anything careless, forgetful, or frivolous; it was the vigour of his confidence in God that worked this prodigy. He used to say that we do not have the grace to bear the cross as a future prospect and that if we knew how to master our imagination in this regard our soul would be one hundred times stronger. He practised this himself and remained calm and peaceful in the hands of his Master: "Let the day's own trouble be sufficient for the day" (Matt. 6:34).

(Abbess Cécile Bruyère on Dom Guéranger in her Notes)

Faith is the beginning of our salvation; by it we come into contact with God. Without it we should remain in darkness; if our faith is lively we are full of light; if it is weak then our entire soul becomes languid. Thus the Apostle says, "Without faith it is impossible to please God" (Heb. 11:6).... Aspire constantly after supernatural things, and strive to appreciate and judge all things from the standpoint of faith alone. It is that of God himself, who has mercifully placed his own light within our reach to prevent our minds from going astray and our nature from falling into error....

Faith must be our element, our nourishment, our joy, our delight; for it is first and principally through faith that God communicates himself to us and makes our life partake of heaven.

The life of those docile to grace will be gradually opened to the divine light, and all things will appear under a new aspect. The world and this present life will be transformed in their sight. They will clearly see the all-in-all of God and the nothingness of the creature. The goodness of God, the honour and happiness in renouncing one's self for him, the insignificance of the sacrifices involved in following him will be revealed to them and fill them with contentment and a holy liberty of spirit....

Let it be understood that the faith so necessary to us does not consist merely in that intellectual conviction of the truth of Christianity acquired by study and experience. It is true that we must employ our intelligence to the degree granted by God to ground our unshakeable conviction on the facts of divine revelation and on the reality of the mysteries by means of which God has deigned to put himself in contact with us; but it is easy to see that in practice this faith is not sufficient to sanctify us. The devils and the damned have this faith and it neither saves nor converts them. It is the virtue of faith, not the more or less learned deductions of doctors, that converts and saves. Christians believe because they will to believe, because they are humble before God, because they know that God imparts his light to the simple of heart, and that the faith of the intellect remains barren when it is no longer the faith of the heart....

Finding us, then, united by the bond of sincere submission to his Spouse, the divine Saviour will diffuse in us this spirit of faith that will become a reservoir of all graces, the source of a supernatural enlightenment that will guide and confirm us in all things, and prepare us to behold for all eternity and without cloud, that indescribable light whose faintest rays we shall have prized so dearly even in this world.

(Règlement du Noviciat, 1856)

Faith is a light intended not only to shine before us; it ought likewise to guide our steps and lead us to another virtue essential to the Christian, the goodness of hope. Without this virtue, the Christian does not exist. But he whose soul abounds in hope can truly by said to be on the way that leads to his end. Hope is that supernatural and unshakeable trust in God, that he will graciously bring us to a happy eternity, provided we profit by his grace, and that he will always grant us his grace in proportion to our needs, provided we ask for it in humility.

Strive to realize that the goodness of God toward his creatures, being infinite and manifested by works of the most sublime mercy, demands this confidence in him, by which we render him justice. The power of this sentiment is such that the Apostle does not hesitate to say that the Christian "is already saved by hope" (Rom. 8:24).... Assured on the one hand of the all-powerful goodness of God who delights in saving and sanctifying his creatures and leading them to eternal happiness, and convinced, on the other hand, that humble and confident prayer obtains all things from the heavenly bounty, you will feel the happiness of hope the more you become little before God. This virtue will procure for you a joyful heart, interior sweetness, a most profound peace, the anticipated possession of the infinite happiness which awaits you, and finally, the courage to conquer self in all things; and enlightened by faith, you will approach nearer to God, whom you are called to possess by love.

(Règlement du Noviciat)

I should like to see something a little more personal in "charity toward one's neighbour." God doesn't exist on his own, and we haven't completely done our duty toward our neighbour if we only love God in his creature. We must also love that creature who is our sister and whose company will be one of our joys in heaven. Let us be more simple and more devoted—we will lose nothing.

(Letter to a Carmelite prioress)

The Lord, says Sirach (17:14), "gave commandment to each of them concerning his neighbour." The monastic life brings us near to God in devotion and love; so monks, entering into the spirit of their vocation, should be carried away by a holy zeal for the welfare of their neighbour, which is the great and eternal preoccupation of God, for which end he delivered up even his own Son. Let no one imagine that the monastic life consists exclusively in working out our own perfection, regardless of the sanctification of our neighbour. Let us rather bear in mind that the good works performed in the Church affect the entire mystical body of Jesus Christ through the communion of saints. Accordingly, the intentions of each one of the faithful ought to extend beyond his own person.

(Règlement du Noviciat)

The love of God is the whole Christian life. The other moral and theological virtues only prepare us for and lead us to the love of God. St Augustine says, "Love and do what you will." He who truly loves God is safe against sin, because sin is contrary to the love of God. To love God is the easiest and sweetest of all the commandments, though it is just the one that is violated most frequently and imperceptibly. Love of God brings us into the possession of God himself. It is by love that heaven is heaven. It is the prime necessity of our being, because we can be happy only in loving the good, and this is God. This love is a holy debt, because God loved us first, continually works in us by his love, and awaits with generous patience the return we owe him.... Let us act in all things with the conviction that, as

Christians and religious, we have a lofty and all-embracing duty to fulfill in this world, namely the duty of loving God before all things and continually, with a love proportionate to the grace bestowed on us for the purpose of loving him.

(Règlement du Noviciat)

Notes

1. St Augustine, *Confessions*, Book I, 1.

2. Cited in Dom Savaton's Life of *Dom Delatte*, pp. 300-01. No date is given.

3. The vessel used for exposing the Blessed Sacrament for veneration.

CHAPTER SEVEN

"That my joy may be in you" (John 15:11):

Fullness of Joy

"It is a remarkable religion in which joy is a precept," remarked Dom Delatte, "in which the command is to be happy, in which cheerfulness is duty." The message of Christianity may be summed up in "joy"; it is part of God's revelation to us in Christ. The Gospel story begins and ends in joy. It is "good news of great joy" and "peace on earth" (Luke 2:10, 14), and peace and joy are often interchangeable terms for the ultimate blessing of salvation, summed up in Abbess Cécile Bruyère's use of the word "beatitude." Joy is the distinguishing atmosphere of the Christian life, "the perfect expression of the soul consecrated to God" (Abbess Cécile Bruyère), "the normal, persevering attitude of the baptized" (Dom Delatte). There is no virtue, no circumstance, no occasion that is not to be illumined by joy. "Be alleluia from head to toe," Dom Guéranger used to tell his monks. A joyless life for the Christian is even a kind of blasphemy for Dom Delatte.

Christian joy springs from the fact that "we are so rich, so saturated with God," as Abbess Cécile puts it. In creating and reconciling the world through his Son, God has given us everything, himself. And the writers suggest that through joy we open ourselves to that transcendent realm which is God, "because it lives in that part of us where God reigns and dwells" (Dom Guéranger). Christians have been given joy, as they have been given faith, hope, love, and peace. They have been given reconciliation with God and the fruits of the Spirit. Christian joy, then, is both a gift and a responsibility, an act of virtue, and adoration. Christians are called to live in joy and to communicate joy, the joy of communion in the one body of Christ, the joy of believing, joy in the midst of suffering, joy in spite of suffering. Joy, they insist, is not something determined by our state of mind or situation; it lies deeper than happiness or unhappiness, pleasure or pain. The *raison d'être* of the Christian's joy is to be sought elsewhere, at the point where the finite opens out onto the infinite.

Dom Prosper Guéranger

I fear that the sight of your weakness is making too great an impression on you; God's mercy is infinitely greater than your weakness and poverty. Whenever sadness becomes dominant in the spirit in such a way as to produce discouragement and melancholy, that is no longer compunction, which is gentle, calm, and confident. So what is it? It is a little touch of self-love, combined with the physical state we are in at the time. Nothing else. Therefore we must shake it off, and make an effort to be cheerful. Cheerfulness takes courage, as does everything else; and it is for God that we must overcome ourselves in this way. "Rejoice in the Lord always; again I will say, Rejoice" (Phil. 4:4).... We must pull the ground out from under the feet of that melancholy that is no good for either this world or the next.

(Letter to Dom Piolin, one of his monks, 29 May 1843)

If I were St Francis de Sales I should tell you that God requires that you be charitable toward yourself; certainly not that natural indulgence which is mere cowardice, but real charity, which is entirely compassionate and supernatural.... Meditate on this phrase of the Saviour: "Let no one take away your joy, your peace" (cf John 16:22). That means there is a joy, a peace in us that must never be shaken, by no circumstance, because it lives in that part of us where God reigns and dwells. God is peace, joy, and happiness. Our troubles should never penetrate to that region we have reserved for him. We must always find rest, calm, and happiness, even when everything else is agitated, submerged, unsettled. We have only one task on this earth: to overcome ourselves, to become masters of ourselves, so that our whole soul, in harmony like a first-class piano, can play music worthy of the One who has made us.

(Letter to Euphrasie Cosnard, 30 August 1831)

I often ask for you from Our Lady that deep and sweet peace which comes from an undivided love. That is the hundred-fold promised to those who have left everything to follow Jesus Christ. Keep that peace bravely within yourself, and watch that the enemy never takes it away from you, even for a minute. That peace is the element in which those who belong to God dwell; but if possessing it is a grace, preserving it is a virtue. That is why I often ask God to give it to you; he is so good that he rewards you for preserving your peace. As if peace were not the greatest happiness!

(Letter to one of his monks, 28 May 1843)

We must possess a persevering joy, but to acquire it we must be detached from ourselves. One is only ill-humoured if one is in some way attached to oneself. As far as it depends on us, we must push away the cloud; otherwise, wait with patience. But above all, we must not consider our own will to be of any importance, for it will betray us; there is no fault that does not originate in self-will.

(Quoted by Abbess Cécile Bruyère in her Portrait of Dom Guéranger, October 1867)

It is above all in the matter of gratitude that our heart will always be behind with God.

(Letter to Madame Swetchine, 7 December 1833)

Your sorrows, your anxieties, whose mysteries I sincerely respect, touch me deeply, as you can imagine; and so it makes me very happy to learn that in the midst of all these God has been for you what he always is for those who seek him: calm and rest.... Indeed, why are there unhappy people on earth? People who suffer—God desires that, and he has loving reasons for it;

but unhappy people? However, it is a sad fact; and we are so deeply embedded in the senses, which are so evil, that when it happens that we are, to some extent, in order, we owe an immense debt of gratitude to God; for order is not natural to us except through grace. God is so good to us! I assure you that I understand the Church when she teaches us that in this life man cannot *habitually* love God for himself. The fact is that the gifts of God are so many, so varied, and applied to all our needs with such delicate profusion, that our poor hearts—even those of the saints—under such pressure of gratitude, cannot always find that leisure, that rest, which is called love. The time will come when we will be able to love and give thanks at the same time, to the same degree, and at all times; but that is because we shall be consummated in God and be one and the same thing with him.

(Letter to Madame Swetchine, 6 May 1834)

Receive gladly the peace which our Lord sends you. *Pax vobis*. Realize that this peace is near to you, that it is only a question of enjoying it. Delight in it, in all security and without anxiety. You know that anxiety leads nowhere. What am I saying? That it distances you from God by clouding the heart, whereas peace, by creating rest in the soul, can in all events only draw near to God. Thus you will have peace. Strive to work to establish it, to nourish it; it is not by the head and by reasoning that it finds an entry, but rather by way of the heart and will. Don't think, therefore, that it will follow on an examination of one's troubles. Ah! If, to experience this sweet peace, it were necessary beforehand to judge whether we merit it, what mortal would dare give it entry into his heart? "If thou, O Lord, shouldst mark iniquities, Lord, who could stand?" (Ps. 129 [130]:3). But no, we can surrender ourselves to this peace since we cannot live without it, because we have need of God, because we desire to love him despite our unworthiness. And God who is much more lovable than he is terrible, will rejoice that we have understood him so well; he will love us still more.

(2 March 1832)

Abbess Cécile Bruyère

The measure of our faith is the measure of our joy.

* * * * *

The secret of joy, of security in the supernatural life, is to centre one's attention upon God rather than on oneself.

* * * * *

Goodness, and a fully-developed soul, manifest themselves by joy. The longer I live, and the older I grow, the more clearly I see that joy is the most perfect expression of a soul consecrated to God. The closeness of God is manifested in this blossoming of the soul, this agreeable and simple manner. For the Lord, who is himself severe at times, does not wish us to behave severely. Do you want to praise God perfectly, and to give him pleasing homage? Be resolutely joyful in the midst of everything. Repulse any element of sadness that might tend to insinuate itself into you. That atmosphere of joy should become the habit, the ordinary impetus of your soul. Rejoice, not because things are pleasant, but because it is God who sends them.

(Letter, 1899)

To greet with a smile all God's ways whatever they may be is certainly the most tender expression of love.

* * * * *

We are so rich, so saturated with God, that all our misery can come only from lack of awareness. We possess everything, and it is real ingratitude to behave as if we had not the slightest suspicion of that fact.

(Letter, 6 March 1891)

Come, let us talk for a moment of the ways by which you can always increase in love, that is to say, true perfection.

The One to whom you are united is the source of all beatitude; you cannot touch him, enter into contact with him, without peace, calm, serenity and joy flooding your soul. Your will, which is the point at which you cleave to God, must hold itself so firm that nothing can dislodge you from him. Sometimes God holds you close to himself and then his grip detaches you from all things and yourself; but often he holds you without clasping you, as if to say, "Go away, if you like." But you must never desire to leave him who truly fills you with joy and makes you *beatus*: there is nothing more perfect than being with him.

Serenity is, then, a barometer which directs you accurately, enabling you to gauge whether, through all the ups and downs of life, you are faithful in most perfect love. A serene soul is truly detached, pure, and poor with true poverty. This interior serenity is more a matter of will than you might think.... It is the condition of whole-hearted fidelity. For by it, all self-love, pride, ill-regulated passions are overcome. It gives God complete sway over the soul, which one escapes when one is agitated, even over good things. Serenity preserves right judgement, for the eye of the soul is continuously clear; whereas agitation stirs up dust so that one cannot see the truth. Serenity keeps the light of faith from flickering; it keeps the anchor of a generous hope firmly fixed in the ocean of eternity; it manifests that divine love always gives God first place and that all will be well, since God does not change, that he is always himself, always great and beautiful. Serenity enables us to serve our neighbour as the angels do, without passion or personal interest, with wonderful devotion, free of all egoism.

What more can I say? This willed serenity, the fruit of our union with God, allows us to offer back to God, pure and unalloyed, every suffering he sends; for then the suffering will be like that of Our Lord and Our Lady, endured for us.

But how do we keep this serenity when we, through weakness, commit some slight imperfection or are surprised by some venial sin? Isn't it legitimate to be sad about that?—Yes, if you have consented *willingly* to turn away from God, even in a small matter. But if it was by surprise or awkwardness, a failing unforeseen and promptly made good, then we must hold fast to a valiant, confident, resolute serenity. It is easy to understand

why. These involuntary imperfections, these inevitable surprises, are put right by our very union with God. Now as the
union is expressed by serenity, to hold fast to serenity is to
return to this union and to cast into the divine fire the dust that
was clinging to us. This is to flee the commotion and trouble
which sever our union, to cut away self-love at its root, to
practise a generous humility that never seeks self-satisfaction, to
practise patience: "In your patience you shall possess your souls"
(Lk. 21:19; Douay). In this way, we imitate the suppleness of a
branch which springs back into place when no longer pressed
down by some weight. This is to practise simplicity by involving nothing human, no resentment, in our regret at having
weakened. The serene person sees her imperfection just as it is,
but she knows that regret for such things is expressed above all
by more exact and more perfect fidelity. The serene person is
strong, mistress of herself, magnaminous, persevering.

This serenity is often indicated in Holy Scripture: "Sing joyfully to God, all the earth" (Ps. 97[98]: 4).... "Rejoice in the
Lord" (Phil. 4:4). All the *beati, beatus* express nothing other
than this state in which the soul does not merely practise virtue
but practises it with serenity; does not merely endure trial but
sees it coming with unflappable serenity, which has union with
God as its source. It is probably in this sense that joy is given as
a fruit of the Holy Spirit. We know nothing about joy or
happiness if we do not understand this way of serenity, so well
expressed in the sentence: "A secure mind is like a continual
feast" (Prov. 15:15; Douay).

The devil fears this serenity more than anything else, for it
unsaddles him as nothing else does, and he strives perseveringly
against it. There's no doubt that many of his ambushes have no
other purpose than to unsettle the soul on this point by suggest-
ing the most specious reasons for abandoning it. But with a bit
of practice, the soul comes to realize that, as soon as she gives
way on this point, she loses half her strength, and that the
exterior attacks of the enemy pierce more deeply. The first dyke
has been broken, the waters flood in, confusing everything if the
breach is not closed up....

If the devil suspects that we will easily lose that serenity which he dreads, on account of these little accidents, he will find a way of multiplying them around us, not for their own sakes but for the sadness they bring; for that, being the real imperfection, is just what he wants.

(Letter, Christmas Octave, 1897)

Dom Paul Delatte

Gaudium.... Why joy? We have just noted that love consists in finding one's own happiness in the happiness of the one whom one loves. And so loving God is finding one's happiness in the happiness, the joy, of God; it is, therefore, possessing complete and total joy, for God is immutably happy. The normal, persevering attitude of a baptized person is the high noon of joy; those who belong to God, who live by God, are given over to joy. Since we are with the Lord, and he with us, how do you expect our life not to be a life of joy, of exultation? Ah! If we are really with the Lord Jesus, then there is inevitably joy, hope.... Peace for the present, hope for the future, and as the fruit, joyfulness, happiness, perfect joy. Now, that joy is a fruit of the whole supernatural life, an exercise of the theological virtues. Of faith, because we are here in the sphere of the invisible, of the revealed, and the motive for our joy is entirely in the order of faith; of hope, because in us joy proceeds from the beginning of possession, a participation here and now in the promise; of charity, because of the presence of God and the plenitude that is in him. For the love of goodwill, which is real love, rejoices at the wealth and the plenitude of the beloved object, even if we do not yet ourselves possess it in its entirety.

(Commentary on Psalm 1)

Establish yourself firmly in peace and supernatural joy. It gives honour to God, as I have often said, if those who belong to him are liberated from all suffering, or at least from all inconsolable suffering. I don't think there is a single one that, submerged in him, does not turn into joy. He is faithful. We are his; he is ours. Our eternity has begun. On the surface it appears that the years change, that they succeed one another; but we are already carrying our portion of eternity in the treasury of our faith and our charity. We may not be unchangeable, but we are attached to the One who is unchangeable, and we live in his light. Everything is self-explanatory to us, and we know that we are travelling toward eternal love. *A Dieu.*[1]

(Letter to Émilie Butruille, 29 December 1898)[2]

For us, to be happy is an act of virtue. It is also an act of adoration, because it bears witness to the fact that God, who belongs to us, is everything to us…. Whenever anything troubles us, wounds us, turns us away from God, we should say, "It's nothing." We should not affirm anything but God. To deny thus the things that are in any way hostile to him is to deny and to renounce ourselves. And if you would like to make a little attempt at this spirituality of calm and perfect serenity, you will soon discover how effective it is.

(Letter to a nun of Sainte-Cécile, 7 May 1913)

I believe that the most complete, the most profound, and the most filial homage that we can pay to God in the course of our supernatural life is quite simply to be happy in his presence, in a joyfulness that nothing can alter, that nothing can disconcert. The tenor of our entire life should show God that there can be no sadness where he is.

(Cited in Via Clarescente)[3]

Sadness, as you can see, has something blasphemous about it. To know that the supernatural life is all that we have just said it is, and to have so little heart as to allow oneself to fall into any kind of sadness in the midst of these divine splendours! Joy is the blossoming of our soul in the purity, in the light, of God.

(Cited in Via Clarescente)

Peace is, at times, silence. Then the gift of God no longer has a name in any language. It is an absolute tranquillity, a joyful

availability of one's life, the elimination of passions, of all violence. I call it, with reason, "a joyful availability of soul," as if
the soul had become totally supple, total docility in order to
receive the impulsion, the movement of God; it is a disposition
whereby the soul lends itself to every divine action.

(Commentary on Hebrews 12:14)

Pax, peace, is order, self-abandonment, supporting oneself quietly and gently on God as if we were resting on his heart, where
nothing can touch us because we are in his arms. Peace implies
the idea of a perfect connection, of two things closely united,
linked, leaning one upon the other; of two spiritual beings so
intimately united that no human effort is able to separate them.
Pax Dei, the peace of God: it isn't a calm one feels, nor a state of
soul one perceives, nor a psychological disposition in which one
might succeed in establishing oneself. It is not only the peace
that comes from God, it is the peace that is God. One should
translate *Pax* as "Deus"—"for he is our peace" (Eph. 2:14).

(Conference, 1909)

"All this I tell you that my joy may be yours and your joy may
be complete" (John 15:11). It seems that the Lord is joyful, and
this joy at the moment when the Lord is speaking to us, has a
particular character: in a few hours, he will be on Calvary. And
yet there is joy in the heart of the Lord; he says, "my joy." That
is an instruction: I think it is a duty for each one of us to be
joyful. It is a remarkable religion in which joy is a precept, in
which the command is to be happy, in which cheerfulness is a
duty.

(Conference on John 15, 1902)

Notes

1. See Chapter 2, note 4.

2. Émilie Butruille, a sister of several monks and nuns of Solesmes, entered
the Abbey of Notre Dame, Wisques in 1907, dying three years later in 1910.

3. *Via Clarescente*, an unpublished *florilegia* compiled at the Abbey of Wisques
(see Preface).

CHAPTER EIGHT

"To you I lift up my eyes" (Ps. 122):

The Life of Prayer

To forget ourselves, and to live in habitual recollection, zealously
to plunge our souls into the very beauty of the mysteries, is to be
interested in every aspect of the supernatural economy according
to the inspiration of the Spirit of God who alone can teach us to
pray. The words of God, of the saints, as we repeat them over and
over again and enter more deeply into their meaning, have a
supreme grace to deliver the soul sweetly from preoccupation
with itself in order to charm it and introduce it into the very
mystery of God and of his Christ. Once we are there, we have
only to look and love in all simplicity.[1]

This text from Dom Guéranger contains the whole programme
of Solesmes' approach to prayer, in all its freedom, simplicity,
and breadth, nourished on Scriptures and the liturgy, the mysteries of the faith and the living word of the Church. Following
monastic tradition, it is a way of prayer in which sacred reading,
reflective meditation, vocal prayer and contemplative prayer all
have their place and are part of a continuous whole, in which
these various forms of prayer are not only means to an end but
contain something of the nature of an end.[2] It is a prayer that
knows no conflict between "active prayer" and "prayer of simplicity," between public prayer and personal prayer, between
liturgy and contemplation. "One of the most beautiful books
on mental prayer and contemplation that has been written,"
affirm Jacques and Raïssa Maritain, "is by an author whose
whole life was consecrated to the *opus Dei*—Madame Cécile
Bruyère, Abbess of Sainte-Cécile de Solesmes."[3]

Solesmes' devotion to the sacred liturgy, then, in no way
sacrifices contemplation; for these writers, contemplation is part
of the liturgy in the fullest sense. The liturgy, which Dom

Delatte calls "organized contemplation," is the Church's contemplation, the song of the Spouse to her Bridegroom as she gazes on him. The liturgy itself asks the faithful to tend toward contemplation, to cultivate interior recollection, and to practise loving attention to God; and participation in liturgical life is one of the best preparations for union with God by contemplation. "For the contemplative," writes Dom Guéranger in his *Liturgical Year*, "liturgical prayer is sometimes the source, sometimes the result of the Lord's visits." The worship rendered to God by the Church is an exterior worship, but it is also, as Abbess Cécile Bruyère insists, a worship in spirit and in truth, in which the interior movement of souls and the work of divine grace are of the utmost importance. For Solesmes, the liturgy is the great school of prayer, comprehending the whole prayer life of the Church and of all Christians. Dom Guéranger never used the expression "private" prayer; for him, Christians always pray as members of the body of Christ and of the communion of saints.

Our very capacity for prayer begins with the Trinity. "The first move," writes Dom Delatte, "can only come from God. For the spirit of man to adapt himself to conditions which are so new, it is necessary for God to show himself as Father, for us to belong to the Son, and to be guided by the Holy Spirit." Prayer acknowledges that we are children of God; it is because we are children that we are able to pray. Prayer, then, is a privilege, a miracle of God's love granted to his children, giving them access to him through his Son in the Spirit "who alone can teach us to pray." "The precept of prayer can only be given," Dom Delatte adds, "because God reveals himself to us as the centre, the focal point, the ocean of all graces." Thus praying Christians, by virtue of their baptism, do not have to strive laboriously to enter a region alien to them;[4] when they pray, they enter into the truth of their existence, which is not their truth, but God's.

Prayer leads us into the depths of revealed truths, what Dom Delatte calls "true mysticism." If God has revealed himself in the Incarnation, the Redemption, the Eucharist, the Church, then dogma is necessarily part of Christian prayer. Far from being barriers to contemplative prayer, these truths make prayer possible and "introduce us into the very mystery of God and of his Christ," as Dom Guéranger said above. Through meditation and contemplation, "the long, continuous, intentional gaze directed toward God," as Dom Delatte defines it, supernatural realities become "concrete and vivid"; they become the rich totality out of which our soul is nourished. Prayer, then, does not dissolve doctrinal formulas but renews itself on the entire objective world that is God's world, on every aspect of the supernatural economy. Prayer is the practical expression of our faith. "Doctrinal truth," writes Abbess Cécile Bruyère, "is the very root of our prayer."

From these texts we see that in prayer we should not look for a method or a system, but cultivate an attitude, a habit, a way of "looking": "we have only to look and love in all simplicity" (Dom Guéranger). This looking at God develops our sense of the supernatural, of the richness and mystery of God; conquers our persistent preoccupation with self; enlarges our horizons; expands our spirits. In such a prayer of adoring attentiveness, we allow ourselves to be transformed and transfigured: "By the very persistence of our inner gaze," writes Dom Delatte, "his beauty penetrates and transforms us." Dom Delatte reminds us that our primary duty in prayer is to receive, and that God acts on our life, gives himself, in proportion to our adoring love and humble receptiveness. In using this image of looking, Solesmes also shows a predeliction for the teaching of St Paul and St John, who both relate the idea of gazing with being children of God. Moreover, from this "looking" spring all the other dispositions of prayer: adoration, contrition, gratitude. And this prayer will transform our vision of the world, enabling the soul to "see all things in God, that is, in oneness; and it sees this oneness in all" (Abbess Cécile Bruyère, *The Spiritual Life and Prayer*).

Abbess Cécile Bruyère

Happy is the one who remains silent, in order to listen to nothing but God.

* * * *

To live the contemplative life is to reflect God in the depths of one's soul because one is ceaselessly gazing at him; and, while we look at him, he is imprinting himself upon our soul.

(Conferences)

Apostles, in order to work effectively, need to be great contemplatives. Everything begins to crumble when people desire action only. The conversion of a soul is, essentially, the work of God. If God must be the first to act, since, as the Church says, grace *praevenit et sequitur*,[5] then he must be the first object of our activity. The contemplatives decide God's side of the question. Once that is done, the rest is child's play. All the missionaries say so.

In any case, prayer is the first of the missionaries. When St Stephen was being stoned, Saul was there "approving his murder"; but the prayer of the deacon landed right on him and achieved what words had not achieved. And if there had been one St Paul fewer in the Church for the spreading of the gospel, that would have been quite something!

(Letter, 1890)

The spirit of prayer is the continuous acceptance of God's sovereignty over us and within us.

* * * * *

To make the Divine Office the whole of our prayer and suppress private prayer would render us absolutely impersonal. It is, indeed, a great mistake to isolate the individual, instead of making him a member of the one body that is the Church, but to absorb him into a great whole where he can no longer function personallly would be a sort of pantheism (I use too strong a word to make myself understood). I have as much a horror of that as I have of egoism. Truth lies in between the two. To reject personal prayer is, to my mind, to annihilate the human personality in a way that is both unlawful and dangerous. It is, moreover, quite contrary to Holy Scripture and tradition....

Personal prayer, I think, is absolutely necessary for creating and maintaining a continual tendency toward supernatural things and the awareness of their reality.

The Divine Office is the time for ideas, and in order to celebrate it perfectly, our intelligence must make an effort at the same time as our voice: *ut mens nostra concordet voci nostrae.*[6] But the time of private prayer is quite different. Then we must be willing to "sit down," like sheep which are grazing in a field, or like a dog which sits down at the feet of its master. To be with the Master, at his disposition, tranquil, even without ideas, as long as our will is wholly in accord with the Will of God—that is true prayer. We think we waste our time like that, but we are quite wrong. Think about the relations between people who love one another; it would be tiring to talk all the time; and to stay still, without a word, often expresses better the depth of their love. It is the same with God and especially with him, since he sees our most intimate thoughts. Simply place yourself before the divine Sun like a little daisy or sunflower. This may appear to be idleness but it is true contemplation.

(Letter, 1 May 1898)

"And he told them a parable, to the effect that they ought always to pray..." (Luke 18:1). This interior, wordless prayer is nothing other than a very simple exercise of charity.

Do you want to belong entirely to God? *Tu solus Dominus.* You alone are Lord. One must desire to belong to no one else but God, and everything follows. To live a contemplative life is nothing else but this intimacy extended to all our activities.

This atmosphere of prayer should penetrate our whole life, from the moment we wake until the moment we fall asleep; and even when we fall asleep, it is in the arms of God; it is a continuous prayer, and even when it seems that everything sleeps, this prayer penetrates our whole being, just as incense penetrates the objects that receive it; its perfume remains on the altar in the flowers and the vestments. That is a good image of the perfume of prayer which a nun should exude. One doesn't achieve that ceaseless prayer of one's whole being by means of the effort of one's brain, but by the harmony of one's will with that of God, by the unconditional handing over of one's life to him.

To hand oneself over to God means to say: "Lord, take me; guide me; protect me." So often in the Psalms we call God "*susceptor*," or else we ask him to take us under the shelter of his wings. That is the true atmosphere of prayer; it is not a specific act; it is a state one calls forth in oneself by seeking it constantly, by ceaselessly returning to it.

(Letter)

A soul should never absent itself from God, since he never absents himself from us.

* * * * *

We musn't be surprised that God should desire to be actively addressed in prayer, in order to admit his rational creatures to close union with him; for that is both the final end of his works and the guarantee of the supernatural prosperity of the Church. Let those who love the Church ponder that for a moment. If they wish to work for her, the most effective way of doing so is to possess the knowledge of the saints, and to be able, through it, to bring pressure to bear upon the centre at which human events unroll. It is thanks to that powerful intervention that Moses won battles for his people: "Whenever Moses held up his hands, Israel prevailed" (Exod. 17:11).

Holiness of life and the spirit of prayer achieve everything in the world; and when the Lord does not find that element on this earth, he bewails it as if he could no longer exercise his mercy. It is in these terms that he speaks to Ezekiel: "And I sought for a man among them who should build up the wall and stand in the breach before me for the land, that I should not destroy it; but I found none" (Ezek. 22:30). That is certainly the secret behind many revolutions among empires. One can understand, then, that private interest as well as social interest call for an increase in the number of souls truly united with God. Undoubtedly such an increase is a grace; but, once again, it is nonetheless promised to prayer that is ardent and generous.

(The Spiritual Life and Prayer)

Prayer has no boundaries or, better, a soul that abides in God can reach all things.

* * * * *

You must not become tense during prayer, but relax and be at rest.

* * * * *

You can find our Lord everywhere, and there is no prayer so valuable as renouncing one's own will.

(Conference, 25 March 1884)

In the work of our transformation, and the way to accomplish it in its entirety, there is one condition, without which one can attain only to a merely philosophical or human perfection, quite inadequate for a creature called to a supernatural state. That essential condition is prayer. Just as the face-to-face vision of God establishes the soul in the possession of the Good and in perfection, so our prayer, our attitude of soul before God in the course of this life, creates in us a determined direction, a supernatural impetus, according to the measure of its intensity. It is not for us to choose our own ways of arriving at supernatural perfection; to pray or not to pray is not a matter of choice in attaining this end. On the contrary, nothing is more important than prayer, as we learn from certain sayings of the saints, words which, at first sight, seem to be merely pious exaggerations, although they are strictly true.

Doubtless, the choice of such and such a method of prayer is of secondary importance; but the practice of faith, the persevering search for union with God, cannot be neglected without real detriment to the soul. One cannot seriously strive after perfection without taking some means of knowing the divine pattern according to which we are to be shaped. "Look and make according to the pattern shown you on the mountain" (Exod. 25:40). It is in this sense that Psalm 44 says: "Hearken, O daughter, and see" (Ps. 44[45]:11; Douay). Indeed, faith comes first by hearing, then it enables us to see the truth by a light of its own which penetrates intellect and will. In this world our relationship with God cannot stop at pure formality; our hearts must really turn toward him, through the impetus given by our intelligence; we must rediscover the secret of that intimate conversation with the Lord which Adam knew in paradise.

In view of all this, it is interesting to note how the study of dogmatic theology transforms the soul much more effectively than the study of moral theology. Distinguished missionaries have observed this in the case of their pagan converts. The study of dogma transforms profoundly, raising the soul to the highest regions and showing it the pattern of what is true, good and beautiful.

Thus we cannot be too strongly encouraged to study to know God in order to be transformed, and to have little regard for what is commonly known as "blind and simple faith."

In an age like ours when people strive indiscriminately to learn everything, know everything, penetrate everything, how can they leave behind the queen and mistress of all the sciences, that which throws its light on all the others? How can Christians neglect the only study that makes for the real advancement of the soul, to cultivate exclusively the knowledge of things around them? The knowledge of God is necessary for our intellectual and spiritual progress. There are certain weaknesses and failings which this knowledge does away with altogether; the soul makes room within itself, sets itself in order, when it knows the God from whom the moral law comes, and who promulgates it within the soul by conscience and the Church.

If knowledge of doctrinal truth is so necessary, it is because it is the very root of prayer and the safeguard against many illusions of the imagination, the corrective to pious daydreaming and false mysticism. It is really presumptuous to expect, by an immediate light from God, that knowledge, when we can and ought to acquire it for ourselves as part of our work in this world. To stop deliberately at the vague notions about the truth into which our baptism has initiated us is culpable laziness. God may be waiting for the work done in the sweat of one's brow before completing by his grace the measure of knowledge necessary for the development of the supernatural life within us. For infused knowledge has two forms: either it teaches what is unknown, or it can enlarge and make fruitful what the mind has already acquired by study.

The "sublime ignorance" of which theologians speak has nothing in common with ordinary ignorance: the former disdains one kind of knowledge for a higher, whereas the latter cannot disdain what it does not possess. It remains true that, as long as God himself does not directly intervene to instruct us, one of our principal duties is to cultivate in our minds those truths which he has revealed to us and without which no intimacy can be formed with him. "If you continue in my word, you are truly my disciples, and you will know the truth, and the truth will make you free" (John 8:31-2).

Our freedom, then, is bound up with the truth, the truth known and lived, which will put right all our imperfections, reverse all our failings, correct all our faults, as the Church teaches us in this prayer:

"O God, who, through communion in this venerable sacrifice, hast made us partake of the one supreme Godhead: grant, we beseech thee, that, having come to the knowledge of thy truth, we may obtain it by a worthy life."[7]

Personal prayer brings the soul into direct contact with God and is the way we will become perfectly likened to that divine principle which is to transform us and make us worthy to enter the eternal dwelling places.

(The Spiritual Life and Prayer)

Dom Paul Delatte

What do you mean by saying, "Prayer is absent"? I don't believe it. There is a prayer of attitude, which is worth more than all the formal prayers; it seems to me that prayers that are definite and of a tangible form are all summed up in a direction, an attitude of one's life. Movement tends toward rest, words toward silence, acts toward being; and our soul is made up of its works. Where there is faith and the cultivation of faith, prayer is always alive. Peace has that character when it is deep-seated. Ask yourself whether, at the moment when the soul seems to be totally indolent, it would not spontaneously move toward any work or any sacrifice demanded of it by God. Well then! The depths are tranquil and therefore remain unperceived.

(Letter)[8]

I have been thinking about your problem. I really do think that one can create a turn of mind—no, of soul—that carries us toward God. I think that habit makes us turn back to him as soon as our thoughts cease to be unavoidably occupied elsewhere. There are certain flowers that turn with the sun.

However, we musn't expect such a disposition to be created in an instant. It may happen quickly, but God likes us to have some of the credit for what he accomplishes in us. He appreciates our efforts. The frequent acts that create in us first a habit, a need, and after the need a real necessity, these acts are movements of perfect charity that give God too great a joy for him to deny them to himself even for the sake of an excessively rapid accomplishment. More than four-fifths of the work is done as soon as we manage to grasp that, for us, there is nothing but him in the world. We must tell him so, and we are not forbidden to tell him so with tears. Then it is a good thing—without any singularity—to love to be silent, to love to hear nothing, to love to see nothing. Then it will happen, little by little, in the same way as we grew up. And yet it happens quickly; I promise you that it does happen, my child, and that our soul is already awakened to true realities.

(Letter to a young nun, 3 August 1903)

In his treatises on the states of prayer, in particular the ones that were not written out but only sketched, one can see clearly that Bossuet's single thought—and it is a magnificent one—was to demonstrate that the prayer of beginners, the prayer of those who are making progress, and the prayer of the perfect are nothing other than the exercise of faith, hope, and charity, of the three virtues that belong specifically to the Christian life and that unite us to God. In every prayer, this is what I intend to say: "O God, I think as you do, I receive with joy every part of your thought on this, or on that, and on everything you have thought good to tell me." Faith consists in making our thought an image of that of God; hope, in making our will an image of that of God, in time and in eternity; our charity consists in loving as God loves, and for the same ends. And in never giving the lie by our lives to any part of what we say to God in our prayer. To speak to him as one speaks to a person who is present, and to take up before him the attitude he desires, one can always make use of the gospel, which is itself the thought, and the promise, and the tenderness of God, and speak to him as one talks to a friend.

(Letter to a young girl, 17 March 1905)

We must keep our whole soul assiduously held in the contemplation of this beauty (the glory and the perfection of the Lord). What a sweet marvel! As long as we have consented to the required renunciations, that beauty of the Lord, which is so attractive, is also active. Through the assiduity of our interior gaze, it penetrates and transfigures us. It is said that certain types of marble reach the point, after a long period, of fixing the light within themselves and becoming phosphorescent under the action of the sun. Our souls are not as hard as marble.

(Commentary on 2 Corinthians 3:18)

Look, but look with all your eyes and all your soul; look in the same way as Raphael's little angels, submerged in the light. The supernatural beauty on which we set our eyes with so much love enters into us little by little, penetrates and transfigures us. Face to face with the light we become light. We are deified and come to resemble more and more the One whose glory we contemplate.

(Retreat, 1899)

Let us keep our eyes fixed on those realities that cannot be seen: "we look not to the things that are seen but to the things that are unseen" (2 Cor. 4:18). My desire would be that that should be engraved at the centre of your life. It is impossible to gaze upon God without being transformed into him. Every kind of cowardice, of laxness, disappears; in the supernatural life, everything is done in a most efficacious way to the extent that we consent to gaze upon God. This constant company draws us to imitate the beauty on which we gaze: "seek the things that are above" (Col. 3:1).

(Commentary on 2 Corinthians 4:18)

Contemplation is not study, not reflection, not a specific act of prayer; it is often done with no definite thought, no precise emotion; it is rather a concern, a preoccupation, an occupation, a contact, a muffled awareness of the supernatural realities that are around us, within us; a long, continuous, and intentional gaze directed toward God. And the supernatural realities, instead of being distant and abstract as they once were, become concrete and vivid. They make up our society, the atmosphere of our thought. There is no effort; it is a general attitude of our life. Indeed, it is so natural that the soul returns to it in a certain sense by its own weight, as if to its centre, as soon as it ceases to be called upon from without by duty or by charity.

(Notes on the Spiritual Life)

The precept of prayer can only be given to us because God reveals himself to us as the centre, the focal point, the source, the ocean of all graces. "Every good endowment and every perfect gift is from above, coming down from the Father of lights" (James 1:17). So we only have to ask: "in everything by prayer and supplication with thanksgiving, let your requests be made known to God" (Phil. 4:6). Do you need something? Stretch out your hand. That is all you have to do. If you feel the lack of this or that, ask, ask. If you think it is urgent, ask with still greater insistence.... We don't pray. I believe that we don't ask, that that is our mistake, and also the reason for the ineffectiveness of certain prayers. When we need something, our first thought, our first idea, is to find help in human skill; while the first disposition of every soul, when it feels itself to be poor, should be to turn toward infinite riches and stretch out its hands: "Truly I say to you, if you have faith and never doubt, you will not only do what has been done to the fig tree, but even if you say to this mountain, 'Be taken up and cast into the sea,' it will be done" (Matt. 21:22). And the Lord adds: "And whatever you ask in prayer, you will receive, if you have faith." An interesting comment on the efficacy of confident prayer. It is not only the Son of God, it is also all those who, relying on him, address themselves to God with confidence and without hesitation, whose prayer will be granted by him. You will obtain from God what you ask of him with confidence. God is a Father to you; no one is so much a Father to you, and you have only to stretch out your hand.

(Cited in Domus Orationis)[9]

There is nothing that obliges us to ask for a great deal in the supernatural order so much as awareness of the infinite tenderness of God. For, if we do not ask for the infinite, it will always seem to him as if something were lacking in our prayer. Our prayer, when it is addressed to God, is never complete unless we ask for God himself.

(Domus Orationis)

There is nothing that transforms souls like the truth. The truth transfigures us. Certain texts of St Paul say it all: "We are being transformed from glory to glory" (2 Cor. 3:18). It is a transformation by light; the Lord works through his doctrine. The truth changes us.

(Retreat, 1894)

The work of the intelligence is not to dig in like a drill, to push ever further, to make one's instrument produce all sorts of new sounds, to make the strings vibrate. The truth is a satisfying food, and God enlightens the soul that can see better because it possesses a truth it loves.[10]

"We will devote ourselves to prayer and to the ministry of the word" (Acts 6:4). It is unbelievable how much light certain passages of Scripture contain to determine what one might call the hierarchy of our duties. What is the origin of God's victories? Agitation? Oh, no! Their origin is calm, silence, prayer. I believe that we are never more powerful than when we address ourselves directly to God. Note that even when it is a question of preaching the gospel, the apostles give the first place to prayer, and so we too will attend firstly to prayer, and we will persevere in that prayer. There we have the lever which suffices to shift the inertia of the world; we have the all-powerful instrument for gaining all the victories of God.

(Retreat, 1889)

Dom Prosper Guéranger

Try to live with God, without any mental effort, but as with a friend, for there is no bitterness in his company.

(Letter to a monk)

At this word "contemplation," some may perhaps become dismayed in the mistaken belief that the element signified by it is only to be found in the rare conditions of a life passed in retirement and far from contact with mankind. That is a serious and dangerous error, which too often stops souls in their flight. Contemplation is the state to which, in some measure, everyone who seeks God is called. It doesn't consist in those phenomena the Holy Spirit chooses to manifest in certain privileged persons, and which he makes use of in order to prove the reality of the supernatural life. It is simply that relationship of greater intimacy that grows up between God and the person faithful to him in its action. For that person, if he puts no obstacle in the way, are reserved two favours, of which the first is the gift of Intelligence, which consists in the enlightenment of the soul, henceforth illumined by a light from above.

The light does not take away faith, but it clarifies the eye of the soul by strengthening it, and gives it a more extensive view of divine things. Many clouds, which had their origin in the weakness and coarseness of a soul still uninitiated, now disappear. The delightful beauty of those mysteries, of which one had been aware only vaguely, now reveals itself; inexpressible harmonies, whose existence one had never suspected, appear. It is not the vision face to face, which is reserved for the eternal day, but all the same it is no longer that feeble glimmering that previously guided our steps. A whole ensemble of connections, of appropriatenesses, which appear one after the other to the spirit's eye, brings a certainty that is full of sweetness. The soul spreads itself before these new clarities, which enrich its faith, increase its hope and develop its love. Everything seems new. And when it looks back, it compares and sees clearly that it grasps the truth, which remains the same, in an incomparably more complete manner.

(The Liturgical Year: Eastertide, 1841)

There is that spirit of pride that is the enemy of prayer because it says "prayer is not action"; as if every good work of ours were not a gift from God, a gift that presupposes the request and the thanksgiving one makes for it.

(Preface to The Liturgical Year, 1841)

Meditation has a twofold purpose: to recall to the intelligence truths that are well-known, but too often forgotten; to extract them from the silence and obscurity in which they sleep, and thereby to give them a power of action they cannot have except by means of our reflections and our memory. Meditation, therefore, will consist of recollecting oneself, of considering attentively a supernatural truth whose impression has become weakened, and which no longer governs our existence effectively enough to imprint upon it its form and its mark. So long as people have not made supernatural truths familiar, or even whenever they feel their impression weakening, their point becoming dull, or their efficacy lessening, meditation will be an indispensable necessity. One cannot see unless one looks. It is only by means of meditation that one takes, or recovers, possession of the truth.

Experience shows clearly that in any work of the mind, ordered and persevering reflection restores our intelligence to the possession of ideas it had forgotten; and meditation upon supernatural truths can also restore them to our conviction, even when they have been ignored or forgotten for a long period.

(Cited by Abbess Cécile Bruyère in
The Spiritual Life and Prayer)

If one comes to prayer with no more than a few vague ideas about God, one shouldn't be surprised to find oneself pouring with sweat at the effort.[11]

* * * * *

Notes

1. Quoted in Thomas Merton, *The Silent Life* (London, 1957), p. 64.

2. Cf Dom Delatte, *Commentary on the Rule of St Benedict* (London, 1921), pp. 306-7: "It is to contemplation and union with God that the monastic *lectio divina* tends. The hours which St Benedict would have us devote to it every day are essentially hours of prayer.... Contemplation itself is endangered as soon as it claims to be self-sufficient."

3. Jacques and Raïssa Maritain, *Liturgy and Contemplation* (London 1960), p. 18. The expression *Opus Dei* refers to the Divine Office, the Liturgy of the Hours. St Benedict called the Office the "work of God," the work of which God is the beneficiary, the work at which he is the principal theme and agent, the work performed for his glory.

4. cf Dom Delatte, *Commentary on the Rule*, p. 307: "In order that prayer may become an easy matter it is enough to realize the treasure which baptism has given us, and with St Paul's help, understand what it means to be redeemed in Christ and to live with his life."

5. Collect for the twenty-eighth Sunday of the year: "O Lord, we pray that thy grace may always precede and follow us...."

6. *Rule of St Benedict*, chapter 19: "that our mind and voice may be in harmony."

7. At the time of writing, this was the Secret (Prayer over the Gifts) for the eighteenth Sunday after Pentecost. It is now used as the Prayer over the Gifts for the sixth week of Eastertide.

8. Cited in Dom Savaton, *Dom Delatte*, p.319.

9. *Domus Orationis*, an unpublished *florilegia* compiled at the Abbey of Wisques (see Preface).

10. Cited in Dom Savaton, *Dom Delatte*, p. 284.

11. Cited by Dom Soltner, *Solesmes et Dom Guéranger*, p. 84.

CHAPTER NINE

"Worship in spirit and in truth" (John 4:23):

Adoration, Thanksgiving and the Liturgy

The names of Dom Guéranger and Solesmes are forever linked with one of the great movements in nineteenth-century Church history: the restoration of the liturgy. The liturgy is the centre of Solesmes' life, the true source of its spiritual life and apostolate.

Dom Guéranger realized, first of all, that the liturgy is the fundamental catechesis of Christian doctrine and that its celebration is the means best able to stimulate and nourish the highest and purest spiritual life. And he realized that the liturgy should be a source of spiritual vitality and provide a framework for the whole Christian people in the Church. His *Liturgical Year* (1841), a day-by-day commentary on the seasons and feasts of the Church, drawing on Scripture, patrology, theology, and tradition, and imbued with the perceptions and love of a contemplative, contributed much to a real understanding of the rites and prayers of the Church and to their appreciation. Composed by a monk for whom the liturgical life was life itself and who was inspired with an intense desire to make it possible for all to enjoy the same experience, it offered, in the words of Cardinal Manning, "the fruit of that spirit of prayer and retreat characteristic of Benedictine life, a prolonged meditation on the wonderful order of divine worship." Both this work and *Les Institutions liturgiques* (1840) met with immediate success. Half-a-million copies of the *Institutions* were sold in fifty years.

For Dom Guéranger, the liturgy is not only prayer, but "prayer considered as a social act" (*Institutions* 1,1); the liturgy is "the highest, the holiest expression of the intellect and thought of the Church." Now, in Dom Guéranger's view, this prayer of the

Church was menaced by a certain individualism. The nineteenth century was a period of intense spiritual life; but in its abundance of ascetic and mystical literature, he perceived a diminishment of that other facet of Christian life, the mind of the Church. His study of history, patristics and theology had shown him the necessity of associating the faithful with the life of the Church. But that could not be done until new life had been given to the liturgy, "that totality of symbols, chants, and actions by means of which the Church expresses and manifests its religion toward God" (*Institutions* 1,1). Far from doing away with individual piety, Dom Guéranger's aim was rather to make sure that it was nourished on the objective content of Christian faith and the sacraments.

The liturgy as seen by Dom Guéranger in his youth had been overlaid with fanciful interpretations and developments foreign to its nature. Since the Renaissance, liturgical ceremonies often resembled operatic shows and were more concerned with performance than with prayer to God. In the *Institutions Liturgiques*, Dom Guéranger gave a lively and picturesque description of liturgical vestments, of "chasubles lined with stiff buckram and looking from the back like violin cases; those equally strange copes ... making the wearer look as though he were shut up in a sentry box."

He went on to consider national, local and private usages and rites among the factors responsible for liturgical decadence, and advocated a return to that liturgy he held to be the most faithful to tradition, the Roman liturgy. The liturgies which Dom Guéranger criticized were not ancient Gallican liturgies. The missals and breviaries in use in most French dioceses at the beginning of the nineteenth century were compiled in the seventeenth and eighteenth centuries. "One felt," he wrote, "that they were the work of a particular age, a particular person." Because the decrees of the Council of Trent had never been promulgated in France, French bishops claimed the right to make many liturgical decisions in their dioceses. The French Revolution, moreover, had turned liturgical diversity into liturgical chaos. It was not unusual to find, within the same diocese, priests following three or four different liturgies. Dom Guéranger believed that a return to the Roman liturgy would free this diversity from the abitrariness and errors that he found so detrimental to the life of the Church in France. He felt that many of the innovations—the alteration of collects and other texts of the Mass, for example—reflected Gallican and Jansenistic tendencies.[1]

Polemic and controversy were far from his mind, but in the following ten years he was subjected to bitter criticism and found himself ranged against the greater part of the French hierarchy. Dom Guéranger was not in principle against diversity, but rather against the profusion of missals and breviaries that did not have Rome's approval and that in his judgement could not be called the prayer of the Church. While insisting that the texts of the liturgy embody the rule of faith and be the principal instrument of the Church's tradition, he pointed out that this did not mean that texts were unchangeable or had to date from apostolic times. Liturgical texts embody the tradition of the Church; they are not themselves that tradition. The only invariable text the Church has is the text of sacred Scripture. The Church can change the text of the liturgy. What Dom Guéranger objected to in the local liturgies of the dioceses of France was that they had been produced without proper authority, and some at least were of doubtful orthodoxy. And far from claiming that everything was perfect in the Roman books of the day, he envisaged the eventual reform of the Roman Breviary. Ten years later, after his ideas had gradually prevailed, he himself became alarmed at the speed with which the dioceses of France were beginning to adopt the Roman liturgy. Writing to Dom Laurence Shepherd in 1857, he noted that "the French are fond of extremes; at one moment they reject the Roman liturgy altogether, and now that they return to it, they would adopt even those appurtenances that Rome no longer observes in practice."

For Dom Guéranger, the source of the liturgy is to be found in the very heart of the Trinity: God contemplating himself, loving himself, praising himself. But liturgical expression, properly speaking, implies the Incarnation. The "totality of symbols, chants, and acts" that make up the liturgy has to be understood in the light of the Incarnation; according to the economy of this mystery, invisible realities are made known to us by means of visible realities (cf *Institutions* 2, 182). Moreover, the liturgy is not merely the official regulation of external worship but Christ's own worship of the Father, which was begun on earth with the Incarnation, is carried on in the Church, and continues forever in heaven. The perfection of our adoration, worship and thanksgiving is realized in Christ, for in him man's response to God's word is identical with that Word itself. The whole of Christian life, all Christian prayer, is thus able to take on an atmosphere of thanksgiving, praise, and adoration in union with Christ. This adoration is in fact the highest act of religion, the very heart of the life of prayer, directed at God for and in himself.

Those Christians who live the liturgical year fully are living at the heart of the Church, experiencing the mystery of Christ ecclesially. "What the liturgical year works in the Church in general," wrote Dom Guéranger, "it repeats in the soul of each member of the faithful who receives attentively the gift of God" (Preface to *The Liturgical Year*). The Fathers condensed this idea in their concept of the *anima ecclesiastica* or *vir ecclesiasticus*, expressing a life having all the dimensions of the Church. "This inseparable union of the Church with God," Abbess Cécile said, "is none other than that contracted individually with God by the souls that make up the Church. The soul that has attained to union with God is an exact miniature of the Church...." The liturgical year is centred on Christ and his saving mysteries that he might be formed in the individual Christian. To live the liturgical year is to grow into the full stature of Christ, and each successive year brings with it a new growth.

By his restoration of Gregorian chant, by his fidelity to the authentic spirit of the liturgy, by his strenuous efforts toward unification, Dom Guéranger paved the way for the rediscovery of the liturgy as true prayer. And by the same means he led the way toward the realization that the liturgy is something we are not only to see and hear, but in which we are above all to take part, in a traditional and collective glorification of God. "Liturgical prayer," he insisted, "would soon become powerless were the faithful not to take a real share in it." In an almost prophetic passage, Dom Guéranger expressed his longing to see again "those ages of religious fidelity to divine worship" when the whole Christian people would follow all the rites "with an intelligent and religious eye" and would feel itself lifted up thereby "to the contemplation of things invisible" (*The Liturgical Year*). As Pope Paul VI recognized,[2] Catholics in our day owe much to Dom Guéranger who more than anyone taught that "sublime language spoken by the Church to God in the presence of men."

Abbess Cécile Bruyère

The true adorers are those who live in God, for God and with God, continuously in the only attitude which can befit an intelligent creature whose activity is ceaselessly turned toward God: it is these whom popular language calls "the saints."

Saints are people like any others; it is just that they have taken seriously the conditions of their creation and the final end God had in mind when he created them. They have used faithfully, and in the measure granted to them, all the graces the Lord has placed at their disposition. The very tenor of the Gospel narrative demonstrates with great clarity that the true adorers are born to the supernatural life in the baptismal font, by becoming Christians. For our Lord unveils the divine plan before the Samaritan woman at Jacob's well, first offering her a mysterious water that is within the reach of every person and is destined to quench their thirst for ever. So the true adorer is born in us at baptism, and we are then given all the energies that can make of us the ones whom the Father seeks....

The act of adoration in spirit and truth, made possible to Christians through their baptism, does not however make them adorers unless that act is not a passing and rare one in them, but an almost permanent disposition, a sort of professional state and constant attitude.

True adorers are those whose soul, freed from all multiplicity, restored to perfect simplicity, has reached the point of total harmony within itself, in a harmony with no dissonance, having wiped out by a sustained effort all dividedness, all disunity, all contradiction, to enter again into the first unity of its being. The simple soul has a single gaze, love, direction, desire, end: one gaze, it sees only God; one love, it loves only God; one direction, it tends only to God; one desire, to please God; one end, to possess God. It neither relives the past nor anxiously forecasts the future; it peacefully concentrates all its powers in the unity of the present hour; and in the present moment it sees only the unity of God's good pleasure. The simple soul lives in happy detachment and admirable indifference: times, places, tasks, successes, events in general, whatever they are, never disturb the peace and security it receives from the total abandonment of itself to God's good pleasure.

(The Spiritual Life and Prayer)

Whatever else may have been the motive of the Incarnation, it at once brought this result: it associated with the liturgical act rational creatures, elevated to the supernatural state, and for whom the Son of God would condescend so far as to make himself not merely a holocaust, but a victim for sin, blotting out their faults, making reparation for all their errors; in such a way that these creatures cooperate thenceforth in his own sacrifice, as the members of one and the same body of which he is the head.

(The Spiritual Life and Prayer)

Silence is one of the laws of adoration; it is at the same time the path by which the Lord comes and the result of his coming.

* * * * *

Remember that this new celebration of the mysteries of our salvation is a way for us to assimilate them more completely, a way that presents itself a limited number of times in a human life. There is no doubt that the important thing for us is the fact we have been redeemed; and yet it is no less important that we should be careful to incorporate within us the fruit of the Redemption.

* * * * *

The liturgical cycle is a lived creed. It is at the same time a complete treatise on the spiritual life, which can be adapted to each soul according to its needs.

* * * * *

Our temples must have a chant, or they would be mournful. But we have a chant, an incomparable chant. The Second Person of the Blessed Trinity has come down to earth; the Word was made flesh. What is the Second Person of the Blessed Trinity? What is the Word? He is at one and the same time a Cantor and a Chant. The unique Cantor who gives a voice to the entire creation; a Chant that never ends, for God does everything through his Word; a Chant we repeat unceasingly, for it is always the Word of God that the Psalms repeat.

(Conference, 12 October 1888)

"The glory of the Lord filled the temple" (2 Chron. 7:2). Seek for that interior temple where the Divine Majesty resides, and to which love gives us access. That tender and devoted love is a permanent act of adoration. Take your rest there, and do not even make efforts to be at rest. The law of love—when God puts us in this state—is to abandon totally to him the government of our whole being, body and soul.

(Letter)

The heart becomes an altar where God alone dwells, and offers to his Father a sacrifice of adoration, of praise and of love.
(Commentary on The Ascent of Mount Carmel)

When God chose to come forth from his eternal repose and create that which his mind had conceived before anything was begun, he sealed his works with the stamp of his likeness. He, who is absolutely and perfectly beautiful, has given to what he has made a beauty manifested in order, harmony, and seemliness.

Music is one of the created images of uncreated Beauty. The Father eternally begets his Son, who is the Word, and that Word is uncreated music, ever vibrant and resonant; music equal and consubstantial with its Composer, fruitful music, which by loving its Principle with an ineffable love, produces the Holy Spirit. That Spirit proceeds from the reciprocal love of the Word who is brought forth and the Father who brings forth; he is that love itself.

Dom Paul Delatte

The final end of all things is that God should be glorified, that he should be adored, acknowledged as God, treated as such; it is that we should tell him so, should sing of it to him, that our whole life should be a sign of it for him. That is the adoration in spirit and in truth desired by God, demanded and sought by the Father; his plan, his final intention: "But the hour is coming, and now is, when the true worshippers will worship the Father in spirit and truth, for such the Father seeks to worship him" (John 4:23). And even all supernatural purity is ordered to this end—to be in a condition to serve God as is his due: "... how much more shall the blood of Christ, who through the eternal Spirit offered himself without blemish to God, purify your conscience from dead works to serve the living God" (Heb. 9:14). One isn't good for the sake of being good; one isn't pure simply in order to be pure; one doesn't establish supernatural beauty in oneself for the mere pleasure of establishing in oneself the supernatural beauty that comes to us from the blood of the Lord. No. The point, the intention, of all purity and all supernatural beauty is to pay to God, to the living God, a homage more worthy of him: "purify your conscience ... to serve the living God." If we do not understand that, we shall not understand our life; neither our Christian life, nor our supernatural life, nor our monastic life, which is, in time and in eternity, a liturgical life.[3]

* * * * *

171

Adoration itself is of a higher order in proportion to the dignity of the adorer. And when is it that the Father is truly glorified? It is when from our whole life the Lord gathers this fruit: our adoration. And when is that adoration the most exalted, the most perfect there is? When we are completely the Lord's disciples, taught, guided, formed, determined by him; when, liberated from ourselves, there is nothing left in us but him, and when he has definitively taken over all our life, thoughts, words, desires, emotions, affection. Isn't that what it means to be disciples of the Lord? And precisely there is to be found the glory of the Father: when, from our souls, belonging fully to the Lord, there rises to him the homage of adoration, an adoration which is complete because it is that of Christ in us. So we have nothing else to do but to form in us what one could call the "tool" of adoration: ourselves.

* * * * *

Do you know what would be needed to restore the Christian people to what it once was? It would simply be necessary for the liturgy again to take its proper place. If people began to pray together, at the foot of the same altar, before the same God, if they sat down at the same table and fed on the same bread, if they allowed the same life to penetrate their marrow, it is certain that the Christian people, which was created in that way, would recreate itself.

For the liturgy has the triple effect of honouring God, of sanctifying man, and of uniting men among themselves. And this is something to which insufficient attention is paid, and which is nevertheless considerable: Christian gatherings have the effect of preserving, of increasing, of promoting without limit the Christian spirit.

* * * * *

All the baptized understand the ceremonies of the Church when they are carried out with dignity. These things work like a divine charm, like a sacrament of tenderness and faith. One cannot escape from them, one cannot remove oneself from their influence, one cannot say good-bye to them. Ah! That is true preaching: the sight of this prayer, the profound action of sacred symbolism, the edification that is born from the devotion and conviction of liturgical formulas and movements. How greatly we need it! How effectively these liturgical realities raise us above the earth and its interests, its small, petty passions! It is by means of liturgical prayer that souls are formed; it is by means of liturgical prayer that a Christian people is formed.

(Conferences on the Spiritual Life VI: Benedictine Life)

But what then is the real secret of liturgical prayer? The reason for its greatness? It is that the Christian people is brought together in our Lord Jesus Christ who is the cause of the unity of a whole mystical body. He includes everything; he should be in all; he is the only moral agent. He is hierarchical. He is all-inclusive; it is through him that our sacrifice will pass. God who is in us, outside us, next to us, God who desires to take every-thing, who desires in some sense to be in our acts whenever we act, hope and love, God will certainly be—and even *a priori*, without consulting the Gospel—in that act of ours called prayer.

* * * * *

At the sacrifice on Calvary the Lord was alone; at the sacrifice of the Mass, the Lord cannot be alone; all souls must be with him. We cannot exaggerate the importance of this intimacy we have with our Lord Jesus Christ. If we really understand that, if we understand the part we play in the Holy Mass, we have the whole secret of the liturgical life that should be ours. Then we understand that we not only immolate ourselves with the Lord, but that we eat the flesh of that victim in order to be that victim ourselves, in order to be the Lord throughout our lives—*non mutabor in te, sed tu mutaberis in me*.[4] Let us remember all that is implied in Holy Communion: a community of life that permits us to be, following the Lord and through him, true adorers, and thanks to our perfect union with him, we are transported with him before God: "we pray that your angel may take this sacrifice to your altar in heaven…."[5] We are taken up whole and entire;

this leads to the total disappearance of ourselves, the vanishing of every personal thought. It is the daily work of transformation into that victim we have eaten, so that his life may pass into us and absorb our life. Do you see, once again, what adoration is? It is the disappearance of the creature in the face of God. It is the definitive entry, the transforming entry, into the sacrifice of the Mass. Then our sacrifice is spontaneous: "Freely will I offer you sacrifice" (Ps. 53[54]:6). We go to it with our life in all its entirety united to the Lord. No delaying, no inertia, no thoughts of our own, because the Lord reigns within us: the whole of the human will disappearing before him, all that we are vanishing before him.

* * * * *

Christians should live in thanksgiving. Whoever we are, if we desire to study our lives, if we desire to flick through, so to speak, this interior Bible, this interior revelation from God that each one of us has in our past life, we will understand very well that really there are only two things to say to God: "Forgive me" and "Thank you." Forgive me for what I have done, Lord; thank you for all you have done! "Always and for everything giving thanks..." (Eph. 5:20). That is the Apostle's lesson to the Ephesians, because gratitude is the essential duty of the Christian life, the basis of that life. Just like our joy, just like the cultivation of our faith and of our charity, our gratitude should be something continuous, regular, as spontaneous and habitual as our very breathing. And it will be so from the day we realize what we are, what we have become, to whom we belong, of whom we are members, from whom we have the blood that flows in our veins. That blood is divine blood; it is the blood of the Son of God. If we realize all that, our gratitude will be the normal, instinctive, spontaneous, and almost necessary expression of the awareness we bear within us of the graces and gifts of God.

* * * * *

It would be a mistake to exclude exterior worship on the pretext that the Lord demands spiritual worship. To conclude that there is no longer any place for ritual worship would run counter to the Lord himself and many passages of Scripture. Our Lord Jesus Christ loved, and loves, exterior worship, even though he loves it when it is vivified by the spirit.

There is another thing. To look upon God as Father, to adore him in spirit and in truth, is the formula for a revolution in religious life; it is a new attitude to be taken, and it does not belong to us, however bold we may be, to take up that attitude before God, if God does not give us the sign to do so and does not put his hand to it himself; the first move can only come from him. For our spirit to adapt itself to conditions so new, it is necessary for God to show himself as Father, for us to belong to the Son, and to be guided by the Holy Spirit. In a word, it is necessary that the figures and shadows that had reigned until the Incarnation should be succeeded by the reality. Then, and only then, everything becomes possible. If God shows himself as Father, giving his only Son for us, then adoration becomes easy.

(Commentary on John 4)

The duty of all the baptized is to tend with all their strength toward adoring God in this inner sanctuary, in this centre where he resides, and where he desires to be found by us. It is in our soul, the Holy of Holies. It is not in the first stage of our supernatural life that we will enter it. All the work, often painful, of purification and illumination leads us to it. As happened symbolically in the Old Testament, it is not the lot of everyone to enter it. There, there is no more suffering, no more dryness, no more noise. It is not that there is nothing for the soul to do, since, its ideal being so lofty, it can always grow. But everything takes place in peace, in silence; it is definitive rest and peace. The vexations of the world have ceased; there is no other desire, no other prayer, but that which God himself inspires, and it is from the centre of the soul, from the sanctuary of the soul and from God that all the dynamism of life springs.

(Conferences on the Spiritual Life, 1899)

From all eternity God bears within himself his glory and his jubilation. The uncreated glory of God is his Word. The uncreated jubilation of God, his personal exultation, is the Spirit of God. We also know that eternity is the place of praise, the authentic place of songs and hymns: "... when the morning stars sang together, and all the sons of God shouted for joy" (Job 38:7). We have picked up some of its echoes: *Sanctus, Sanctus, Sanctus; Gloria in excelsis Deo*; and also in the songs of the Apocalypse. We must accustom ourselves to these ways. Earth has followed heaven, and even after sin, it has not forgotten how to sing to God.

(Retreat notes)

The whole work of creation is not appreciated by all in the same way. For a traveller, the world is an immense expanse, dotted with shining stations and a lengthy business to traverse. For an astronomer, it is a whole population of stars and planets, which his telescope studies with curiosity. For a naturalist, it is the universal theatre where life in its various forms is unfolded. For a physicist, it is the field of activity of material forces. For a child, it is a vast plain, with a blue skull-cap of the same size, where it rains, hails, thunders, and is hot in turn; where a big round lamp walks about; where in the evening, at bedtime, a crowd of twinkling little flowers appear, which seem to be looking at you in chorus. For Christians, the world is a concert in praise of God. Only Christians are entirely right. After them comes the child! The world has absolutely no other function, no other purpose: to sing of the glory of God, to express God. Whatever does not express God does not exist, could not exist. Isn't there a contradiction in a being that does not express Being? That necessity is so imperious that God cannot go against it.... All beings express God and speak to us of him according to the measure of their nature and their limited perfections, which are only pale reflections and fragments of their existence, which is entirely borrowed, which is never possessed, but always received. In such a way that the first act whereby creation, were it conscious, expressing its feelings before God on the day it woke from nothingness at his word, would be an act of adoration, of self-abnegation, of sacrifice.

(Letter)[6]

Christian life was once the generous school alike for martyrdom and for eternal life. We must preserve as much of that as we can. When supernatural ways became tepid, when the habit of contemplation fled to the Thebaids and monasteries, experience, the guidance of the Church, the wisdom of monastic legislators contributed together to form this body of prayers, readings, and ceremonies that came to be called the liturgy: it is simply organized contemplation. If contemplation is not merely a word, it is our intelligence and will employed in a constant and loving attention to God, to his works, and manifesting to him their adoration in defined and precise forms. It must be that the Lord should be able to gather from this earth the homage that is his due and that, if it has become rarer, should be carried out with greater care.

God has made all things for his glory alone; and never is his glory better obtained than by interior acts of the spirit and the heart. The *Quis ut Deus*[7] is said in a low voice; the *Ecce ancilla Domini*[8] made no sound. What glorifies God is the intelligence and will cleaving to him and manifesting that to him. We shall do no more than that in eternity. In the meantime, even in this world and in the regions of shadows and mystery, we practise for our eternity.

(Retreat notes)

Dom Prosper Guéranger

Adoration is an act whereby we acknowledge our nothingness lovingly before God; we give to him what we have received from him; we declare and proclaim him to be worthy of all praise from all creatures. Nothing is more important; and I should like to add that this act should turn into a habit. It cannot be a passing thing. One cannot think that it is appropriate at one moment and not at another. For by the very fact that God exists and we exist, as soon as we think of him, adoration should arise in us at once. In this sense, adoration cannot be an effort: it comes, so to speak, by itself. But take particular note of one word in my definition: I said that adoration is a loving act. It is therefore not something sterile, dry, in which the heart has no part. There is within us what one might call an attraction that causes it to arise: the creature puts itself in its place and is happy to be there, and God finds it to his liking; it is beautiful in his eyes. If he has been familiar with certain of his creatures, it is because they had acquired, from adoration, something that enraptured and seduced him. And so there is nothing more important, nothing wiser, nothing truer than adoration.

(Retreat, 1874)

What God desires is to be able to have dealings with you; he doesn't want to look at you from a distance, but rather to consider you as belonging to him. And he has a method for that: he has put at our diposition a region in which we can have our ears open to hear the Lord. The Holy Spirit has said in the Old Testament: "I will lead her into the desert and speak to her heart" (Hos. 2:16). Don't regard that as phenomenal, as being the lot of those favoured souls who have gone so far as to receive the honour of canonization. No, it is to all of you that this word is spoken; people are constantly called, and God begins to speak to them. Whether that lasts a long or a short time, we must adore, even it were only for a minute. God is happy. He jumps for joy, if I may speak so. If you have more time, then you are blessed. But often it is like a flash that comes upon us, and when the soul seizes the awareness of God who comes like this in passing, then it is close to him; and the proof is that another flash follows the first. Then the soul can be relied upon, it is in its element; and if you want the proof again, it is that the soul acts upon that light.

In adoration, then, there is sweetness and ease; and I would add that everyone is capable of it, even those who have the least education. As long as one knows God, one can adore, and God has put at the disposition of everyone the means to know him.

And so, it isn't a question of something wise or clever; … it is a thing God expects of you and in which you will find your soul's rest.

(Retreat, 1874)

The soul that gives itself over to adoration opens all the treasure houses of God. It cannot see all the affection, all the confidence united to that act of adoration, but that is not necessary; and since it has such good relations with God, everything God deigns to grant in answer to the holy fear it has of him is to that person's advantage. The soul that, on the other hand, does not possess this fear sees God on one side and it on the other, so that when it can think about God it does so, but outside these times when it returns to him, how is its life filled? What has it been? How has it lived? What has God been to it? We must hasten to take our proper life before God, or else familiarity will quickly engender a facility in forgetting God....

In all this I am not talking about failings due to character, about defects that show themselves differently in each one of us and which even originate, sometimes, in temperament; for we can serve God with any temperament. I'm talking about the will. As long as the will is not endangered, there is no danger; but if the will is defective, we must beware. If we say to ourselves: "I used to think more about God, I used to control myself—how is it that is no longer so? Have I guarded my treasure as I should have done? I should have made efforts to that end, but since then I thought I could spare myself those efforts; I saw things more or less clearly; a little cloud rose up between God and myself, and I was quite comfortable under that cloud; I let slip the thought of God." We must be on guard against this, for "in him we live and move and have our being" (Acts 17.28).

(Retreat, 1874)

The liturgy is something so excellent, that to find its principle it is necessary to seek it in God; because God, in the contemplation of his infinite perfections, praises and glorifies himself

179

ceaselessly, as he loves himself with an eternal love. However, these diverse acts accomplished in the divine essence did not have a visible and truly liturgical character until the moment when one of the three Persons took human nature, and from that moment the duties of religion were rendered to the glorious Trinity.

(Institutions liturgiques)

The liturgy is the highest and the holiest expression of the thought and intelligence of the Church, simply because it is carried out by the Church in direct communication with God, in confession, in prayer, and praise.

(Institutions liturgiques)

And so the liturgy is not simply prayer, but rather prayer considered in its social aspect. An individual prayer, made in an individual name, is not liturgy. However, the formulas and signs of the liturgy can legitimately and appropriately be used by individuals, with the intention of giving greater power and efficacy to their work of prayer, as when one recites set prayers, hymns, responses, in order to rouse oneself to devotion. This type of prayer is even the best as regards vocal prayer, because it associates to the effort of the individual the merit and the consecration of the entire Church.

(Institutions liturgiques)

For persons of contemplation, liturgical prayer is sometimes the source, sometimes the result, of the visits of the Lord.

(Preface to The Liturgical Year, 1841)

Prayer, for us, is the first of all good things. It is our light, our food, our very life, since it puts us in relation to God, who is light, food and life. But of ourselves, we do not know how to pray as we ought; we must turn to Jesus Christ and say to him as did the Apostles: "Lord, teach us to pray" (Luke 11:1). He alone can loose the tongue of the dumb, make the mouth of infants eloquent, and he accomplishes this wonder by sending his Holy

Spirit of grace and prayer, who delights in coming to the aid of our weakness, supplying for us and in us by sighs too deep for words (cf Rom. 8:26).

And on this earth it is in the Church that this divine Spirit dwells. He descended upon her like a mighty wind at the same time as he appeared under the expressive form of flaming tongues. Since then he makes his dwelling in that blessed Bride; he is the principle of her movements; he prompts her requests, her desires, her canticles of praise, her enthusiasm and her sighs. That is why, for eighteen centuries, she has not kept silent by day or by night; and her voice is always tuneful, her words always go straight to the heart of the Bridegroom....

The prayer of the Church is therefore the most pleasing to the ear and heart of God, and therefore, the most powerful. Happy, then, are those who pray with the Church, who associate their particular desires with those of that Bride, so dear to the Bridegroom, whose wishes are always granted. And that is why the Lord Jesus taught us to say "our Father," and not "my Father"; "give us," "forgive us," "deliver us," and not "give me, forgive me, deliver me." ... For if this prayer made in union with the Church is the light of the mind, it is also the fire of divine love in the heart.

But this liturgical prayer would soon become powerless were the faithful not to take a real share in it, or not to associate themselves with it in their hearts. It can heal and save the world on condition that it be understood. Open your hearts, children of the Catholic Church, and come and pray the prayer of your mother....

The liturgical year, whose plan is traced out for us by the Church herself, provides the most sublime drama that has ever been offered to us. The intervention of God for our salvation and sancification, the reconciliation of justice and mercy; the humiliations, the sufferings, and the glory of the God-man; the coming of the Holy Spirit and his workings in humanity and in the faithful soul; the mission and action of the Church—all are there expressed in the most vivid and striking way.

Each mystery has its time and place through the sublime

succession of anniversaries. A divine event happened nineteen hundred years ago; its anniversary is kept in the liturgy, and comes each year to renew in the Christian people the consciousness of what God accomplished so many centuries ago. Human ingenuity could never have devised a system of such power as this. And those writers who are bold and frivolous enough to assert that Christianity has no longer an influence in the world, and is now but the ruin of an ancient thing, what would they say at seeing these undying realities, this vigour, this endlessness of the liturgical year? For what is the liturgy, but a ceaseless affirmation of the works of God, a solemn acknowledgement of those facts, which took place once but whose reality is imperishable in man's remembrance, and are every year renewed by the commemoration he makes of them?

This renewing power of the liturgical year is a mystery of the Holy Spirit, who ceaselessly animates the work he has inspired in the Church, in order to sanctify the time assigned to humanity to make it worthy of God. This renewal also brings about an understanding of the truths of the faith and the development of the supernatural life. Every single point of Christian doctrine is not merely expressed during the course of the liturgical year, but also inculcated with the authority and unction the Church has been able to instil into her language and rites, which are so expressive. Thus the faith of Christians becomes clearer year by year; the theological sense begins to form within them; prayer leads them to knowledge. The mysteries remain mysteries; but their splendour becomes so vivid that the heart and mind are enraptured by it, and we come to the point at which we can get an idea of the joys which we will receive from the beauty of those divine things, when the glimpse of them through the clouds is already such a delight to us.

(Preface to The Liturgical Year)

Notes

1. Dom Guéranger was the sworn enemy of both Gallicanism—which asserted more or less complete freedom of the Church in France from the ecclesiastical authority of the Papacy—and Jansenism, which he called "the

greatest enemy of the whole economy of the relationship of the creature with God" (Letter to Dom Guepin, 1874). "Whereas Gallicanism represented a form of anti-Roman spirit on the institutional plane, Jansenism was a form of anti-Romanism on the spiritual plane. The Jansenists were able to use the Gallican movement of independence and promulgate their teaching" (see Dom Cuthbert Johnson O.S.B., "Prosper Guéranger: A Liturgical Theologian," *Studia Anselmiana* 89, Rome, Pontificio Ateneo S Anselmo, 1984, page 173, and the whole of his chapter, "The Local Liturgies of the French Church").

2. "Epistola summi Pontificis Pauli VI ad Congregationem Solesmensem Ordinis Sancti Benedicti," *Notitiae* 11 (1975), pages 170-2. "... The new springtime the Church is experiencing today by means of the liturgical renewal is as it were the fruit of that seed which Dom Guéranger worked to scatter with a patient heart and at the price of so many labours." See general introduction above.

3. Unless otherwise indicated, the following texts from Dom Delatte are taken from *Domus Orationis*.

4. St Augustine, *Confessions* VII, 10: "You shall not change me into yourself [as bodily food], but into me you shall be changed."

5. Words from the Roman Canon of the Mass, now Eucharistic Prayer 1.

6. Cited by Dom Savaton, *Dom Delatte*, pp. 112-3.

7. See Chapter Eleven, note eight.

8. "Behold the handmaid of the Lord" (Luke 1:38).

CHAPTER TEN

"Behold your Mother" (John 19:27):

The Vocation of Mary

Writing to Madame Swetchine in the early days of the priory in the midst of difficulties of every kind, Dom Guéranger avowed, "When I see Our Lady, my heart leaps for joy, while my head and imagination remain firmly anchored, as if on the unshakable rock of Confidence" (7 December 1833). Solesmes has always had a singular devotion to the Mother of God. The Congregation keeps 9 July, the date of its origin, as a feast of Our Lady under the title *Mater Providentiae*. On that day in 1837 Dom Guéranger was praying before this Roman Madonna of the Via delle Batteghe Oscure as the cardinals made their way to the Quirinal to decide the fate of Solesmes. The first monastic clothings and first five professions at Sainte Cécile took place on the feast of the Assumption. The Congregation itself is dedicated to Mary under the title of the Immaculate Conception.

Of all the Marian mysteries, the one most associated with Solesmes is that of the Immaculate Conception. In 1823, long before his work on the definability of the dogma, Dom Guéranger received what he called a special light into the privilege of Our Lady's Immaculate Conception. Until then, by his own account, a certain rationalism had affected his appreciation of this mystery, which had not yet been defined as a dogma. On the morning of 8 December, while meditating on the feast of the day, the Conception of the Blessed Virgin Mary, he found his reason and his heart irresistibly drawn "to believe Mary immaculate in her conception": "I experienced a sweet joy in my acquiescence; no transport, but a gentle peace coupled with a sincere conviction.... It was one nature disappearing to make room for another." He saw this mystery's profound connection with the Incarnation. If Mary was preserved from the stain of original sin, it was because she had been chosen by God from all eternity to be the Mother of God's Son. Her freedom from sin is based on her position in the salvation that embraces the whole Church. She is free from sin only because of Christ's work, because of her unique proximity to and cooperation with the saving mystery of Christ. "The Son's love," observed Dom Guéranger, "protected the Mother."

To give Our Lady a place in our devotion and our love is "to embrace in an act of faith the whole of Christianity" (Dom Delatte). One of Dom Delatte's favourite titles for Mary is "*notre educatrice*." By this he meant not merely our teacher, but our whole pedagogy, our supernatural education, who reveals to us the truth about Jesus, the truth about the Church, and the truth about us. She remains "the eternal means and method of God, the authentic way by which God comes to us." Through Mary we penetrate more deeply into the mystery of the Incarnation. The great Marian dogmas—the Immaculate Conception, the Assumption—at once protect and reveal the original faith in Christ as true God and true man. She unites in her person the mysteries of the faith and the mystery of the God who intervenes. For these writers, the vocation of Mary has not ceased with the mysteries of the Incarnation and Redemption, any more than these mysteries themselves have ceased. Mary is still our Mother in the work of sanctification and supernatural education.

In Mary, too, the whole Church is outlined and completed. "By herself, for an instant," writes Dom Guéranger in his *Liturgical Year*, "she was the Church of Jesus." In her is anticipated the Church's worship, pondering these things in her heart; "the fruit of the liturgy is to make our whole being Marian," notes Dom Delatte. In her is anticipated the Church's total offering to God, her role as Bride, Mother, and Virgin, her mediation, and her participation in the mystery of the cross.

Mary shows us what we should be before God, standing as she does in unconditional faith, hope and perfect obedience, that unreserved "Yes," which enabled her, in St Augustine's phrase, to conceive Christ in her soul before she conceived him in her flesh. Or as Abbess Cécile Bruyère puts it: "The soul can produce only what it possesses." In Mary we see all that God desires in our response—body and soul.

Finally, Mary shows us what we will be before God. Her perfect beauty and purity, "the mirror of the sanctity of God himself, as far as this is possible for a creature" (Dom Guéranger), are a living image of the beauty and purity that will be required at the end of time by all the redeemed. Mary, immaculate from the very moment of her conception, is "a first pledge of the divine mercy" already given us of what the whole Church will be.

Dom Paul Delatte

To love Our Lady and to give her, not the first place, but an incomparable place in our devotion and our love is to embrace in an act of faith the whole of Christianity. If Jesus Christ is not God, Our Lady is no more than an ordinary woman who has given birth to an ordinary child. If Jesus Christ is not man, Our Lady doesn't even exist, since he who is not man has no need of a mother. If there is no union between God and man, the same alternative reappears. And so, to have veneration, devotion and love toward Our Lady is at the same time to place our beloved Lord in the reality of his double nature; it is to profess that he is man, to profess that he is God, to profess that his whole doctrine is the truth and that his Name is above all names. Look at this demonstration from all angles; it is there, and not in one or another arrangement of the decrees of God, that we will find the secret of her greatness and the doctrinal basis of the devotion we have toward her. There is an entire theology of Our Lady, with much better reason than there is a theology of the Angels; and nowhere better than in her can we see God.

(Letter to a Benedictine nun)

Unlike every other creature, who only receives from God, Our Lady's condition was that of giving to God. The Son of God is her Son, and therefore under an obligation to her. By her free consent and her maternal cooperation, she gave to God a place in his own creation.

(Conference, 1917)

There are certain acts of faith that are central, such as the act of faith in the beauty of Our Lady. God is nowhere more visible than in the Blessed Virgin: "A woman clothed with the sun" (Rev. 12:1), clothed with God, with the light of God, with the beauty of God, as with a garment. Such a lovable summary of the whole of divine Reality: God brought closer, made more accessible. For fear that we might be terrified when faced with him, the Lord appeared to us in his Mother: he came to us through her. Sheer beauty, sheer liberty, sheer tenderness. We feel that the infinite tenderness of the Father who is charity and who is able only to love has expressed itself in the Blessed Virgin. Isn't all the splendour of the soul of Mary a revelation of God, and a theophany?

(Homily on Our Lady, no date)

The Church would not have made such a magnificent display, from her Immaculate Conception until her glorious Assumption, if the Blessed Virgin had been no more than a means, a lovable but temporary piece of ingenuity the Lord made use of in order to dwell among us, the instrument through which the Incarnation came about: a tool one uses only for a single day. Our Lady remains the eternal means and method of God, the authentic way by which God comes to us. It is not on a single occasion but always that Our Lady is Our Lord's path toward us. She is the Mother of Jesus Christ in his individual nature, and also in his mystical body, the Church. *Christus venit semper.* Christ always comes, but he always comes by the same path, by the same means, in silence and through his Mother. She it is who introduces us into his presence. God repeats himself. The paths of the Incarnation are such that God does not wish to know of any others. It is by Our Lady that the union of God with human nature was consummated; and it is only by her that the union of each one of us with God will be achieved. "They found the child with Mary his mother" (Matt. 2:11).

(Conference, 1915)

In the Loreto litany we say to Our Lady: *Mater, Mater....* They aren't just formulas we say to edify ourselves and to give her pleasure. There is something else, a far deeper truth: we belong to that family. We call her Our Lady, our Mother—and so she is. All we have to do is live our lives with that realization. There is no Christianity without that, and I believe it is the failure to appreciate the relationship that links us to Our Lady that is at the root of our repeated falls, our delays, our procrastinations, our insensitivity, our illusions, our infidelities.

(Conference, 1914)

If we would pay her due honour, we must look upon her as the agent of our supernatural education; it is only at that price that she is Mother.

(Conference, 1917)

Basically, holiness is nothing but a well-made supernatural education, a completely successful supernatural education, and according to the Church, Our Lady cannot be without her part in it.

Don't say to me: We're too grown-up, we can run our lives now. We're never grown-up to God, nor to our mothers, nor to the Mother of God. We are always little to her: "My little children, with whom I am again in travail until Christ be formed in you!" (Gal. 4:19). She brought up her Son, and she will bring us up too. One doesn't resist one's mother; her maternal teaching enters us through her influence, through gentle and powerful suggestion; and that influence is sovereign because it is continuous and beloved: "Happy is the man who listens to me, watching daily at my gates, waiting beside my doors" (Prov. 8:34).

(Conference, 1916)

We should allow a Marian temperament to form in us. To be gentle as she was, loving as she was, peaceful as she was, simple as she was, abandoned, as she was, to all that God wishes and desires. There should be no moment of our lives that cannot be brought under her sweet influence. Let us ask the Lord to place in our soul, in our heart, in our body, all the dispositions, all the tenderness, all the self-abandonment, that were in his most holy Mother. He will do it if, in her, we seek him alone. Doesn't a child always look for its mother's face? The fruit of the liturgy is to make our whole being Marian, to bring to the realization in us the stamp of our Mother, to make our whole being crystalline in such a way that from the centre to the surface there may freely circulate in us the light and life of the little Child she has given us. We shall never more perfectly resemble that Son, the divine model, than on the day when the beloved features of his Mother are imprinted upon us and he will be able to recognize them. That is the fruit of the gift given on the Cross on the evening of Good Friday: the fruit of the Pasch.[1]

* * * * *

One cannot escape from the Marian character of these passages (chapters 8 and 9 of Proverbs and chapter 24 of Sirach) by saying that it is interpretation and accommodation, that they apply to the Incarnate Word, and that it is only by a sort of violent twisting that they are applied by the Church to the Blessed Virgin. I have never felt satisfied with that reply, even when I made it myself. The Church doesn't indulge in word-play, and the liturgy doesn't amuse itself with riddles and puns. And when it is a question of lives that have, in the mind of God and in reality, ties as close as those of the Lord and his Mother, united in a single decree of predestination, the sense people call, with a touch of disdain "accommodated" is, in itself, one of the multiple facets of the literal senses, and must be so for us. When Wisdom says of herself, "I am the mother of beautiful love, of fear, of knowledge, and of holy hope" (Ecclus. 24:24; Douay) and so on; above all when she says to us priests, "Come, eat of my bread and drink of the wine I have mixed" (Prov 9:5), tell me, who can distinguish whether it is Wisdom Incarnate or whether it is the Blessed Virgin who is speaking to us: the bread kneaded by my virginal hands, the scented wine that is the blood of the God-man?

(Conference, 1917)

Abbess Cécile Bruyère

Our Lord Jesus Christ, who could justly appreciate the tenderness of his Mother, knew how necessary she was to us, and would have felt that he had not given himself wholly if he had kept her for himself only. She is necessary to us, not as the author of grace, but as the channel through which grace comes to us. Mary is not our final end, for God does not wish any creature to be our final end; but she is the wholly lovable way that leads us to it.

(The Spiritual Life and Prayer)

"Behold the handmaid of the Lord" (Luke 1:38). When someone is resolved to acquiesce completely to the will of God, you may be sure that she will reach the summit. People search for methods of spirituality! Take up the Gospel of the Annunciation. If that was enough to make a Mother of God, it will be enough to make a perfect Spouse of our Lord.

(Conference, 25 March 1884)

Yes, between Our Lord and Our Lady there was a perfect harmony, a similarity between their souls; in eternity we will be struck by their mutual resemblance. When one considers Our Lord, it is impossible not to admire his Virgin Mother; if we are looking toward one, we will be looking toward the other. And so, when we become like the Son, we shall by that very fact be like the Mother. Let us come right up to her today, the better to see the little Child. Like all mothers, she has a marvellous gift of understanding, knowing what her Son wants of us and knowing what we are. We can indeed say to her: on this feast, which belongs to you, we have only one desire—to resemble as far as possible your divine Son, to walk in his footsteps, because we know that on the day when we come to resemble him, we shall possess all things....

He has united her to himself, and in all his mysteries she accompanies him to the very end: "Near the cross of Jesus there stood his mother" (John 19:25). It was indeed necessary that she should be there, since it was she who formed the Lamb, the Priest, the Victim. In the mystery of the Ascension, of Pentecost, the foundation of the Church, she is there again, as an essential part....

As for this title of Mother, we must not think that the Lord has given it to her for his childhood needs. No, she is ever his mother, and in the splendour of heaven she is all-powerful, always heard; because she is his mother the Lord is happy to pay her homage.

(Conference, Christmas 1891)

Just as Mary's maternity toward us does not consist simply in feelings, dispositions, a motherly devotedness that is truly incomparable, but is based on realities and not only on feelings, just so we must become aware of the links we have with her, which rest on a doctrinal ensemble far deeper and more resistant than sweet and devout feelings. We abase the honour paid to the Blessed Virgin by reducing it to a devotion; and we lessen our love of her by failing to elevate it to the level of a doctrine.

(The Spiritual Life and Prayer)

Devotion to Our Lady is not a devotion of the sort that one may have to the saints. The affective side of it can't be manufactured; it must be given by God. This devotion is part of our faith.

(Conference, Christmas 1891)

"Whoever does the will of my Father in heaven is my ... mother" (Matt. 12:50), said the Lord in the hearing of his Mother. If a creature who has been laboriously sanctified can bear such a title, what must we say of Our Lady? How is it that a soul can receive such a title from the Son of God? It is when it has arrived at perfect identification with the will of the eternal

Father, when by its holiness it becomes that sealed fountain, that enclosed garden of which the Holy Spirit speaks to us in the Song of Songs. The soul can only produce what it possesses. God was the sovereign Master in Our Lady; she was consequently like no other, just as she was virgin like no other. All this is a teaching of great value for us and demonstrates what it is that God seeks in the human creature.

(Conference, 1885)

It is because God rested in her as in no other creature, that Saturday is consecrated to the Queen of heaven, to Our Lady, the Immaculate Virgin. For he chose for the place of his rest not only the soul of Mary but also her virginal body, as it is said: "He that made me rested in my tabernacle" (Ecclus. 24:12; Douay). But at the same time, no creature has entered into God's rest as has Our Lady, Mary. From the first instant of her Immaculate Conception, this truly exceptional creature turned toward God, and disregarding all things and herself, she never for an instant looked away from God. She went through everything, but she took her rest only in God. All the words she ever spoke reveal this fixity at the centre. Nothing either troubled her or elated her. Her most holy life unfolded in a constant sanctification of the seventh day and in the rest of God. This is the whole secret of her life and the whole manner of her lofty sanctity, calm, silent, ordered, profound. The joys of Bethlehem, the anguish of Calvary, were to her soul what the waves whipped up by the wind are to the deep waters of one of those lakes one meets in high mountains, unexplored lakes, where no living thing is seen, unless it be the mighty eagle. Lakes so deep that one cannot reach the bottom, so far down into the earth's crust do their waters penetrate. The surface may be disturbed, but what can touch those unfathomable depths?

(Conference)

The work of our sanctification is a work God desires, and he desires it in a permanent way for each of our souls. Now if God desires us to become holy, he gives us the grace for it, and we have only to reply, if we wish to be in harmony with Our Lady:

"Accomplish whatever you desire for me, Lord; do in me whatever you wish." We have to juxtapose two terms: nothingness and being, the finite and the infinite. These two terms must be brought together into harmony because they are to come together one day. They came together in Our Lord, since the Word was made flesh; and that coming together must continue in each of us, not by the hypostatic union but by a real union, for St Peter formally declares that we are "sharers of the divine nature" (2 Pet. 1:4). All that is necessary for that is that we should know how God is present and that our soul should be disposed to give everything to God in all simplicity. Why not go directly, openly? What an attitude of directness there was in Our Lady! What a full and entire gift! What a total abandonment of her existence with all its energies, all its powers, all its aptitudes, in order to accomplish to the very last detail everything God asked of her! It is very simple, and it is precisely that absence of difficulty, once the will of God was known, that was the essence of Our Lady's sanctity. Difficult ways are for the unfaithful, for those who want things only by halves, who vacillate all their lives.

Our Lady was the most humble of all creatures; she had the correct understanding of the humility that is so true and so perfect. I say "so true" intentionally, because there is never anything forced about it. When one studies the true nature of Our Lady, the depths into which we see her plunge herself are not in the least exaggerated. "Behold the handmaid of the Lord": yes, because she is a creature; she desires to be what she is by the fact of her creation; she desires it in her will. Not only is she subject to him who made her because she is a creature, but she desires it to be so, she loves it, she brings it before God.

Our Lady, during the whole of her life, remains always in the truth. Truth envelops her entirely, in her words, in her actions, in her whole being. Let us ask of her that we may be so penetrated by the truth. Fundamentally, this is the grace of graces; we do not need anything else, for if we are submerged in truth we shall possess by that very fact all the virtues we admire in Our Lady.

(Conference, 25 March 1898)

The role of Our Lady and Mother has not come to an end with the mysteries of the Incarnation and the Redemption any more than have these mysteries themselves, which continue and become complete throughout all generations until the formation of the last of the elect. Mary is still our Mother in the work of our sanctification; Our Lord came to us through her, and it is always through her that he comes, he who always comes, until the end of time when he will come for the last time as Judge of the living and the dead. Since it is through the most blessed Virgin that the Lord comes to us, she is for us the channel of the supernatural life; it is through her that we receive all non-sacramental graces and all the dispositions that prepare us for fruitful reception of the sacraments.

(The Spiritual Life and Prayer)

Dom Prosper Guéranger

We must cease to be surprised if the Church exalts Mary and her greatness with such enthusiasm. We should, on the contrary, realize that all the praise it could give her, all the homage it could offer her in the liturgy, will always remain far below what is due to the Mother of God Incarnate. No one on earth will ever succeed in describing, or even in understanding, all the glory contained in this sublime prerogative. Indeed, since the dignity of Mary stems from the fact that she is Mother of God, it would be necessary, in order to grasp its extent, already to have understood the Divinity itself. It is to a God that Mary has given a human nature; it is a God that she had as a Son; it is a God who considered it a glory to be subject to her, according to his humanity. The value of such a high dignity in a simple creature cannot therefore be correctly estimated except by considering it in connection with the sovereign perfection of the great God who has thus deigned to place himself in a position of dependence toward her. Therefore let us recognize our nothingness in the presence of the Majesty of the Lord; and let us recognize our lowliness before the sovereign dignity of the one whom he chose as Mother.

(The Liturgical Year: Christmas)

194

After the humanity of our Redeemer, the entire person of Mary, her soul, were formed in the order of grace more highly than all other creatures put together. It could not be otherwise, and one realizes this as soon as one attempts in one's thoughts to plumb the depths of greatness and sanctity represented by the Mother of a God. Mary makes up, by herself, a separate world in the order of grace; by herself, for an instant, she was the Church of Jesus. At first it was for her alone that the Spirit was sent, and he filled her with grace from the very instant of her immaculate conception. That grace developed in her through the continuous action of the Spirit until it had made her worthy, as far as a creature could be, to conceive and give birth to the very Son of God who became also her Son.... The Archangel had not yet come to her to announce that she was to conceive in her chaste womb the Son of the Almighty, when already—as the Fathers teach us—she had conceived this eternal Word in her soul. He possessed her as his spouse, before calling her to the honour of being his Mother.

(The Liturgical Year: Eastertide)

She is not the principal agent, but it is through her that this agent influences each one of the members. Her union with the Head is immediate, as is right, for no creature but she had, or ever could have, such a relationship with the incarnate Word; but everything that enlightens and vivifies us comes through her from her Son.

From this follows the general action of Mary on the Church and her particular action on each one of the faithful. She unites us all to her Son, who unites us all with the divinity. The Father has given us his Son, the Son has chosen for himself a Mother from among us, and the Holy Spirit, by making this virgin Mother fruitful, has consummated the reunion of humankind, and of all creation, with God. That reunion is the final end God had in mind when he created all being. And now that the Son is glorified and the Spirit has come, we know the whole of the thought of God. More highly favoured than all the generations that followed one another before the day of Pentecost, we have, no longer as a promise but as a reality, a Brother who is crowned with the diadem of divinity; a Comforter who abides with us until the end of time to light our path and sustain us in it; a Mother whose intercession is all-powerful; a Church, also a Mother, through which we come to share in all these benefits.

(The Liturgical Year: Eastertide)

Notes

1. Cited in Dom Savaton, *Dom Delatte*, p. 340.

CHAPTER ELEVEN

"To him be glory in the Church" (Eph. 3:21):

The Body of Christ

"This new Congregation will have no other life than that of the Church."

Dom Guéranger in 1837

Solesmes' liturgical renewal was ruled and inspired by a wide and deep devotion to the Church, the actual hierarchical and communal Church of today, acknowledged and loved as the living body of Christ. Some have considered Dom Guéranger's work as inspired by a desire to bring back to life the Church of the Middle Ages, or that of the first centuries, as if the Church of those eras alone rightly understood Catholic liturgy and practice. This was far from being the case. It is one thing, as Dom Guéranger recognized, to single out a period in the Church's history when theology, art, and daily life all gave clear testimony to the essential nature of Christianity; it is quite another to try to remodel the external features of the Church of today according to the external features of that same period. "When will it be," he asked, "that we see once more the wonders of the Catholic centuries? Will it be when we have plenty of cathedrals newly-built in the style of the thirteenth century, and plenty of imitations of the art of the Middle Ages? No" (*Institutions liturgiques* 2, p. 283). For Dom Guéranger, to look to the early centuries of the Church's tradition is to find the clue to what is of enduring value, "their spirit of faith and keen sense of the supernatural" (*The Liturgical Year*: Christmas). To study tradition was, for him, to observe "the continual and ever-growing life of truth in the Church." In both his *Monarchie pontificale* (1870) on infallibility and his *Mémoire sur l'Immaculée conception* (1850), he shows that the Church's faith, as experienced and professed by all the faithful, is the main argument in the definition of a truth. The explicit formulation of allegedly new Marian dogmas proves to be nothing more than the definition of something that already existed. A contemporary of Newman, Dom Guéranger was as fascinated as he with the coherent development of the Church's life and thought, the unfolding of God's action in the life of the Church. This is part of "the genius of the Church, which enables her to adapt to the needs of the times, and she, like every inhabitant of this world, is subject to the law of salutary progress.... The Church, the mystical body of Jesus Christ, is subject to the law of development" (*Institutions liturgiques* 3, pp. 492-3).[1]

In an almost prophetic passage, reproduced here, this Benedictine warned of the danger of dividing the Church into periods, "for the Church, as regards its teaching, is always the same, no matter what period we are considering.... For believers, the Church of their time answers for the doctrine of the centuries of the past and those of the future." It is in the Church of today that we encounter the living Christ. Every choice for or against a particular council or teaching destroys the whole binding tradition, which can exist only as an indivisible unity. In his *Institutions* Dom Guéranger expressed this by saying that even if St Gregory the Great returned today, he would be obliged to accept the liturgy he found the Church to be using (*Institutions liturgiques* 4, p. 555). There is but one, unique Church that journeys toward her Lord, "rich with all the riches of the Lord" (Dom Delatte), ever dispensing the treasure of the faith he has entrusted to her.

Dom Guéranger's understanding of the need and value of unity was founded upon an existing state of disunity. The Catholic Church of the Restoration was firmly Gallican in character, attached to the alliance of throne and altar, suspicious, sometimes hostile to Rome and the Pope, and allowing the government free rein in Church affairs. It was against this background that Dom Guéranger affirmed the Church's universality, her unity, her tradition, and her liberty, because her existence and her rights come from God alone. The pages of *The Liturgical Year* devoted to the champions of ecclesiastical liberty—Hilary, Gregory VII, Anselm, Thomas Becket—are intentionally full and firm in tone.

His strong attachment to all things Roman, however, was not naïve, sentimental or blind. When in 1856 he narrowly missed being raised to the cardinalate, he wrote to his friends: "You will never know the happiness one feels at not being made a cardinal. I think I would have died of boredom, etiquette, and above all, exile. The Bon Dieu did well in doing what he did, and our Holy Father, the Pope, too. I love this excellent Pius IX very much, but I love him more from afar than from near." In the event, in what was to be one of Dom Guéranger's greatest sacrifices, it was Dom Pitra, one of his monks, who was summoned to Rome by Pius IX in 1858 and made a cardinal five years later.[2]

The mystery of the Incarnation, the permanence of the economy of the Incarnation, is at the centre of Solesmes' teaching on the Church. In an autobiographical note of 1829, Dom Guéranger wrote, "I understood that the dogma of the Incarnation must be the centre upon which everything else should turn, and that the dogma of the Church must be seen in relation to that of the Incarnation." In both cases, God is being faithful to the logic of his choice: taking a natural body, operating in a mystical body. More than an organization, the Church is a living organism; she is "Jesus Christ, living, radiating, continuing, prolonging himself through regenerated humanity, whose Head he is," as Dom Delatte puts it. This is the ultimate source of the Church's life and unity.

Indeed, there has never been Christianity without the Church; to be a Christian, as the New Testament writers recognized, and to be a member of the Church are one and the same thing. "As a Christian," affirms Dom Delatte, "I stem from the Church alone. Those who do not understand that do not possess a sufficient awareness of their nature as a Christian and as a child of God." The complete Christian mystery forms one body with that of the Church. In order to understand their faith, Christians need to understand the Church, indeed, to become Church. "The soul that has attained union with God," writes Abbess Cécile Bruyère, "is an exact miniature of the Church, one, holy, catholic and apostolic." It is in this way that we have access within the mystery of the Church to the mystery of God. Visible and invisible, organized society and mystical participation, unfolding in time and already possessing something of eternity, the Church is "the most perfect model of the spiritual life" (Abbess Cécile Bruyère).

Dom Prosper Guéranger

For us Catholic Christians, the Church is a divine institution that has no reason for existing and abiding on the earth except in the promises of Jesus Christ, and in the continuous and immediate existence of the Holy Spirit; that is why we place the Church in our Creed. For if the Church is a society, she is at the same time a dogma. Her permanence, without alteration or adulteration is the miracle of history; and it is enough to compare her with anything founded by men to realize that she is not human.

(from l'Univers, 14 December 1856)

If one could specify a period, however short, during which the Church had ceased to be under the influence of her divine author, during which she had been deprived of the direction of the divine Spirit he had poured forth upon her, that would be the end of the promises of Jesus Christ; the whole edifice of the Faith would crumble from the foundations.

It is easy to understand that it need not be necessary for a member of the faithful, whose personal existence will not stretch the length of a single century, to interrogate all the ages that have preceded him in order to know what the Church teaches. The Church of his time answers for the doctrine of the centuries of the past and those of the future. Otherwise how would he be able to form for himself a sufficient appreciation of a teaching that covers so many generations? He believes the Church (*credo Ecclesiam*), and with that faith he is in an intimate relation with the divine Word and with the Holy Spirit, who do not for a single day abandon that Church which they have deigned to make their necessary instrument for the salvation of the human race.

And so, the method of splitting the existence of the Church into periods is a dangerous one. For the Church, as regards her teaching is always the same, no matter what period we are considering. Tradition is the Church herself, believing and professing this doctrine or that, and the witnesses we find in the monuments of her existence are of value only in that they represent the thought and teaching of this society whose beliefs never change. If in a certain century the professions of faith appear more developed than in another, this only means that that Church, under the influence of the Holy Spirit who guides her, has considered it appropriate to make more precise, for the sake of the unity of her children, what was within her from the very beginning; and we know that she is divinely assisted in this work of development. What does it matter if, as a result of the destruction of the monuments of past centuries, we cannot always establish the exact progress of such-and-such a dogma through the ages? Our zeal for collecting the witness of the Fathers should not become sluggish for all that; but, when these beacons are lacking, isn't the Church there to supply for them with her clear and radiant light, of which the Fathers represent only a few scattered rays, of value only because she is their source? The Church, ever divinely assisted, ever watchful, ever pure, ever "without spot or wrinkle," believing today what she believed yesterday and what she will believe tomorrow, but perceiving it and teaching it with ever greater clarity and precision.

(Mémoire sur l'Immaculée conception, 1850)

Just as the holy sacraments, the secular remedy for the human race have been passed on and will be passed on even to the final generation of our race, even though those who were the first to receive the majestic power of conferring them disappeared eighteen centuries ago, so, in the same way, Christ has willed the permanence of his vicar here below. With this end in mind, he has rendered Peter immortal in the successors he gave to him.... No mere mortal invested him with his power. Christ himself established it in advance when he said, "You are Peter." These words are said to Peter in his entirety, to the Peter who lives even to the consummation of the age.... Such is the power of these divine words which Christ has uttered once and for all the ages to come.

(Monarchie Pontificale, 1870)

Peter is not the Church, the Church is not Peter; but as St Ambrose put it, where Peter is, there is the Church.

(Monarchie Pontificale, 1870)

What you have said to me about the axiom of Vincent of Lérins, *quod ubique*, etc,[3] is absolutely correct. This catholicity of times and places must be understood of the implicit presence of dogmas, and also of their period of development. There are some that have always been explicit, for example the divinity of Jesus Christ; others that have been believed in an undeveloped state, in germ, for centuries, but developing later and demanding, in their new state, the explicit adherence of faith. That is what the same Vincent of Lérins calls *profectus fidei*.[4] Numerically speaking, there are no more dogmas now than at the beginning; but from our point of view there have been ramifications that allow us to grasp the ensemble, which previously had not been so completely perceived. It is like the action of spring on the trees of a forest.

(Letter to Philippe Guignard, librarian of the city of Dijon, 17 March, 1868)

The dogma concerning Mary and that concerning the Roman Pontiff are closely related. They both have their origin in the mystery of the Incarnation. The Son of God needed a mother; and after the Ascension, he needed a Vicar on earth.

(Monarchie Pontificale)

202

We French are still far from that respect for authority that makes us resigned to the mistakes it can make, because we know in advance that authority, being exercised by a man, is necessarily subject to humanity's weaknesses and errors. One always imagines an impeccable authority, and that does not exist. Even God has not willed to give that prerogative to the Head of the Church; he is satisfied with making him infallible in the teaching of faith.

(Letter to Leon Landeau, 27 February 1852)[5]

Abbess Cécile Bruyère

The Church is the type and model of the contemplative soul. She is first Rachel before she is Leah; she shows herself to be Mary before she becomes active like Martha; she gives to the exterior only from her own inner fullness....

The Father desires the beauty of this splendid Virgin; but that beauty is not merely exterior—or rather, the external is only the shining forth of the internal radiance: "All the glory of the king's daughter is within" (Ps. 44[45]:14; Douay). And so it is with all the power of the Holy Church; all the beauty of her passage through the ages; all the splendour she sheds as she passes, even upon human things: literature, the arts, the sciences; the life she communicates to everything connected with her; everything, even the progress of civilization, everything proceeds from within, that is, from her close union with God. This exuberant power appeared in her from the very start, and the unbelievers who misjudged its origin said: "They are filled with new wine" (Acts 2:13).

(The Spiritual Life and Prayer)

This inseparable union of the Church with God is none other than that contracted individually with God by those who make up the Church. The soul that has attained to consummated union is an exact miniature of the Church, one, holy, Catholic and apostolic; the more that soul identifies itself with its Mother, the more surely it will win the heart of the One who has done all that can be done in this world for his collective spouse, and who, in the accomplishment of his designs, has only one model.

(The Spiritual Life and Prayer)

Nothing is achieved in the Church without the shedding of blood: that of the heart or that of the body.

* * * *

The Church lives only by the devotedness of her children, and God himself is not willing to do anything in this world without persons who consent to give themselves unreservedly. Of course, I do not intend to underrate the incomparable beauty of martyrdom, but often, when I think of our Father Abbot Guéranger, it seems to me that some martyrs would undoubtedly look with admiration at those long years spent among such temporal and spiritual bustle without our having seen him ever attempt to distract himself or escape from them by going and making himself a life outside to compensate for the troubles inside. What a lovely fidelity is this daily perseverance in *multa patientia* (2 Cor. 6:4), in a generosity nourished not by the sublimity of the actions but obscurely and continuously living the *abnegere semetipsum.*[6]

(Letter, 28 January 1890)

The power of the Church consists of echoing on earth the marvels of heaven, imitating them and reproducing them as well as she can and with the means her Spouse has given her.

(The Spiritual Life and Prayer)

Dom Paul Delatte

The Lord has been pleased to affirm that it is his own voice that is heard in the Church: "He who hears you hears me" (Luke 10:16). And so the Church has, like the Lord, the words of eternal life; when she teaches all nations, when she educates her children, she has the authority of Jesus Christ himself, and in that work of supernatural education she pursues, the Lord is with her until the consummation of the age.

204

That is essential. The Apostle said, if you have ten thousand instructors in Christ, you have only one father (cf 1 Cor. 4:15). And we have neither several instructors, nor several mothers in the order of the supernatural life: our mother is not science and she is not criticism. Our mother, the one who, after bearing us and feeding us, forms our soul and our heart by supernatural education, is the Church. God has given us to her alone. In the supernatural order, I do not receive my teaching from science, or from criticism, or from philosophy; none of these instructors has divine investiture; God does not speak through any of them, and none of them can claim to form me for eternity. As a Christian and from the point of view of the formation of my thought, my heart, and my life, I stem from the Church alone. Those who do not understand that do not possess a sufficient awarenesss of their nature as Christians and as children of God. If I had lived with our Lord, in his time, if St John the Baptist had directed me toward the Messaiah, and if it had been granted to me to receive his thought, his doctrine, his teaching from his divine lips, I would not—unless I had taken leave of my senses—have consented to cast doubt on the word of the Lord, on the pretext that Renan, Loisy or Herbert Spencer[7] wanted to contest the truth of it. "Godless men have dug pitfalls for me, men who do not conform to thy law" (Ps. 118[119]:85). God forbid that I should compare the teaching of our Lord Jesus Christ with the ephemeral theories that rise up against him! And so I need only listen to the Church, for when Jesus Christ departed from us, he left his Church, to whom he sent his Holy Spirit.

(Conference, 1914)

And what would have become of Our Lord himself without the Church? Our Lord would have been no more than a dazzling meteor, which appeared for a few years on earth; a brilliant phenemenon—and an extraordinary one—whose disappearance would have plunged the world into a darkness deeper than the former one. But it was not in such a way that the plan of God was conceived and realized. Our Lord jealously desired to remain eternally with us, and he gave us the Church, as he gave us the Eucharist.

(Retreat, 1899)

It is important that we should grasp this: Our Lord wished to establish not simply a religion, but a society. I beg you to keep this point of view firmly before you. States, governments, the liberals of today, to whatever category they belong, *légistes* or others—or even Catholics—will have none of it. They would be quite happy to recognize Jesus Christ as the founder of a religion, but not of a society. However, the Lord did not come simply to bring to the world a religion, to create individuals who are baptised: he came to create something supernatural on earth. It is by virtue of our naturalization, or rather, our supernaturalization, of our entry into that society he founded on earth, that we become children of God. One cannot become a child of God unless one becomes a child of the Church. The two things, it is true, are historically simultaneous, and yet there is a sort of logical priority that requires us first to belong to the Church as a society, so that through her we may then belong to God.

(Retreat, 1899)

We belong to the Church, we belong to that incomparable unity, that society, that immense family. It is indeed only by virtue of that belonging to the Church, and through her to Jesus Christ, that we enter with Jesus Christ into the uncreated family of the Blessed Trinity. But if that is so, then we must become conscious of our life and of our insertion in the body of the Church.

It is not enough to see God in that supernatural creation, to believe in that divine work, to admire its details and its functioning. It isn't enough to break with other conceptions of the order of things, and to recognize in a Platonic sense that everything gravitates around God, that the universal centre of all things is not the sun but the glory of God, and that it is for the Church to procure that glory. We have our place and our share of the activity in this immense Body, and we have absolutely no right to be unconcerned about it....

I cannot understand Christians who are conscious of what they are in the Church, Christians whom everything reminds of the organic solidarity that unites them to the Church, I cannot, as I say, manage to understand how such Christians could close in on themselves without having in their heart a constant preoccupation for everything that concerns the holy Church of God.

No one can go in two directions at once. There is no middle way between the apostle and the apostate; you are one or the other; it is necessary to make a choice.

But perhaps you will say to me: "What can I do about it, with my petty little life? How am I, with my poor supernatural energy, how am I to shift the immense inertia of the entire world?" Note, the Church is sustained only by the holiness of her children. St Dominic and St Francis, in the time of Pope Innocent III, supported on their shoulders the Lateran Basilica. Look what St Benedict did for the Church, or what Dom Guéranger did for her, simply by writing his *Liturgical Year*. Do you see what weight a life can have? No doubt, you don't have that sort of strength, but think about it: God's victories are always won by inner acts. It is by inner supernatural acts that one moves the world. And do you realize what the weight of a supernatural act can be?

There are physicists who have claimed that not a single atom can begin to vibrate in the universe without the echo and repercussions of that vibration being felt in the entire world, so close, so real and so profound is the organic correlation that exists among all the atoms of the universe. How accurate that theory is for the natural world, I don't know; but I believe in the dogma of the Communion of Saints, and I know very well that by virtue of the profound correlation that exists among all the members of the mystical Body of Jesus Christ, we cannot perform, in the secrecy of our heart, the most straightforward, the simplest, the gentlest supernatural act without there being an echo, a repercussion from that act throughout the whole supernatural world. Look at the significance of a supernatural act, the

Quis ut Deus? ("Who is like God?") of St Michael.[8] Look at the repercussions in the supernatural and historical world of that inner act—for it certainly was inner, since the angels have only intelligence and will.

I know that the inertia of the world is immense, but I also know—and that reassures me—that the Idea is invincible, that an idea never dies, that an idea always triumphs.

(Retreat, 1899)

It is in the Church that this life of our Lord circulates; it is to his Spouse that our Lord Jesus Christ has entrusted it. He has given her everything: his blood, his body, his merits. He has established her as the perpetual dispenser of this treasury of active sanctification, of this wealth of merits he has placed in her hands: the Holy Sacrifice of the Mass, the sacrifice of praise, the Faith, Tradition, Scripture, the power of sanctification and the supernatural gifts, the power of government and authority—it is to her that he has given these things.

And note the degree of unity that exists, in this area, between our Lord and the Church: so true is it that he has placed all his treasures in her hands that no sacrament can be validly conferred unless the minister has the intention to do what the Church does, and so that in this way it is truly the Church, rich with all the riches of the Lord, who always acts directly.

(Retreat, 1899)

What gives things their beauty is God; it is the reflection, the manifestation, the presence of God within them; and faith is precisely that superior understanding within us which makes us see the truth and beauty of God where they are to be found. Now, there is some of God in the Church, and as Jesus Christ subsists through God, the Church subsists through Jesus Christ. The Church is Jesus Christ, living, radiating, continuing, prolonging himself through regenerated humanity, whose Head he is; the Church is the Incarnation perpetuated throughout the ages; the Church is the Redemption being offered and realized in all generations.

(Retreat, 1899)

Notes

1. As Bride of Christ, as both virgin and mother of all those who are born in the Spirit and whose life she sustains with Christ's own life, the Church is profoundly "she." This understanding of the Church as a feminine reality derives from the whole of New Testament teaching, as well as from the teaching of the Church Fathers. This is not to give way to some sentimental impulse or to empty titles and analogies: as these texts make clear, it expresses a reality which bears inseparably upon God and humankind.

2. One of the most learned men of his age, Jean-Baptiste Pitra (1812-89) is perhaps Solesmes' most famous son. A professor at Autun, the young priest of twenty-eight had just deciphered the third-century "Inscription of Autun," when he presented himself at Solesmes on 15 August 1840, making profession on 10 February 1843. A month later he was appointed prior of the ill-fated Saint-Germain de Paris, where he was one of the chief collaborators in Abbé Migne's Greek and Latin Patrology. After the collapse of the Paris foundation, he was engaged from 1846 to 1850 in scholarly research, copying out thousands of hitherto unpublished patristic and ecclesiastical works, while travelling throughout France, England, Belgium, Holland and Switzerland in search of funds to sustain Solesmes' precarious finances. A lover of his monastery and the monastic life, it was a great trial for him to be away so much. "Let me be always exiled, provided I am the only one!" he wrote to his abbot before crossing the Channel. "Provided that at this price, you will be happier with my brothers! It is your troubles that weigh me down most...." It was his unrivalled acquaintance with the Byzantine Church that led Pius IX to call him to Rome in 1858, from where he was sent to Russia for seven months to study the law of the Russian Church. Raised to the cardinalate in 1863, he also supervised the edition of liturgical books in the Greek rite and served as Vatican librarian.

3. "In the Catholic Church herself, one must take great care to hold fast to what has been believed everywhere, always, and by all, *quod ubique, quod semper, quod ab omnibus creditum est*; for it is that which is truly and properly catholic, as the force and etymology of the word itself show, which embraces the universality of things." This is the famous "canon" provided by the monk St Vincent of Lérins (died before 450), as a guide in determining the true Catholic faith and tradition.

4. "The essential characteristic of progress, *profectus*, being that each thing grows while remaining itself."

5. See Chapter Twelve, note 2.

6. "Let him deny himself and take up his cross and follow me" (Matt. 16:24).

7. Alfred Loisy (1857-1940) was a French Modernist biblical scholar who treated the Gospels merely as catechetical and cultural literature, having only a slight historical basis. Ernest Renan's (1823-92) *Vie de Jésus* repudiated the

supernatural element in Jesus' life and portrayed him as "the gentle dreamer of Galilee." Herbert Spencer (1820-1903) was the leading exponent of agnosticism in nineteenth-century England.

8. Tradition holds that St Michael's name, which in Hebrew means "Who is like God?" was the war-cry of the faithful angels in the battle fought against Satan and his followers. His name is mentioned four times in Scripture: Dan. 10:13ff; 12:1; Jude 9; Rev. 12:7-9.

Chapter Twelve

"Shepherds after my own heart" (Jer. 3:15):

The Art of Spiritual Direction

When a person of somewhat rigid character said to Dom Guéranger that, having the task of guiding others, he found it repugnant to use any artifice in leading them toward God, the Abbot of Solesmes smiled and replied: "Our Lord is constantly using his ingenuity with us. Do you consider that artifice? Certainly not; it is love. And so, love those souls and you will be skilled with them, without being humanly calculating. Love alone will give you inexhaustible resources with which to lead them to God."

Both his impact within the monastic world and his activity in the wider affairs of the Church have tended to overshadow the warmth and charm of Dom Guéranger's character, his tender regard for individuals. For the abbot of Solesmes, each person was a world, a special creation; and the work of spiritual direction an exercise of docility to the Holy Spirit, a question of humility. "When I get to heaven," he used to say, "God will not ask me whether I have written books, but whether I have taken care of the souls entrusted to me." "People are so used," wrote Dom Delatte in his life of Dom Guéranger, "to seeing in the abbot of Solesmes the tireless champion of the Church's rights that they do not think of the fervent monk, the enlightened director of souls, of the superior wholly devoted to the good of those in his charge, who were truly his children."

Both Dom Maurus Wolter and Dom Laurence Shepherd were deeply impressed by the family spirit of the Solesmes cloister. The family character of the Rule derives from the vow of stability, which binds each monk to his own particular monastery, and from the life-long tenure of the abbatial office. It had been something of a triumph for Dom Guéranger to have obtained permission for life abbots, since triennial superiors had been the norm. Moreover, the growth of pre-revolutionary abbeys, increased educational and parochial responsibilities and centralized congregations had tended to withdraw the father of the family from the life of the house. It was no small part of Dom Guéranger's genius to have recovered the immediate and ever-present paternal government of St Benedict's abbot. For he was himself above all a father, firm and gentle, continually setting before his monks, nuns, and guests the highest spiritual ideals, while showing a tender and even humorous patience with human weakness. Dom Laurence Shepherd noted how accessible Dom Guéranger was to his monks; many years later Dom Delatte would affirm in Chapter that all were free to enter his cell at any moment without knocking, a custom he maintained even after his resignation.

This family spirit embraced not only their own communities and Congregation, but all those who came within the bounds of their monasteries. The robust rector of Kerentrech, the Abbé Schliebusch, recalled the affectionate exclamation that greeted his visits to Solesmes: "Here is one of the children of Solesmes!" As a consequence of their ability to "plumb the depths of the heart" (as one retreatant described Dom Guéranger), by their power of sympathy and affection, and the clarity and virility of their direction, these writers exerted an influence over a large and varied circle, which included princes and dignitaries of the Church, the foremost spirits of the Catholic revival,[1] men and women, old and young, mayors and marble-cutters.[2] To enumerate all their friends and guests is an impossible task: the number of Dom Guéranger's correspondents alone exceeds three thousand. But what is striking in their correspondence is the way they give themselves whole-heartedly to the smallest child as to the most illustrious prince of the Church. Two days before he died, Dom Guéranger was still giving catechism lessons to a small girl; while Cardinal Pie promised Abbess Cécile Bruyère "to make known to you all the great needs of my soul.... You will help me to become more pleasing to God and prepare me for a less severe and humiliating judgment when I go before him." Abbess Cécile marvelled at Dom Delatte's "fresh enthusiasm for souls, your wonder at their beauty, the captivation they inspire in you, often from the first moment. That both rejoices and surprises me." At the same time, she recognized that, as a young abbot, he could perhaps be too demanding of souls, in a letter that throws vivid light on her own methods:

> You are not aware of your own strength, your influence, others' need of you; if you were, you would make more allowance for those who form the greater part of the human race: the weak and unsteady, who have more need of a doctor or a father than a professor of logic.... Mon Père Abbé, you would be more at home among the angels, good or bad, because your ways of thinking, your habits, belong more to them than to humankind. Except for those who have enough courage and affection to follow you, the others leave you along the path because of their little legs. There is only one thing to do: it is to take them into your great arms.

This is an image characteristic of Solesmes' spiritual direction: not so much bending down to one's weakness as lifting one up to the level of strength.

At the root of this attitude was a charity that made them see each person as unique in the world, and an understanding of spiritual direction that derived from the character of a Benedictine abbot. In his two chapters on the abbot, St Benedict supplies a profile of the personal qualities that should characterize the abbot's dealings with others, insisting on mercy, discretion, and avoidance of excess. The abbot is to teach his children not only by words of counsel but also by the pattern of his whole life; he is a living model and exemplar, providing them not only with words but also with a personal relationship. He must so temper his commands and his correction that "the strong may have something still to wish for, and the weak nothing from which to shrink" (ch. 64). He must therefore have consideration for the varying strengths and qualities of individuals, and for the needs of the old and the sick. He should strive rather to be loved than feared, and to profit his brethren rather than preside over them. He must be patient, adaptable, flexible. "Dom Guéranger," wrote Abbess Cécile Bruyère, "was in his spiritual works what he was in the direction of souls, that is to say, supple, very forgetful of himself." The action of the abbot or abbess, noted Abbess Cécile, is like that of "the sun, as it causes the things of nature to grow, developing everything according to its own shape and colour." As Dom Guéranger wrote in a letter (12 January 1867) to a superior:

> Above all, one must guard against the desire to force everyone into the same mould. There are so many ways that lead to God, so much diversity of graces, that one must, like St Paul, make oneself all things to all men, enter into each person, without forcing them to enter into oneself. Be small, and full of tender charity, and everything will turn out as it should; it will be no longer you who speak but the Bridegroom.

And again like St Paul who, in his role as apostle, compared himself to both a father and a mother (cf Gal. 4:19; 1 Thess. 2:7-13), Dom Guéranger recommends to Dom Maurus Wolter, the young prior of Beuron, to be "like a mother" to his children and showed himself "maternal"—the word is G. B. de Rossi's[3]—to his friends and guests. Dom Delatte, too, habitually addressed a mother—and grandmother—whom he directed for fifty years as *mon enfant*; it was his favourite expression. (He used *mon fils*, "my son," only for Mère Rosalie, Prioress of the Servants of the Poor at Paris!) If holiness is "nothing but a well-made supernatural education" (Dom Delatte), then the art of spiritual direction is a parental and expert training and cherishing of the spirit.

Tender without being sentimental, combining great firmness with understanding, their varied, unrigoristic, and persuasive direction of souls was characterized by breadth and a Gospel-like simplicity. The emphasis in their direction is on God's intimate action and on the humble acceptance of the ordinary circumstances of life, helping their pupil souls to find there the raw material for holiness and an opportunity of approaching nearer to reality. Adapting themselves to every temperament and aiming at a more abundant life for each, they do not hesitate to remind people of the forgotten truths of Christian faith in all their purity, of the greatness of God's gifts, of the reality of our union with him, and of the universal call to perfection. Any diminishment of either God's promises or his demands, however hard and costly, they do not allow, even among the widely differing states of life: each one can and must claim eternal life.

Dom Prosper Guéranger

When I get to heaven, God will not ask me whether I have written books, but whether I have taken care of the souls he has entrusted to me.

(Cited by Abbess Cécile Bruyère in
Portrait of Dom Guéranger)

You are the last of all, and you have been made the first. The only way you can compensate for that is by the most loving compassion toward each one. The same gentle and supernatural affection will be given to you in return; and I know of nothing that gives greater joy to the heart of our Lord than the exchange of divine charity between the souls he has thus brought together. Use all your capacity for zeal and discretion to make them love one another ever more.

(Letter to a Superior, 26 March 1867)

Being a superior is simply a question of the heart. The law is always the same. One fine day our Lord passes by a soul and says to it: "Do you love me more than these?" (cf John 21:15). And if the soul replies with sincerity, "You know, Lord," the Lord replies in his turn, "Feed my lambs." After that, one must keep to the response one has made to the Lord, and everything becomes fidelity to God, love. It is from God that one expects everything; it is for him alone that one works; the question is very much simplified.

(Cited in Portrait)

One must be the very humble servant of souls; I know nothing but that.

* * * * *

Pray hard that I may be a good shepherd, entirely given to his flock for love of the Chief Shepherd, but also for love of the sheep themselves.

* * * * *

When I am occupied with a soul, our Lord grants me the grace to see nothing but that soul in this world.

* * * * *

The spirit of the Holy Rule is that the Abbot should always have a word ready on his lips and should always be ready to give his children a light on everything. He isn't asked for eloquence or brilliance, but a simple, fatherly word. For that purpose, acquire the habit of gathering everywhere like a bee—in the Divine Office, in what you read, in your thoughts, and even in conversations—in such a way that your spirit, always vigilant, renews and enriches itself ceaselessly. But in fact, the real preparation is above all union with God and the true spirit of prayer; for then your intelligence will profit doubly. Our Lord himself will renew you, will refresh you, blessing your reading, your work, giving fruitfulness to your mind which will never be empty—any more than your heart is—for those who require from you their spiritual nourishment.

(Cited in Portrait)

Take care of your health; you need it, and it doesn't belong to you. Encourage in every way you can a holy liberty of spirit among your monks, and do everything to make them love their state of life more deeply than anything else in the world.

Make yourself lovable always and in all circumstances. Be a mother rather than a father to your children.

Imitate the patience of God, and don't demand that spring bear the fruits of autumn.

Be always accessible to everyone; avoid etiquette and ceremony. Come as close as you can to the familiarity you have seen practised at Solesmes.

Adapt yourself to everyone, and don't try to adapt others to yourself; for God has created us all different, and you are the servant of all, like our Lord Jesus Christ.

Take scrupulous care of the health of each one, and don't wait for a serious illness before giving a dispensation.

Establish the observance progressively, and don't be afraid to retrace your steps if you have gone too far.

Don't be worried about any relations with the world that your monks may have, if they have the spirit of their state and if it is a question of the glory of God and the salvation of souls.

Remember that the spirit of faith is the only basis of the monastic life.

Inspire the love of the sacred liturgy, which is the centre of all Christianity. Have your monks study with love the *Acta Sanctorum Ordinis*, the Annals, and also the history of individual monasteries.

Make sure that they study theology, especially St Thomas, canon law, and Church history.

Finally, strive to increase in your sons the love of the Church and of the Holy See.

> *(Letter to the first Prior of Beuron, Dom Maurus Wolter,*
> *5 May 1863)*

Yes, you are right to say it: those who love our soul are indeed precious, even more than those who love our heart, all the more because, like God, they could not love the one without the other.... When he decides to direct us, his direction is certainly as valuable as that of men who can, after all, only introduce us to him. The simplicity of heart you possess is a marvellous disposition for hearing his voice, and once that voice has been heard, it is only at a cost to us that we can resist, if we have integrity; for God said to the apostle on the road to Damascus, it is not easy, it is hard to resist the word one hears, that word that is like a goad. There is a lovely phrase in the psalms: cast the care of yourself on the Lord and he will lead you, he will feed you (cf Ps 54[55]:22). In a word, he will be your director.

> *(Letter to Madame Swetchine, 7 December 1833)*

Beak! So you've been pecking people's heads off again! That had better not happen to you any more, or you'll be plucked. You know that I don't like the devil—and neither do you. As you say, I have to turn you into a bird of paradise—but you are so thin! One would think you ate nothing but lizards. If I can't fatten up your body, at least I'd like to fatten up your soul; cooperate with me in that, and follow the diet I'm giving you, or else—well, again, I'll pluck you! Beak, Beak, Beak, keep well, keep good, and keep thinking of your father who is praying for you. Be obedient, my dear child; that is the only way you will find life.

(Letter to a young monk, Père Louis David,
nicknamed "Bec" ["Beak"], 25 March 1840)

You are making things difficult for yourself by felling the branches when you should be directing the axe at the trunk and the roots.

(Letter to Reverend Mother Elizabeth de la Croix,
Prioress of the Carmel at Meaux,
23 December 1860)

Prudence, self-possession: all that is very difficult for a nature as ardent and personal as yours. Nevertheless, they are necessary, and our Lord will give them to you. They will come after humility and through humility.

Consider yourself the last of all; strive unceasingly against your nature; never hurry things along. Keep yourself united to your prioress in a spirit of faith, and you will come in the end to do what Our Lord expects from you, or to put it better, he himself will do what you have to do. Shield yourself from all overexcitement; learn to be patient, unified, kindly, especially toward those whom you do not like.

(To the same, 13 April 1861)

When you learn to keep silence and see the good side of things, then you will have made great progress.... Every foundation is imperfect and full of wrangling: people and things need to settle, then the Lord acts.

(To the same, 17 August 1861)

Wage war, first, on self-will and pride. Seek submission and humility, and that constantly. Don't let yourself off anything, and you will have peace: in peace, Our Lord will work in you, and you will come in the end to respond to his love.

(To the same, 17 May, 1862)

Calm, reflection, gentleness should characterize all your ways. See everything, reflect much, act little, and never under the influence of passion.

Don't forget, my dear child, that you have been made the servant of all; thus, as long as it is compatible with your duties as superior, forget yourself, efface yourself to give pleasure to those whom you are guiding. Strive to be loved rather than feared. That's a maxim of our Father St Benedict. Recall unceasingly your young age, humble yourself before God, pray unflaggingly that his Spirit may be always in you and preserve you from the outbursts of nature; the recompense for your humility will be that you will be pleasing to God and to men....

You have understood well, and I do not doubt it, that having received a share in being a father, you are bound to pray much for your little flock, collectively and individually, at the altar, at the Divine Office, at prayer; always have present before you the needs of each one. There you will find, my dear child, your great help in doing good, the light you need to discern it, the consolation you need in the obstacles and contradictions that you will experience. Do not forget me in these prayers at the feet of our Lord, and know well that I do not pass a single day without commending you will all my heart to the Divine Majesty.

(Letter to Dom Menault, named superior of
a priory in 1854)

Abbess Cécile Bruyère

I dreaded the irrevocability of the [abbatial] Blessing. I dreaded the honours attached to the title; I was very aware that the obscurity for which I so much longed would be impossible.... It pleased Our Lord that the Blessing should change my whole being. And he has allowed my soul to see, with intense clarity, the total detachment to which it is called. Until then I had felt that the love of God would make me undertake anything; but from then onward I saw that the second commandment was like the first, and that I must be to my neighbour—through the Lord and for his sake—what I was to him. I felt that I must give my time, my thoughts, my whole life to souls, and that the Blessing would put the seal on that complete holocaust to the honour of God....

God is faithful, that is certain.... I have only failed in my commission when I have ceased to lean upon the divine gift and relied instead on myself. Otherwise the grace I received gives me the discretion and equity necessary "to adapt oneself to many different temperaments" (*Rule of St Benedict*, ch. 2). Imperfection comes when I begin to seek myself, to begrudge my time and labour, in a word, to have a life of my own again. The love of God lies in devotedness... it is after all, the gift of oneself, and is not the formula for it: "My beloved is mine and I am his" (Song of Songs 2:16)?

(Letter)

How beautiful it is to be an abbot on Christmas Eve. There are things only an abbot can see in it: "Lo, I come ... to do thy will, O my God" (Ps 39[40]:7). What an honour it is for a creature to have so great a resemblance to the Son of God, that nothing falls outside the sovereign domain of God in that body and soul which are wholly given over to him. One is unaware of all this as long as God has not possessed us sufficiently to give us to others.

(Letter to Dom Delatte, 24 December 1890)

I feel as if I am only one thing for everyone: a sort of all-purpose

220

utensil, which is never out of use, even though it is cracked and dented by wear and tear.

(Letter)

Dom Paul Delatte

If it is true that abbots make their monks, it is certain that monks make their abbot, and that the monastery is a school of mutual sanctification....

The abbot has a greater compensation of which St Benedict does not speak: the profit he wins from constant contact with good souls. This contact is the most wholesome there is, and resembles a sacrament. It is partly because such souls are to the abbot an encouragement and an example, but chiefly because they are for him a sort of anticipated vision of God. The greater the effect and the nearer to its cause, the more perfect is the knowledge we get of the cause; and here the effect is not only that work of God—a spiritual soul—but also all the means God takes to transform it and unite it to his beauty. Thus the abbot finds there a real theology. And until the day when he comes to contemplate God face to face, he will nowhere see him more clearly than in souls, in the living crystal of their purity. He will not find it hard then to keep very close to our Lord....

(Commentary on the Rule of St Benedict, 1913)

People need confidence, and this can only be given with kindness and confidence. Point out what is amiss but with gentleness and affection, asking our Lord to supply what is lacking. One thing helps souls very much: it is the belief that they will do well. They will tend, with God's help, toward the good that is shown them when we assure them that they possess the supernatural resources within them to achieve it. This does not mean that certain ingrained defects do not leave traces for a long time, but when a person is wholly given up to God, even these disappear, and there remains nothing but a scar, beautifully healed by the hand of God. A time comes when only God remains in the soul. You can never go too far in the direction of peace, calm, joy, supernatural prayer. All that is the fruit of charity; and the theological virtues, which unite us to God, know no extremes.

(Letter)[4]

This soul needs to be both calmed and reassured. Quiet, pacify, and moderate with sound doctrine whatever is over-eager and effervescent. The first taste of heavenly wine often produces this exhilaration. Remind her that what is happening is the development of what the Lord has built up since her baptism. She is late! Let her read the four spiritual letters of direction written by Bossuet to a young lady of Metz, and also by Bossuet, "Manière courte et facile de faire l'oraison en foi et de simple présence de Dieu." We must never be carried away by excessive emotions and impulses, which can affect health and upset balance. In all this, we have nothing to do ourselves: the only safe way is to allow the Lord to work within us, without allowing ourselves, with a sort of intemperance, to drink in long draughts. Besides this over-avidity, what I would like to restrain is the curious seeking after experimental presence, its way of working and its necessity. Here we are not in a land where we may make discoveries or conquer at will. Exaggerated seeking of this kind would lead almost inevitably to the error of naturalism or to simulation. "In silence and in stillness the devout soul goeth forward and learneth the mysteries of Holy Scripture" (*Imitation of Christ*, I, 20). The higher these things are the less we should bring ourselves to them. Our Lord will lead us to them, if we keep ourselves in fidelity, attentiveness, humility. I am always afraid lest the gifts of God may either be lost or spoiled by a mixture of human reactions. That said, you must reassure. Tell her that spiritual things are incomparably more true and much greater than she can imagine. Then add that there is no illusion when we let ourselves be guided. One is secure in the way of obedience.

(Letter)

Let us be what God has made us. It is in the realm of our moral and spiritual life above all that we must not give ourselves a role, act a part, create a façade, or imitate anyone. God does not issue second editions. He is rich enough always to create something new. We do not have second-hand souls, or minds, which have already been used.

(Letter)

Notes

1. Montalembert, Lacordaire, Louis Veuillot, Alfred de Falloux, Joseph de Maistre—to name but a few. It was after a retreat to Solesmes and with Dom Guéranger's encouragement that Lacordaire decided to restore the Dominican order in France.

2. The marble-cutter was Léon Landeau, one of Dom Guéranger's closest friends. They first met in 1836: while crossing the yard of the marble works near the monastery before dawn, Dom Guéranger tripped over a sleeping man. It was the young manager, a descendant of a long line of marble-cutters from Sablé. Despite his many responsibilities and cares, Dom Guéranger found time to offer spiritual guidance, bless his marriage, baptize the children and follow their education, marrying each in their turn—and to begin once more to baptize and catechize the following generation. He could see the roof of the marble works from his cell, and each year he presided over the workers' annual feast.

3. Giovanni Baptista de Rossi (1822-94), the founder of Christian epigraphy and explorer of the Catacombs, whom Dom Guéranger met in December 1851, at the beginning of the young archaeologist's career. Their correspondence shows Dom Guéranger entering into all of de Rossi's interests, scholarly, human, and divine, encouraging and stimulating the young man with all the generosity and zeal of his nature. "He has been to me," declared de Rossi, "what St Philip Neri was for Baronius." When Dom Guéranger was in Rome for the approval of the Proper of the Congregation in 1856, de Rossi took him to the Catacombs where he celebrated the first underground Mass on 26 April 1856 in the crypt of St Cecilia in the cemetery of Callixtus, surrounded by de Rossi, sixteen of his *fossores*, three religious, and four English Catholics.

4. This and the following two extracts quoted in Dom Savaton, *Dom Delatte*, pp. 316, 326, 308.

CHAPTER THIRTEEN

"The lines have fallen for me in pleasant places; yea, I have a goodly heritage" (Ps 15[16]:6):

In the School of St Benedict

"Half of Europe was converted by religious who lived the contemplative life."—Dom Guéranger

Guided by his sense of the Church and of the Rule of St Benedict, Dom Guéranger desired that the monastic ideal of Solesmes be ordered toward the contemplation of Christ in the mystery of the Church, in fidelity to a living tradition, received, passed on and made present. "He was a true contemplative," said the bishop of Poitiers, Monsignor Pie, of Dom Guéranger. "He has what every Benedictine ought to have: the constant and exclusive preoccupation with God." The monastic ideal represented by Solesmes is essentially a contemplative one; worship and prayer are the raison d'être of its life. It belongs to that category of institutes described by Vatican II as "totally dedicated to contemplation" whose members "give themselves to God alone in solitude and silence, and through constant prayer and ready penance. No matter how urgent may be the needs of the active apostolate, such communities will always have a distinguished part to play in Christ's Mystical Body where 'all the members have not the same function' (Rom. 12:4)."[1]

The "contemplative life" does not mean the personal contemplative prayer to which all Christians are called; nor does it refer to certain states of prayer that are generally considered exceptional and quite independent of any kind of institution. The contemplative life, like every human life and every Christian life, is a "mixed" life, consisting both of contemplative elements—which could be summed up in the classical ascending series of reading, meditation, prayer and contemplation—and of active elements—work, manual or intellectual, the service of others on every level. But it is a life in which these active elements are subordinated to and determined by the contemplative elements. It is this subordination that limits the kinds of work undertaken and the conditions in which the work is done.

The contemplative monastic life does not constitute a Christian life different from that of others in the Church; it is simply "the excellent fruit of Christianity" (Dom Guéranger), "a form and modality of the same life, the Christian life" (Dom Delatte), faithful to the ideal that comes from the gospel. It is, however, a state of life, an actual existence completely oriented toward prayer and ascetical activity, and in which everything is organized to foster both. Wherever the gospel is preached, wherever the Church spreads, there are found those who wish to live out its message more fully, to dedicate themselves to a deeper understanding and more thorough observance of Christ's commands and counsels. "The monk," wrote Dom Guéranger, "is simply someone who takes his Christianity seriously."

In an unpublished, incomplete Life of St Benedict, dating from around 1860, Dom Guéranger sees St Benedict as profoundly conscious of being an heir to a tradition that plunges its roots into the gospel itself: "Monasticism is a form of Christianity as old as the Church herself. It was born in the East with our faith." And because he understood the gospel in its broadest sense to include the Old Testament as understood in the light of the gospel, he finds the monastic life anticipated there in all the patriarchs and prophets who have pre-figured Christ, model of monks. "What then is monasticism," he concludes, "this great thing which the ancient world seems to have been labouring to bring forth, and which, as the Fathers of the Church maintain, is the excellent fruit of Christianity? It is the state in which man, raised again from the fall by Jesus Christ, strives to re-establish in himself the image of God by effective separation from all that can cause sin." This search for evangelical perfection makes the monk a kind of sacrament in which the mystery of salvation is revealed and communicated. In this sense, the monastic life, like the Church herself, is a prolongation of the Incarnation: "God has done nothing greater than the Incarnation, of which the Church is the prolongation. Now the Church has a heart: the religious state. That is the most complete manifestation that there can be here below of the mystery of the Incarnation, by its exact reproduction of the life of Christ."

Dom Guéranger considers the life of St Benedict to be the pattern of the monastic life not only in its double mystery of separation and communion, but also in its profound expression of the paschal mystery. The life of St Benedict both represents Christ's dying to the world and shows forth the new life in the Spirit, initiated by the resurrection of Christ: first, the hermit in the desert, "conforming himself to Christ in the tomb"; then "the hour of resurrection," the founding of twelve communities, "that he might appear as the type of the resurrected life that his disciples profess in the service of the Church and of the faithful." The full prophetic meaning of the monastic life is, then, to be understood in reference to the whole mystery of death and life contained in Christ. St Benedict's life offers an example of the "mixed" life, or rather, a "unified" life, an active life flowing by a kind of necessity from the contemplative life, separation from the world, and the exclusive search for God producing of themselves powerful effects for the good of souls. "All contemplatives who really understand the nature of their calling are a living treasury of truth, teaching, and grace," insists Dom Delatte, "are truly apostolic," truly missionary by their very existence in relation to the mystery of Christ.

In describing the nature of the monastic apostolate and recalling its decisive influence in the formation of Europe, these writers show that this was a contemplative apostolate, belonging to the essential nature of the contemplative life, and they specify its primarily spiritual task. The influence of the Benedictine life was not that of a centralized body, organized for a particular purpose in the Church; it was the influence, rather, of scattered centres of intense Christian life, faith, and culture, outside the demands of a particular period. Monasteries are "powerful preachers," notes Dom Delatte, not so much by what they do as by what they are. And insofar as St Benedict wrote his Rule for communities wishing to lead a life of prayer and work in seclusion, the wide-ranging influence that Benedictines have sometimes had on the Church and the world was not something deliberately sought or anticipated, but a by-product of the discipline, spirituality, and temperament created by the Rule. Their fruitfulness for the good of the Church sprang from the very conditions of monastic life defined by St Benedict—a communal life, a life of stability within the walls of the monastery. As Dom Delatte points out, if the activities of missionary monks took them out of the cloister, one of their first goals was the establishment of new centres of monastic life: "The evangelist was the monastery itself, preacher with a hundred voices that were silent neither by day nor by night." It was not, then, the apostolate of a single monk, but of a whole monastic community, whose role consisted less in action than in a presence, a silent, eloquent preaching of the true Christian life, in which prayer, the liturgy, and good works were the various expressions of a single Christian reality. The aim of these "entrenched camps," as Dom Delatte describes them, was not to spread the faith by going outside the monastery, but to attract, to draw in, by implanting a religious life and culture able to transform a people profoundly from within. The monastery was the medium and the message. Its work, "in the freedom of the Holy Spirit" (Dom Guéranger) was, above all, a contemplative one that merited the name of an apostolate. With Dom Guéranger, one can say in all truth that "half of Europe was converted by religious who lived the contemplative life." [2]

A spontaneous expression of the vitality of faith, springing directly from the gospel, arising in response to no specific apostolic task, monastic life has its own way of realizing and signifying the Church's mystery, especially in its power to create a sign of communion. It is the fact that each Benedictine monastery is a family that has given its predominant characteristic to its service of others; its power for good is far more that of a community than that of the individual. Through the permanent and local character of the bonds of Benedictine community life, through the position of the abbot, through the common life in Christ, celebrated and realized sacramentally in the liturgy, the monastery is a real family. It also represents and realizes concretely an *ecclesia*, as Dom Delatte shows, a microcosm of the great *Ecclesia*, "that immense family of the Church in time and in eternity," into which baptism introduces us. The text that most perfectly expresses this ideal of sacramental communal life has passed from the liturgy of the monastic family into the liturgy of the whole Church, from the humble washing of the brethren's feet by the weekly servers to the rites of Maundy Thursday:

> Where love is found to be authentic, God is there.
> The love of Christ has gathered us together into one....
> Let us fear and love the living God,
> And love each other from the depths of our heart.
> Therefore, when we are together,
> Let us take heed not to be divided in mind.
> Let there be an end to bitter quarrels, an end to strife,
> And in our midst be Christ our God.

> (*Ubi caritas est vera, Deus ibi est.*
> *Congregavit nos in unum Christi amor....*
> *Timeamus et amemus Deum vivum,*
> *Et ex corde diligamus nos sincero.*
> *Simul ergo cum in unum congregamur,*
> *Ne nos mente dividamur, caveamus.*
> *Cessent iurgia maligna, cessent lites,*
> *Et in medio nostri sit Christus Deus.*

Dom Prosper Guéranger

Benedict expressed the spirit of the Rule, which is effective separation from the world, by living out its total reality in his own particular way. But after conforming himself to Christ in his tomb, the hour of resurrection had to arrive, so that he might appear as the type of the resurrected life which his disciples profess and put at the service of the Church and the faithful. First, the hermit in the depths of his cave; later, as the abbot of twelve monasteries, he saw the field of the apostolate open before him. Such in fact would be the destiny of Western monasticism, the legislator and model of which he was called to become. First, the desert, the hidden and crucified life of the cloister; later, the apostolic ministry among pagan nations, works of sanctification and Christian civilization among barbarian peoples who had just come to Christianity. We come at last to possess Benedict in his entirety, and in him the complete idea of his mission.

* * * * *

In St Benedict, one senses a tranquillity and harmony of the soul's powers. It is this that gives him that accuracy of glance, that discretion which tempers all things and reconciles the inviolable demands of law with human weakness. From the depths of his soul, moved by grace that finds no obstacle, comes a kindness toward people that is at once tenderness and sympathy. A humility, whose accent penetrates every action and accompanies every word, bears witness in him to the presence of the great God whose sovereign holiness inspires this sentiment. It is this that holds in check all that in sinful, fragile humanity would tend to assert itself and dominate. Finally, the sustained habit of contemplation causes him to see everything in the divine light, so that his plans and actions bear ceaselessly the stamp of a higher direction which all sensed and no one could resist.

* * * * *

Prepared by God himself, full of God, united to God, the monk will be fruitful, and fruitful in an incomparable way. This love of his brothers, of the Church who inspires his prayers, his labours, his penances within the cloister, will be poured out on human society; and history has borne witness to the degree of life the Church has had throughout the centuries, in proportion to the esteem that has existed for the religious state, from the numbers of its representatives, and from the actions which they have performed.

(Life of St Benedict, 1869)

The unifying element of the monastic community lies in the word. The monastery is a school, and the spirit which animates all within its walls proceeds from the word of God in all its forms, through the teacher whom the monks' chapter has chosen for its guide.[3]

* * * * *

God has not gathered us into the monastery to be poor, chaste, and obedient, and to stop at that.... Inertia must not follow the three great sacrifices one has made. It is like a horse, perfectly harnessed, all ready to go into battle. But as long as he has not set out, of what use to him is his beautiful gear?... Let us be very careful, my brothers, of becoming people of conscience. You remember what Father Faber said, "One cannot imagine a conscientious seraphim." We must guard against becoming the conscientious seraphim. He fulfils his duties conscientiously, but he lacks heart, the eagerness to run toward the goal.

(Conference, 1862)

The theological virtues, if they are practised to their full extent, blossom into poverty, chastity, and obedience.... If we do not have faith, we will not have poverty; if we do not have hope, we will not have chastity; if we do not have love, we will not have obedience.

(Conference, 1865)

You must always tend toward perfection. That is why, in your profession, you promise conversion of life.[4]

(Conference, 1869)

The monastic life, being of its nature a separated life, demands that those who profess it spend their life in the enclosure of the monastery. This separation from the world should be real if we are to accomplish this word of Jesus Christ: "Every one who has left father or mother...." And again: "Come, follow me." The monastic spirit is a spirit of retreat, expressed by religious enclosure. The brothers will therefore consider the monastery their dwelling-place until death and will come to love their withdrawn life; so that if after profession, obedience may occasionally authorize them to go out into the world, their love of enclosure will not diminish. They will regard the separation from their relatives as the essential living out of the teachings of Jesus Christ.

* * * * *

The monastic life is also a life in common, and the spirit of God has designed it thus that the monks may find a powerful help in the example of their brothers, and a high degree of merit in the practice of fraternal charity.

The brothers will thus highly esteem this family life they are called to lead, and will strive to appreciate its advantages and foster its spirit in themselves and in others. They will rejoice to see others participating in the graces of which they are the special object; and they will love one another as brothers who have been called together by the same vocation. They will take pleasure in one another's company, mindful that it is the Holy Spirit who has chosen and united them for one and the same end; let the joys as well as the sorrows be common to all....

This family spirit, stemming from respect for the ways of Providence in their lives, should not diminish the religious affection that they should have toward all other rules and constitutions approved by the Church. They will pray fervently for the preservation and growth of all the various religious orders, and will take a lively interest in them.

(Règlement du Noviciat, 1856)

Only write down what has been approved by usage. In this way we avoid red-tape, indecisions, contradictions, and those frequent rearrangements that take away all respect for the written text. The early Fathers wrote their Rules only after they had been proved by abundant fruits of holiness; St Benedict was no exception. He handed on to us only the fruit of accumulated experience. The monastic life is a life of traditions, and the day when greater numbers of laws are written down is precisely the day when they will be least observed.

(To Abbess Cécile Bruyère)

What makes for the strength of the Jesuits would be our danger. Each monastic family takes on the physiognomy of the country where it establishes itself. Fervent and flourishing abbeys develop of themselves; nor are others reformed simply by way of authority. A monastery is a living being, a being founded on tradition and raised up by doctrine, by the prayer and devotedness of a few, by the generous imitation of a fervent environment, by returning to its native air and the conditions of its origins.

Such is the fourteen centuries of our history. The day we become centralized will be the end of all possible reform; living spontaneity will be destroyed, only to be replaced by an administrative machinery, perfect in its own way, which might imitate the life, but which would not be true life.

(Letter to Dom Maurus Wolter of Beuron, 1869)

In its essence, the Benedictine order is not an active army, but a school of contemplative life; and the monks who are dedicated to seeking God in the silence of the cloister, in the celebration of the Divine Office, in work, obedience, mortification and stability, do not need that centralized organization that is necessary for the active militias of the Church, in order that each member of these armies may be engaged in the various useful works to which he is vowed by his vocation. Those who enter these orders seek an active way of life to procure the glory of God; the monk seeks the busy leisure of the cloister to dwell with God.

(Letter to Dom Maurus Wolter of Beuron, 1869)

I am no partisan of those Congregations that come into being

232

with a plan ready-made in advance; that seems too much like human projects. We seek God's will in our daily living, in the way of life you have seen—study of Catholic tradition, history, and later, biblical exegesis, without excluding philosophy or poetry.... Monks praying and studying, ready for anything God wants; and, as you know, there lies the reason for the enormous duration of the Benedictines for fourteen centuries— they never tied themselves down to a particular kind of work and have been able to render services of every kind in the freedom of the Holy Spirit of God.

(Letter to Père Foisset, July 1833)

Following the example of the martyrs, whose successors in the Church are the monks,[5] let us pray that we may carry off the crown and that the feast of the glorious resurrection of Jesus Christ may find us all dead to sin and living a life wholly spiritual. In that way we will become fruitful and render to the Holy Church the tribute of holiness and edification which she expects from us.

(Letter to his monks, Lent 1844)

Suscipe me.[6] See, he has just torn himself from the earth by the vows. Where will he be going? To God. Again he says: *Suscipe me*. I no longer belong to the earth by any tie; on the other hand, I cannot yet enter heaven. *Suscipe me, Domine*. I take refuge in your arms. You have said, you have promised us, that you will not cast aside the one who leaves everything to follow you, that you will give him life which is yourself, *secundum eloquium tuum*. You have tempted me, called me, drawn me: now take charge of me, do not confound me in my expectation.

(Conference, 1862)

The Benedictine may be learned, but he is monk before all else. He is a man of prayer and religious practices. The chanting of the Divine Office—the service of the angels—absorbs a consid-erable part of his available time, and he gives to learning only the extra hours which God and obedience do not claim. Moreover, he makes his work, whatever its object may be, enter into line with the things he had consecrated to God. Mabillon, Martène, Montfaucon and scores of others fulfilled what it means to be a scholar more than anyone in the world, but they rarely left their choir stall. To desert that would have shown that they preferred the solitude of the human mind for the company of God.

(Preface to Les Origines de l'Eglise romaine, 1836)

Abbess Cécile Bruyère

Taken as a whole, St Benedict's Rule has a special character which must be fully appreciated, lest something contrary to it should be introduced or alter its primitive purity in the government of an abbey....

In fact (apart from vital points of the monastic life), there is a significant absence of over-precise regulations, or anything approaching mechanical or martial organization, or systematic prescription. To explain this breadth, it is held that the ancients were less methodical than we moderns; perhaps it is fairer to say that they were methodical in a different way from us, and that they saw order in a different light. And yet, is that the real explanation for the character of St Benedict's Rule? Is it right to say that its breadth of spirit, its wise liberty, its holy spontaneity is simply a question of period? I don't think so.

The Benedictine Rule is not an indecisive text, vague or incomplete, something we have to define, complete or perfect. Even before St Benedict there were methodical minds, such as St Pachomius, who were capable of making classifications and of giving precise administrative details. St Benedict knew them, and did not follow their lead.... Among patriarchs and legislators, it is he, however, who is closest to the spirit of divine laws which adapt themselves to all ages and all races.

The reticence of the Rule has, in a way, made the perfect life accessible to all; it has widened the entrance, so to speak, with no danger. For, concentrating all its energy on general principles, it can, with no fear of alteration or dilution, embrace within its breadth all of good will, all the baptized, as St Paul says: "For as many of you as were baptized into Christ have put on Christ. There is neither Jew nor Greek, there is neither slave nor free, there is neither male nor female; for you are all one in Christ Jesus" (Gal. 3:27-8). One could almost say that St Benedict had this text in mind when he formulated the conditions for entry into his monastic ranks: "You are the one to whom my words are now addressed, who strip yourself of self-will in order to fight for the true King, Christ our Lord, and take up the strong and glorious weapons of obedience" (*Rule*, Prologue).

When we study the ways by which God draws to him those whom he has created rational and free, great light is thrown upon the spirit in which the Holy Rule was composed. God has given certain precepts to us to be the means of protecting and perfecting us. God's law is like a lighthouse to the mind, showing us the precise places wherein lie dangers that would trammel our perfect liberty and prevent us from tending toward the perfection of our nature and, above all, to our supreme end, God: "The unfolding of thy words gives light; it imparts understanding to the simple" (Ps 118[119]:130). The divine command is also a frontier beyond which the will finds perils and destruction and, in the end, death. Moderate as they are, the divine precepts by which the baptized are bound are sufficient to bring them to the perfection to which they are called, and God never rules us by those ineluctable laws that govern animals, which we call instinct. There is no choice or liberty in that; everything is foreseen and regulated by a sort of absolute necessity. But God trusts to our understanding, and, having instructed and enlightened us and assisted us in our acts, he leaves us to make the decision, in the last resort, by our free will.

Our Father St Benedict, called by God to formulate a law for those who would enter upon the perfect life, made himself, to some extent, an imitator of God in this work, copying the divine approach. The powerful inspiration he received revealed the vitally essential principles for monastic observance; he grasped the precise points that must serve as lighthouses and frontiers beyond which lie all the dangers of so holy a state. Is that not what he was explaining in the following passage:

We must, therefore, establish a school for the Lord's service. In setting out its regulations, we hope to impose nothing harsh or burdensome; but if, for good reason—for the amendment of faults or safeguarding of charity—there seems to be a little strictness, do not take fright immediately and run away from the way of salvation. It must be narrow at the start (*Rule*, Prologue).

Clearly it was a great gift to be able to discern the principal and vital prescriptions at a glance, without being distracted by the details that naturally follow from them. St Benedict, in founding a school of divine service, indicates in his Rule, with supernatural perception, the key points of perfection and urges the monk to a spontaneous following of its ordered course; but he never puts a restraint on human liberty or the play of divine action.

Such a rule, more than all others, calls for an intelligent "engine"; it will not be able to function and bear fruit without it. This great device of the Rule is the abbot. With this living authority, St Benedict can supply for all that he has decided not to say, and that is why the abbot must be chosen not only for the merit of his life but also for his spiritual teaching. This is acquired only by virtue and many years in religion. St Benedict goes on to insist, "He must be learned in the divine law, therefore, in order to know from where 'to bring forth things both new and old'" (ch. 64). One could say that he did not feel sure of the outcome of the Rule he had composed unless there was someone capable of applying it, of making dead words live. Only then would success be assured.

It is perhaps in this creation of the abbot that we find the most pronounced characteristic of the Rule and the reason for its universal success. In our Order, the responsibility of superiors is greater than elsewhere because of the unique position created for them by the Rule, a position in which we can really say: like abbot, like monastery.

The result of all this is that each monastery or "school for the Lord's service" can develop into a unity possessing great variety because of this living authority, just as the sun's action makes natural things grow and develops each according to its own shape and colour. What is revealed in individuals appears in the special usages and customs that are the distinctive characteristics of the collective person. Inevitably, climate, social environment, places and circumstances give a particular physiognomy to the practical application of the Rule, but they do not affect the spirit. So if she is to abide by the spirit of the Rule, a Benedictine abbess should refrain from making such exact, meticulous, precise regulations that her nuns find no scope for initiative and reflection, and that she herself need not interfere with the governing of her house except at rare intervals. We must avoid having everything foreseen and minutely regulated, lest the nuns become bodies without souls, or figures whose movements are artificial, as if inspired by something external and alien. Formalism is not Benedictine; everything in the monastery must be genuine and from the bottom of our hearts.

(Conference)

Our best formation is made when the part played by the liturgy is not limited to the actual celebration of the Divine Office, but when our whole life is grounded upon it, when the content of our prayer, as well as the principles for the correction and sanctification of the soul, are drawn from it. In it will be found the surest commentary on Scriptures, which are the true bread of the spirit after the Eucharist, and the true orientation of our piety. The liturgy is a wonderful school of contemplation; through it, we avoid many of the pitfalls of the spiritual life or come through them with the most extraordinary sense of security.

(Conference)

Holiness is a perpetual profession-day established in our lives. Profession is not only an act of absolute trust; it is also an act of faith. Is it not a wonderful thing that, even before we get to heaven, we can say, "I gather together and take up all my being, all my past, all that I am and shall be, and give it all to God." But that is only a beginning. The consecrated heart must always repeat, "Keep for ever such purposes" (cf 1 Chron. 29:18); take away the human frailty that makes it possible for me to take back, bit by bit, what I have already given.

(Conference, 12 October 1894)

The real social "lever" proper to contemplatives is holiness of life and the zealous carrying-out of the liturgy. That is the vast and fruitful field of our apostolate. Our apostolate, after the example of Mary, Mother of God, consists in seeking after holiness so that our prayer may become all-powerful with God. With that, there is nothing we cannot do in the Church.

(Letter, 1878)

We shall do good, even in the social order, by being saints— Benedictine saints, and never departing from that.

(Conference, 3 September 1884)

The apostolic spirit is, to my mind, the culmination of sanctity, because it is then that it overflows.

(Letter, 12 April 1890)

The monk is the cantor of the beauty of God. To chant God, to praise God, and to contemplate his beauty: this is the whole art of being a monk. He consecrates his life to this; he will worship the beauty of God, and this worship itself will become the most beautiful thing in the world. "Nothing, indeed, should be put before the work of God" (*Rule*, ch. 43). The work of God before all else is the unique work of his life; that is why he withdraws from the world and its distractions, to give himself up entirely to the contemplation of beauty.

(Conference)

"Sing the psalms in such a way that our mind and voice may be in harmony" (*Rule*, ch. 19). So sing that you express what your hearts feel, that every note may carry the accent of love. Express the power of the Word, this efficacious Word that penetrates to the depths of the soul, "piercing to the division of soul and spirit" (Heb. 4:12). All those who hear you should feel that and understand. Your chant of praise will thus find an echo in other hearts, just as the Lord may be heard in your chanting of the psalms.

(Conference)

As for the number of words it contains, the *Suscipe* is restricted, but their meaning opens up a vast terrain. We appreciate the value of the *Suscipe* only when we come to the end of our lives and are received by God. When we first sent up our *Suscipe*, it expressed a movement, an impulse toward God. We extended our arms in the ancient attitude of prayer but also in imitation of the Cross. This is the attitude to which we wished to be conformed. We are tending toward the limitless ocean of God, and our arms are opened wide. In its movement toward God, the human will knows no rest. That is charity. Scripture tells us often what love is; it lies in the will, to will God always. *Suscipe me, Domine*. The constant willing of the soul puts it outside the conditions of time; whether it experiences consolation or dryness, the soul always desires God. In difficult moments, in the struggles with oneself, it always desires God. Among interior and exterior trials of every kind, there is only God for that soul. The intensity of this will toward God increases in the measure in which we mount upwards, climb, for when we stop, there is no longer the *Suscipe*....

I desire you, O my God. This simple formula accomplishes our perfect sanctification. The word "suscipe" indicates that movement; it is really the same thing as the word "traveller," and by it St Benedict desires to show to what we are tending. The vow of conversion of manners is a consequence of that. The more deeply we plumb the meaning of the *Suscipe*, the more we will see that no one has received the gift of going straight to God without effort.

(Conference)

St Benedict prescibes the chanting of the *Suscipe* three time. He loves this triple affirmation in honour of the Trinity.... The *Suscipe* conceals, in fact, a confession of the Trinity. In the word

Domine we see the Father; the expression *eloquium tuum* is synonymous with *Verbum*, designating the Word, the Son of God, who has traced the way by which we go to the Father. And finally, by the words *et vivam* we confess the Holy Spirit who is the principle of life within us, as we say in the Creed: *vivificantem*. We conclude the *Suscipe* by the *Gloria Patri* which is the supreme homage to the Blessed Trinity.

(Explication of the Profession Ritual, April 1892, ms)

Dom Paul Delatte[7]

The word "monk" means not only one who lives alone, but also one who busies himself with God alone, who thus brings his life into unity. This total and exclusive belonging to God is signified by the tonsure and the monastic habit, and that is why, for St Benedict, to renounce the manner of life implied by these exterior signs meant that "their tonsure brands them as liars before God" (*Rule*, ch. 1).

For a long time this was the only form of religious life. Religious life and the monastic life were one and the same thing; to be a religious was to be a monk. The special aim of the religious life is to draw us and bind us to God; and the very name monastic life signifies this glorious belonging to God, the perfect oneness of a life vowed to God, bound exclusively to God. The monastic life expresses that which has been brought back to unity, with no trace of division or diversion, by the very fact of its attachment, its belonging, to God alone.

And in this sense the monastic life is synonymous with the contemplative life. It means to be "monk" by reason of a total singleness of purpose, with solitude and withdrawal from the world as means to this end; it means being dedicated to prayer and contemplation; and because there is one particular form of prayer that is consecrated by the Church's usage, it means belonging to this prayer, to the liturgy of the Church, to the Divine Office. God expects from his creation adoration only "in spirit and in truth." Such has been the ideal of the monastic life, especially from St Benedict's time: "We must, therefore, estab-

lish a school for the Lord's service…" (*Rule*, Prologue).
(Notes on the Spiritual Life, *V: Monastic Life, 1899*)

Contemplation is so characteristic of our Benedictine life that all other elements of the Rule are closely bound up with it. Everything in the Rule is so ordered, measured, determined with contemplation in mind. It is really at the heart of the legislative prescriptions of the Rule. It is organized in the perfection of the divine service and the holy liturgy; everything depends on it. It is why we are separated from the world by our spirit of retreat, our enclosure, and our habit; and it is the reason for our silence, mortification, and work.

We have left the world to free ourselves from its values and ties; we have sought the cloister. Retreat, for us, does not consist in an annual eight or ten days of spiritual exercises, but for the whole of our lives. It goes hand in hand with our enclosure. The cloister is a shelter, a protection; it is not a prison. We do not go out, but more importantly, the world does not come in. Even when, under obedience, we have to leave the monastery for a while, our habit still serves as our enclosure, expresses our spirit of retreat; it reminds us, and it reminds the world of what we are, and protects us from worldly conduct. How we should love the holy habit the Church has given us! The enemy of souls is well aware of what he is up to when he tries to prohibit ecclesiastical or religious dress. I do not think that the habit makes the monk, but it helps to keep him; and wearing secular dress is the first step toward entertaining a secular spirit. Yet, granting this, what is the purpose in our Benedictine life of our separation from the world by our retreat, our enclosure and our habit? Is it for the pleasure of being different? Is it simply a safeguard? A guarantee against vain preoccupations? A means of assuring our own security? Is that what St Benedict wanted for himself and his disciples when, in the words of St Gregory the Great, "he despised the barren delights of the world"? That great monk and great pope goes on to tell us what St Benedict really had in mind: "So he abandoned his home and his father's wealth, and desiring to please God alone, sought the habit of holy religion."

Later he adds, "alone under the eye of God, he dwelt with himself."[8] And as St Benedict "cannot have taught other than as he lived," when he wishes to train his monks in the spiritual craft, he prescribes stability: "Now, the workshop in which we are carefully to perform all these tasks is the enclosure of the monastery and stability in the community" (ch. 4). It is in the interests of enclosure and the spirit of retreat that he wants the monks to carry out their various works inside the monastery: "there should be no need for monks to wander outside, since that is not at all good for their souls" (ch. 66).

Recall how often the Rule invites us to keep silence; it is part of the very fabric of our lives. Here too the purpose of silence, as for our spirit of retreat, is to foster contemplation. I do not think that silence is prescibed as a form of mortification; it is rather a condition of our recollection and fruit of the spirit of prayer. Like our retreat, silence is one of the arts that will bring us closer to God. And is that not the object of our mortification and work, and the reason why they have a place in our life? We do not mortify ourselves in order to destroy or exasperate ourselves. By mortification we put to death everything in us that is rough, everything that stirs up trouble, all those tendencies in ourselves that oppose prayer and union with God. Intellectual work, too, what St Benedict calls *lectio divina*, is only a means by which the intellect enters into the truth of the mysteries of God.

The work of contemplation is, then, the end, the goal, and the gauge of all the vital elements of the Benedictine life. In its essence, this life is entirely directed toward the glory of God, to the work of prayer; and its contemplative character has for its end to render us more capable of offering to God a homage worthy of him. Even external works and duties of hospitality, absences from the monastery, and works of the apostolate and of charity are limited, so as not to detract from prayer and contemplation.

(Notes on the Spiritual Life, VI: Benedictine Life, 1899)

Those who are faithful to this preaching in and through the liturgy are also apostolic. Apart from its sovereign dignity, the contemplative and liturgical life possess a useful role. Enlightener of contemplatives, it also enlightens others who become contemplative through contact with it.... We have only to think of the power of liturgical prayer to form a Christian people, to draw people together, to give them a social conscience, to bring about religious unity, a holy and fraternal solidarity, to make them aware of their oneness before God, before the Church, in the frequenting of the sacraments and in the holy joys of the liturgy. That is what makes a Christian people, that is what brings about true fraternity, true solidarity. It is in the liturgy that one sees the Church's longing to realize the kingdom of perfect love.

No doubt we shall not witness with our mortal eyes the final accomplishment of this work, but it would be childish to expect God to gather together in the narrow bounds of our years here on earth what is ultimately his work. We must be ready to bring all our efforts to bear upon a plan that far surpasses our life. We are workers in an eternal work.

(Notes on the Spiritual Life, VI: Benedictine Life)

All contemplatives who really understand the nature of their calling are a living treasury of truth, teaching, and grace, are truly apostolic. But, you will say, there are, among contemplatives, people who do not write books and never appear in print. That is true, but there are already too many books! Contemplatives write the book of their silent and hidden life. This life is a teaching in itself, and is perhaps today the book most needed by our modern world.

* * * * *

There is a type of preaching that retains inviolably and without ceasing its glorious efficacy. It is the preaching implied by our life, by our integrity, and, if God so wills, by our holiness; the voice of those who remain silent, who speak to God alone and draw down grace upon the world by their prayer. This word can never be contradicted; one cannot deny it. It can be slandered, or people may try to suppress it, but it cannot be gainsaid in a significant way. It is an affirmation of God, of the Church, of the supernatural world, of the invisible world, of eternal life.

People with good minds, and enlightened intelligence, and resolute will, who might have held an important position in the world, who even had, perhaps, a better chance of success than their contemporaries, who might aspire to this world's honours, suddenly renounce everything this world holds dear, to give themselves freely to Someone unseen, and that not for one day only but for a whole lifetime, by a resolute choice maintained hour by hour. To my mind, no word or form of action possesses such power. It is not by what we say to the world, but rather by what we are, that we act upon it.

(Notes on the Spiritual Life, V: Monastic Life)

Monastic history tells us of the work of our predecessors, and how they served the Church of God in all the various works of the apostolate. But if the Church found in our ranks missionaries and apostles who carried the gospel into all the countries of Europe, it is important to remember that the Church took the initiative in entrusting to them their mission, that monks were the only ones in that era of history from whose ranks the Church could find workers, and that the first concern of these monastic preachers, on their arrival in a new country, was to establish monasteries there: so greatly did they desire to steep themselves in the atmosphere of religious life to which they were accustomed, so greatly were they convinced that their preaching would be fruitful insofar as it sprang from the assiduous practice of their rule. The monastery was the centre of life, doctrine, prayer, and witness. It was a conquest, conceived in the Roman sense, by the establishment of an entrenched camp, a taking possession of the land. The evangelist was the monastery itself, preacher with a hundred voices that were silent neither day nor night. Perhaps the imprint of Christianity was in no place more profound than where the monks were the first apostles.

(Notes on the Spiritual Life, V: Monastic Life)

Our life is not founded on study. The monastery is a school, I agree, but a school where one is trained to serve God; one might call it a professional school of contemplation. Everything in the monastery must be directed toward eternity, and the main study for the monk is that which is most apt to sanctify his soul, to adapt him to contemplation and to glorify God, since the merit of the worship depends upon the merit of the worshipper.

* * * * *

We will survive as long as God is first in our lives: we shall abdicate any right to exist if we ever shelter ourselves behind any human pursuit whatever—honour, reputation, or learning—in order to refuse God first place and encroach on the time consecrated to God's service and honour.

(Conference, 1914)

While highly esteeming the solitary life, St Benedict's sole purpose was to write a rule for monks living in community. On the very threshold of monastic life and from the moment of our entry we ask for two things: the mercy of God and a place in the community formed by the monastery. This life in common is not merely an exterior fact achieved by the juxtaposition of individuals following a common rule; it is a way of life that we love, deliberately seek, and that with time will bring about a true compenetration of our lives, an affectionate solidarity. Even progress in the supernatural life can be gauged by this harmonious life of the brethren and its constant growth. The love we have for our brethren is thus a precious sign. The joy of living together under the same discipline implies the elimination of all egoism, self-renunciation, and the restoration of moral health.

We have not, however, defined the special character of Benedictine life by saying it is conventual and cenobitic. A society, a community, can in fact take on a wide variety of forms, like that of a college, for example, or an army. The social groupings of St Pachomius or St Ignatius differ completely, as do those of St Dominic or St Francis. It would not be easy to find a word to qualify each of these forms of cenobitic life, and to identify the precise way in which they differ. But the conventual life proper to the order of St Benedict can be summed up in one word: family life, a community life grouped around the fatherly authority of the abbot, the common life shared among brethren.

All natural and supernatural things are carried out on the level of the family, the domestic family, that family formed by the parish or the diocese, that immense family that is the Church in time and in eternity. It is the most natural form of life, the most supernatural, the healthiest, the sweetest, the most continuous, too, since it is the form of life of society both in time and in eternity.

Somewhere, Newman describes the physiognomy of Benedictines as compared with other religious Orders. He says, finely, that they have a more "childlike" character than the others.[9] There is no need to blush at this evaluation, as if it was underlining an imperfection or some sort of weakness about us. To my mind, this is an honour, it is the attitude of the Lord himself, the effacement of the individual, the uprooting of self-love, the priceless fruit of our contemplative life, the exterior expression of the intimate reality that the monastery is a way of living together entirely as one, where the individual disappears in the whole. In a gentle, tranquil manner all egoism is reduced bit by bit. While this is happening, one's true personality is affirmed. We restrict ourselves only to discover our true selves by bringing our life into harmony with that of our brothers. Just as in choir the first principle is that no voice should predominate or assert itself above the others, but that each should disappear in the whole, so in our common life characters are softened and souls become supple so as to yield to one's neighbour and thus realize fraternal union.

What existed for an instant of time in the primitve church at Jerusalem, life in common, prayer in common, action in common, the absence of any "mine" and "thine," in a word, the supernatural socialism of love, has not ceased to be realized in the Church for over fourteen centuries in our monastic life.[10] It is worth recognizing that the ideal of those who in our day have tried to change the course of human society by promoting communism and socialism, has in fact already long been realized in joy and peace.

St Benedict is for us, as it were, the shadow of our heavenly Father; and I doubt that in any other religious family, the title of father, and fatherly tenderness, are more realized, justified, or more keenly felt. This character of our monastic life has left its mark on certain elements that, at first sight, might seem alien to it. Its influence is especially felt in the domain of poverty and mortification. Anyone looking for new recruits for an army makes a careful selection and accepts only robust candidates. The requirements for a family are less stringent. One is satisfied with certain suitable dispositions. This spirit of discretion and moderation dominates all the prescriptions and counsels contained in the Rule; everything is ordained and determined for the purpose of prayer, which is the centre of our life. In effect, the Rule does not cover everything; no code or constitution can. That is why the cenobitic life has been defined as a life lived "under a rule and an abbot" (*Rule*, ch. 1).

So too, Benedictine poverty is placed particularly under the care and fatherly judgment of the abbot. In the Benedictine sense, one is poor who possesses nothing and makes use of nothing that has not been given by the abbot, to whom it falls, as father of the family, to dispose all things according to the needs and reasonable demands of each one. It would be easy to show how in a Benedictine monastery the paternal authority of the abbot makes itself felt in every domain: work, daily duties, mortifications, exceptions—all come under his authority.

Finally, there is yet another essential element in the Benedictine way of life that portrays clearly its family character. One may change one's regiment but one always belongs to a family. The monastery itself is a stable entity; the monk is a member of this family, he is one of the living stones of the fortress. No more than in human families could monasteries be composed of shifting groups of persons, whose exterior surroundings alone, the buildings, express their continuity and permanence. In principle, the monastic family remains what God has made it, except for those he continues to recruit and those that he has called to eternity. Stability, therefore, is merely fidelity to that blessed place where we are sure to find fullness of life.

(Notes on the Spiritual Life, VI: Benedictine Life, 1899)

Suscipe me, Domine. Grant that I may be really "given" and really "received," truly received because truly given, and that both of us may be able to keep our word. Both my gift and yours rest wholly in your blessed hands.

(Commentary on the Rule, 1913)

Notes

1. *Perfectae Caritatis,* 7.

2. Conferences on Christian life, Solesmes, 1884, v. II, p. 20. Cited by Dom Jean Leclerq, OSB, "Saint Bede and Christian Expansion," in Word and Spirit 7 (1985).

3. Cited in Dom Soltner, *Solesmes et Dom Guéranger,* p. 119.

4. Conversion of life (or of "manners"), together with stability and obedience, form the content of the Benedictine vows. The vow of conversion of life expresses both conversion, the act of becoming a monk, the turning away from secular to religious life; and the commitment to live as a monk, to adopt the monastic way of life. It is generally taken to include, by the very logic of monastic life, poverty and chastity. By this vow, says Abbess Cécile Bruyère, "we stress, in a very energetic way, that our principal work will be to reform ourselves."

5. The association between the monastic life and martyrdom is an ancient one. With the end of persecutions and of the opportunity for martyrdom in the fourth century, the monastic life itself came to be called "a second martyrdom," "a daily martyrdom," "an interior martyrdom," "a protracted martyrdom." The monk was like the martyr not only by his rigorous ascetic practices and heroic endurance but also by his special consecration to Christ's passion.

6. During the profession rite, after pronouncing the vows, the Benedictine novice addresses himself to God in the words of Psalm 118[119]:116, "Uphold me, O Lord, according to thy promise that I may live, and let me not be put to shame in my hope." While the *Suscipe* is not a Benedictine invention, St Benedict did add a three-fold repetition of the verse, concluding with the doxology. In the following selections from Abbess Cécile Bruyère and Dom Delatte, we include their commentaries on the *Suscipe.*

7. As Dom Paul Delatte's classic commentary on the Rule is accessible in English, we present here his monastic teaching as found in his unpublished

"Notes on the Spiritual Life, V-VI: Monastic and Benedictine Life," given to the Solesmes novitiate in 1899. Parts of this work appeared in *Vivre à Dieu* (Solesmes, 1973).

8. St Gregory the Great, *Dialogues*, Book II, 1, 3.

9. Cf "The Mission of the Benedictine Order" (1858) in *Cardinal Newman on the Benedictine Order* (London, 1914), p. 28; *Historical Sketches*, II, pages 372-7, cited in W. S. Lilly, *A Newman Anthology* (1875).

10. The community at Jerusalem grouped around the Apostles presents many monastic characteristics—so much so, that monastic tradition has maintained that the monastic life is only a continuation of the "apostolic life." By apostolic life was meant not a life of missionary, social activity but the life described in Acts, a life apart in which Christians persevere together in prayer, in a common sharing of goods, and in the breaking of bread (cf Acts 2:42).

From the Dedication in Time to the Dedication in Eternity

On learning of the death of the abbot of Solesmes, Pope Pius IX declared, "I have lost a devoted friend, and the Church a great servant"; and he paid a remarkable tribute to the life and work of Dom Guéranger in a Brief[1] addressed to the whole Church:

> Among the men of our time who have been most distinguished for their devotion, zeal and learning ... no on has more right to acknowledgement than Prosper Guéranger. Gifted in so many ways, of wide erudition, he applied himself to the courageous defence of the Church's teaching by writings of extreme importance.

Dom Guéranger died on 30 January 1875, after a short illness and with his mind clear to the last, as he had hoped. Although the preceding months had witnessed a perceptible increase in weakness, he had been active to the end, dictating a short work for oblates, *The Church, or the Society of Divine Praise*; the day before his death, he gave his last conference to the nuns of Sainte-Cécile. Confined to his bed shortly after, he received the last sacraments on 29 January, while his monks chanted his favourite psalm, Psalm 102, "Bless the Lord, O my soul," and the *Te Deum*. His cell remained open to all, monks and friends alike, as he saluted each with a smile and his unforgettable blue eyes. His body rests in the church at Solesmes; his heart, at his request, was placed at the foot of the altar at Sainte-Cécile. Such was the last wish of this father of both monks and nuns.

If Dom Guéranger's death was that of a public figure, Abbess Cécile's death in exile was almost emblematic of her living in spirit apart from the world, her consciousness of being a "stranger and exile on the earth." The last stage of her long illness began just after the dedication of the abbey church in exile, 12 October 1907; it marked the beginning of her final dedication in eternity. Her whole life as an adorer "in spirit and in truth" (her abbatial motto) had unfolded within the framework of the liturgy of the Dedication of a Church. She was born on the anniversary of the dedication of the church at Saint Pierre, Solesmes; that date marked her first consecration to God, the dedication of the sanctuary of her body and soul, at the age of sixteen in the hands of Dom Guéranger; and that of the consecration of the abbatial church at Sainte-Cécile. The dedication liturgy with its themes of time and eternity, of the church as the House of God and Gate of Heaven, as "the borderland between heaven and earth,"[2] of the sanctuary of the soul where God is pleased to dwell, was her favourite. All the activity of her monastic life in preparing a worthy house for God may be summed up in one of the hymns for the feast, *Urbs Jerusalem beata* (Jerusalem, the blessed city):

> Many a blow and biting sculpture
> Polished well those stones elect
> In their places now compacted
> By the heavenly Architect,
> Who therefore hath willed forever
> That his palace should be decked.

Her death on 18 March 1909 in exile was the final dedication, the perfect consummation.

Dom Delatte, who knew himself to be above all a son, died a son. Although he was known as "le Grand Père Abbé" after his resignation in 1920, for the sixteen years that remained to him he lived the life of a simple monk. A stroke on 18 September 1937 left him unconscious and half-paralyzed. He lingered on for two days and two nights, "enclosed in the supreme cloister," as one of his monks recorded: "One thought of the patriarchs, of Moses, of Elijah, preparing themselves in silence and solitude for the vision of God."[3] On 20 September, he entered into what he called "the filial region par excellence."

Our imagination, our feelings, our fear of an unknown future, have taught us to envelop that last moment with dread, observes Dom Delatte in his commentary on the Rule of St Benedict. But death holds no anxiety for Christians who are journeying toward that final meeting with him whom they have sought in faith and love. Our Lord himself tasted that bitter cup with us and for us that he might rob death of its power and "free those who through fear of death had been slaves their whole life long" (Heb. 2:15). For these writers, death is the true communion, the real beginning of all things, the perfect act of charity toward God, the most joyful gift of ourselves to God.

There is another reason for our confidence at the approach of death. Faith, hope, and love, our baptism, the Eucharist, give us access to heaven, to Christ, to God at every moment of our lives. Eternal life is here and now, as Dom Delatte loved to say. And so, in a very real sense, we are moving toward something we already bear within us. "The eternal life that will begin on the day when we enter the vision of God," wrote Dom Delatte, "is the same as that we already bear within us by the very fact of our belonging to Jesus Christ. And it is precisely because we have entered the depths, into the intimacy and tenderness of this life of the Lord, that there is no longer any death for us, simply eternal life that has already begun now." With this final chapter we have come full circle: all the reality Christians bear within them and which sustains them is at the same time coming to meet them. Death will be the unveiling of the reality of Christ in each human soul, "the manifestation, the complete and total flowering of what we already bear within us on earth, the very life of the Lord within us." And it is to this reality that God's judgment is designed to lift us up.

There is a close and necessary connection between what we are and what we shall be, for with the works of our present life we construct our eternity. Dom Delatte used to say: "The smallest actions of our life have their importance, their eternal repercussions." Our whole life is our preparation for death, the preparation God himself gives us; we must fix ourselves now in the dispositions that will make us "precious in the eyes of God." "This present life," observed Dom Delatte in his commentary on the Rule, "is only an apprenticeship, a trial, a novitiate for eternity and it is in view of this eternity that we have to renounce, to learn, and to conquer."

Dom Paul Delatte

There will be incomparable advantages in this meeting with the Lord: on that day we will be true. Father Faber has some ineffable passages in his *Spiritual Conferences*; he shows that on that day we will be really accurate, while we are never absolutely sure during our life that we are true. How much illusion in our lives is there? We can consult and ask questions on this subject, but aren't there certain unrecognized, unknown elements in the depths of our heart? Isn't there a little posing, and, as a result of external pressures, aren't there some deep-seated inaccuracies we do not succeed in getting rid of during our life? It is only by tranquil self-abandonment into the hands of the Lord and of authority, it is only by perfect obedience that we will succeed in eliminating all kinds of posing, of inaccuracy, of illusion; an infinitesimal trace of it may remain in the soul, but that will correct itself.

There are some who during their life are never what they are; the illusion within them is such that it persists until the moment of their death, and includes it. I believe the judgment of God was created exactly in order to make us absolutely true, absolutely accurate; on that day we shall stand in the truth of our being.

* * * * *

Do we have to prepare ourselves for death? First, we musn't wait until the last moment to tidy ourselves up in view of eternity; we musn't say: I'm going to spend my life just anyhow, giving the lie to my Profession by my conduct; and then before my last hour, I shall, like St Maurus, take two years before dying to prepare myself nice and quietly for my death. No—that sort of calculation would be worthless. What is required is not an artificial, planned preparation, but the preparation God himself gives to us. We don't prepare ourselves to die; we prepare to live; death is only an instant, a passage; we prepare ourselves to live eternally. Our entire life should be considered as a sort of novitiate and preparation for eternal life. It is in the exercise of the supernatural virtues that we will find the true preparation for death.

* * * * *

Death, accepted in all its vulgar aspects, death accepted thus, is certainly an act of perfect charity. I believe in my soul and my conscience that death accepted joyfully, with a general tranquillity in the will of the Lord, cleanses our soul like a Solemn Profession; nothing, absolutely nothing, is left; we have given everything. Until then we have given promises; it is easy to give one's life imaginarily, allegorically, by promise; to give one's life in reality is something else. To give one's life in that way, to abandon oneself tranquilly into the hands of the Lord, to accept all the circumstances of death, whatever they may be; I believe that this is an act of perfect charity and that, in the soul that joyfully abandons itself into the hands of the Lord, there remains absolutely nothing except what the Lord has given it: faith, hope, charity, the gift of self-abandonment.

(Retreat, 1894)

Death! It isn't an event, an accident. Eternal life is completely independent of death. Eternal life has already begun for us. As soon as there is no separation, no dissociation between God and the soul, what can it matter to see our prison of clay fall away? Eternal life, that is to say the true life of the soul with God, is independent of physical life, and does not notice the shock we call death. God and the soul do not notice it. It is something that does not make a stir, for, since God and the soul are together and cannot be separated by anything, God holding the soul close, the soul embracing God, God belonging to the soul, the soul belonging to God, what does all the rest matter? If the foundation of eternal life is a total belonging of the soul to God, of God to the soul, if nothing can break the continuity of that essential kiss, the rest counts for nothing.... It is precisely because we have entered into the depths, into the intimacy and tenderness of this life of the Lord, that there is no longer any death for us, simply eternal life, which has already begun now.

The soul withdraws gently; external things enter into the mist of a sort of eclipse for it; it feels drawn elsewhere, it becomes aware of an infinite fatigue.... And then it goes by an unknown way toward God. Don't hold on to it, don't try to bring it back; it is already closer to God than to creation. Leave it alone to follow its path. This is not the time to make it attend to earthly things. Leave it. The hour has come when the Lord will loose its bonds. It will be quite simple. Let the Lord just show himself, he who, until this hour, has remained unnoticed in the inner sanctuary he created for himself within us by baptism. Let him show himself, and it will be all over! The soul will be his alone, in his arms, for eternity.

(Conferences on the Spiritual Life, 1899)

Death is, for me, a region of tenderness and confidence, the region of the filial spirit par excellence.... With my baptism alone, I should have gone to God with confidence, as to a Father, to a Mother; and in fact I am going to him with my soul entirely bathed with, penetrated by the beauty and the Blood of his Son. The soul, when it has passed through death, does not cease to bear God within it; death does not change anything in our relationship with God.

(Conferences on the Spiritual Life)

Then God will be all in us, in me. Then I shall see; that is to say that the only sight, the continuous, eternal and permanent sight that will be before me will be God. God ... light, beauty. And so that nothing may be lacking in that knowledge I shall have of God, so that it may be full and complete, ... God himself will be within me, the principle of the knowledge I shall receive of him. God will be the object, and in a certain sense he will be the subject. God will be at once the beauty I have before me, and in a sense, he will be the "I" that is beholding that beauty. He will be the beauty that is seen and the act of knowledge that sees; he will be the tenderness that is loved, and the heart that is loving that tenderness. He will be at the very root of my thought, so that I may see him; at the root of my will, so that I may possess him; at the root, the centre of my heart, so that I may love him. He will be the beauty I love, and within me, the heart that loves that beauty. He will be the term and the object of my acts; he will be their principle within me. God will be on both sides: he will be at the same time the sight and the seer; and it will be due to God within me that I shall see God in himself.

(Conferences on the Spiritual Life)

O Tenderness, O Beauty, O Purity, who are God, my God, I know that the supernatural life is being with you, but it is to be perfectly with you that I thirst. If you wished it, my God, the flimsy weft of this present life would snap like a thin thread at a movement of your fingers, in an act of charity toward you, and I should be with you who are life for all eternity!

(Commentary on Romans 8)

Abbess Cécile Bruyère

Death seems to me to be the easiest, the simplest of all the acts of our life: the most complete and the most joyful gift of ourselves to God. Doesn't a child fall asleep with confidence in its father's arms, even if it has offended him? Isn't it simpler to let God sort out our lives than to rack our brains? I could say a great deal on the subject.

(Conference)

Jacob, when he had seen to everything, felt the need of strengthening himself by prayer. The state through which he was to pass was to be reproduced in our Lord on the Mount of Olives, when, after he had seen to everything for his disciples, he remained alone "and prayed more earnestly" (Luke 22:44). The struggle of Jacob is a figure of the great struggle of the Lord.

Jacob is here also the type of the soul that, after exhausting and going beyond all ordinary help, finds itself alone before God. There are times when it is impossible to be assisted by others. For many, that moment does not arrive until death; and then it is as if they were hemmed in, everything else fades away, deserts them; and that is the cause of much of the anguish of the dying. Such anguish stems less from the agitation caused by the struggles between the soul and the body, which are going to be separated—a struggle that bears the trace of sin—than from the solitude in which creatures see themselves alone before God. They had always been surrounded by people and things that never allowed them to stand alone before God. It is then that they experience what St Paul says: "It is a fearful thing to fall into the hands of the living God" (Heb. 10:31). But how different it is for souls that have confronted this solitude for a long time and which can find their peace only there, since any contact other than contact with God hinders them.

Castas libertas, a pure freedom.[4] Why not enter into the spirit of the vow of chastity? Why not fulfil this vow with that love which I would call solitary, exclusive? That is not being shrivelled up: this detachment consists in surrounding ourselves with divine things and leaving to the Lord all that we have most at heart; when the soul falls back on itself to find only the Lord— that is the highest point of the vow of chastity. St Michael's *Quis ut Deus*[5] expresses just that. If you wish to be strong, look only to the Lord and his rights over you: it is an honour to be able to sacrifice to him all our holiest and legitimate affections; holocausts are never offered with anything but the best, and we must take nothing back.

(Letter, 1890)

Enthusiasm is not necessary to go straight to God. I do not think the sweet Queen of heaven ever paid God in that coin. Profound adoration which is the perfect flowering of charity: doesn't that spell the ruin of enthusiasm? That is fruit of an inferior world: there is a certain gravity about everything divine.

They say that deep lakes on the plateaux of high mountains have no waves. Waves belong to surfaces; there are none in the ocean depths.

As the soul progresses toward the depths of the Godhead, it is invaded by peace, an ineffable peace that nothing can submerge, neither the thought of our sins, nor our sorrows, nor those of others, nothing in the world, for it is the dawn of eternal life which is beginning to break. We do not yet know the source of that unconquerable peace, but we experience it nevertheless: "Then the peace of God, which is beyond all understanding, will stand guard over your hearts and minds..." (Phil. 4:7).

(Letter of 5 October 1897 to the abbess of Stanbrook,
Dame Gertrude d'Aurillac Dubois, who had
received the Sacrament of the Sick)

Dom Prosper Guéranger

One must admit that it is a great joy to be a Christian! For thus we depart to go to God, and our departure, although it causes our friends great sorrow because it will be a long time before they see us again, does not break their hearts. It is a farewell, but a farewell until we meet again.... Still, death is bitter, and still the days are long once we are left alone, and whoever has no tears is not beloved by God. There is one nature that God has made and that he desires, and one nature that sin has made and that must be sacrificed to God. The world knows only the second, because its heart is of clay, but Christians can, and must, know the other, because they desire all that God desires....

I do not know why, Madame, I am pouring forth commonplaces in such a way; but this sort of commonplace is so true! There is so much real consolation in these words many people repeat in an absent-minded way, and which are, nevertheless, full of an unfailing vitality. One of the things, in my opinion, that shows most clearly the divine origin of our beliefs, is the inexhaustible richness with which they suffice for the needs of the human race. How many millions of heartbroken souls during the last six thousand years have sought peace and courage in the thought of the One who separates only to reunite eternally; and look and see whether the waters of this consoling river are less abundant or less pure for all that. Far from it. God reveals to us, in sorrow, one of his adorable faces, which he has no need to show us when everything smiles for us. Blessed are those who suffer! Blessed are those who weep! That is what he said; and in saying it, in guaranteeing it with his divine Word, he was thinking of you, he said it for you and for all who were to weep and suffer in this world where he suffered and wept himself.

(Letter to Madame Swetchine, 23 October 1833)

Notes

1. *Ecclesiasticis viris*, Rome, 19 March 1875.

2. Dom Guéranger, in his *Liturgical Year*, on the feast of the Dedication of Churches (Time after Pentecost, Vol VI).

3. Dom Savaton, *Dom Delatte* (Solesmes, 1954), p. 353.

4. From the Solemn Prayer of Consecration to Virginity: "By the gift of your Spirit may there be in her ... a chaste liberty."

5. See Chapter Eleven, note eight.

A Chronology

4 Apr 1805	Birth and baptism of Prosper Louis Guéranger at Sablé near Solesmes, in the diocese of Le Mans
Nov 1822	Enters seminary at Le Mans
1826-9	Secretary to the bishop of Le Mans, Mgr. de la Myre-Mory.
7 Oct 1827	Ordained priest
26 Jan 1828	"Conversion" to the Roman liturgy
1830	*Considérations sur la liturgie catholique*
1831	*De l'élection et de la nomination des évêques*
11 July 1833	Restoration of Saint-Pierre of Solesmes
1836	*Origines de l'Eglise romaine*
9 July 1837	Erection of Solesmes to rank of abbey and approval of its Constitutions
26 July 1837	Monastic profession of Dom Guéranger
21 Nov 1837	First four professions at Solesmes
1840	*Institutions liturgiques I*
1841	*Institutions liturgiques II*
1841-1866	*L'Année liturgique (The Liturgical Year)*
1842	Foundation at Paris (Saint-Germain), closed 1845

1843   *Lettre sur le droit de la liturgie à Mgr l'archévêque de Reims*

1844   *Défense des "Institutions liturgiques": Lettre à Mgr l'archévêque de Toulouse*

12 Oct 1845   Birth of Jeanne-Henriette (Jenny) Bruyère at Paris

1846-7   *Nouvelle défense des "Institutions liturgiques": Lettres à Mgr l'évêque d'Orléans*

1848   *Histoire de Sainte Cécile*

27 Mar 1848   Birth and baptism of Olis-Henri Delatte at Jeumont

1850   *Mémoire sur l'Immaculée conception*

1851   *Institutions liturgiques III*

1853   Foundation at Acey, Jura (closed 1856)

Foundation at Ligugé

1856   *Règlement du Noviciat* (published in 1855 and appeared also under the title *Notions sur la vie religieuse.)*

1856-60   Articles in *l'Univers* on naturalism

1857   Dom Guéranger prepares Jenny Bruyère for her first Communion

Sept 1860   Trip to England

2 Oct 1860   H. Delatte enters minor seminary at Cambrai

12 Oct 1861   Jenny Bruyère consecrates herself to God in a private vow made before Dom Guéranger

1862   *Essai sur la médaille de Saint Benoît*

Enchiridion benedictinum (Benedictine texts)

1863   *Édition des "Exercices" de Sainte Gertrude*

1865	Foundation at Marseilles (today at Ganagobie, Provence)
Oct 1865	H. Delatte enters major seminary at Cambrai
29 Sept 1866	H. Delatte is professor at the College Saint-Bertin, Saint-Omer
16 Nov 1866	Foundation of Sainte-Cécile de Solesmes
15 Aug 1868	First five professions at Sainte-Cécile
1870	Dom Guéranger's *De la Monarchie Pontificale*
14 July 1871	Abbatial Blessing of Madame Cécile Bruyère
12 Oct 1871	Dedication of the church at Sainte-Cécile
29 June 1872	H. Delatte ordained priest
7 July 1872	Fr Delatte curate at Notre-Dame de Roubaix
5-10 Oct 1874	Fr Delatte stays at Solesmes' guesthouse; meets Dom Guéranger
1874	Dom Guéranger's *Sainte Cécile et la société romaine*
30 Jan 1875	Death of Dom Guéranger
	Posthumous publication of his *L'Église, ou la société de la louange divine*
11 Feb 1875	Dom Charles Couturier elected second Abbot of Solesmes
Dec 1875	Fr Delatte curate at Saint-Étienne in Lille
Nov 1879	Fr Delatte named Professor of the Catholic University in Lille
Nov 1880	Decrees of expulsion
	Foundation at Silos, Spain
7 Sept 1883	Fr Delatte enters the novitiate at Solesmes

A CHRONOLOGY

21 Mar 1885	Monastic profession of Dom Paul Delatte
1885	Abbess Cécile Bruyère publishes *The Spiritual Life and Prayer*
18 May 1888	Dom Delatte named Prior
1889	Foundations at Wisques
27 Jan 1890	Sainte-Cécile raised to the rank of an abbey
29 Oct 1890	Death of Dom Couturier
9 Nov 1890	Dom Delatte elected third Abbot of Solesmes
8 Dec 1890	Abbatial Blessing of Dom Delatte at Sainte-Cécile
25 Apr 1893	Dom Delatte suspended of his functions
1893	Foundation at Paris (Sainte-Marie)
25 Nov 1893	Dom Delatte reinstated as Abbot of Solesmes
	Foundation at Saint-Wandrille
27 Mar 1894	The Solesmes community returns to its monastery
1894-95	Dom Delatte, *Studium Solesmense: I, De Deo Uno; II, De Deo Trino*
Dec 1895	Foundation of the priory of St Michael, Farnborough
Apr 1897	Foundation at Kergonan (St Anne)
Aug 1898	Foundation of St Michel, Kerganon
1 July 1901	French parliament passes Laws of Association, applicable from 1 October.
15-18 July 1901	Dom Delatte, *Examen de conscience d'un religieux*
Sept 1901	Dom Delatte and his community at

Appuldurcombe, Isle of Wight; Abbess Cécile Bruyère and her community at Northwood House, West Cowes, Isle of Wight

Feb 1906   Transfer of the nuns of Sainte-Cécile to Appley House, Ryde

12 Oct 1907   Dedication of the church at St Cecilia's Abbey, Ryde

1908   Monks transfer to Quarr Abbey

18 Mar 1909   Death of Abbess Cécile Bruyère

1909   Foundation at Clervaux, Luxembourg

Dec 1909   Dom Delatte, *Dom Guéranger, abbé de Solesmes*

12 Oct 1912   Dedication of the church at Quarr Abbey

Nov 1913   Dom Delatte, *Commentaire sur la règle de saint Benoît*

5 Dec 1920   Dom Delatte resigns

22 Apr 1921   Election of Dom Cozien, fourth abbot of Solesmes

1921   Dom Delatte, *L'Évangile de Notre Seigneur Jésus Christ*

31 Aug 1922   Return to Solesmes

1923-27   Dom Delatte, *Les Épîtres de Saint Paul*

21 Mar 1935   Dom Delatte's golden jubilee of monastic profession

20 Sept 1937   Death of Dom Delatte

The Congregation of Solesmes

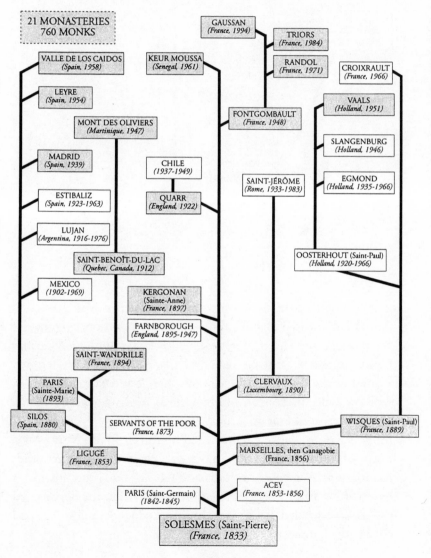

**21 MONASTERIES
760 MONKS**

GAUSSAN
(France, 1994)

TRIORS
(France, 1984)

RANDOL
(France, 1971)

CROIXRAULT
(France, 1966)

VALLE DE LOS CAIDOS
(Spain, 1958)

KEUR MOUSSA
(Senegal, 1961)

LEYRE
(Spain, 1954)

VAALS
(Holland, 1951)

MONT DES OLIVIERS
(Martinique, 1947)

FONTGOMBAULT
(France, 1948)

SLANGENBURG
(Holland, 1946)

MADRID
(Spain, 1939)

CHILE
(1937-1949)

EGMOND
(Holland, 1935-1966)

SAINT-JÉRÔME
(Rome, 1933-1983)

ESTIBALIZ
(Spain, 1923-1963)

QUARR
(England, 1922)

LUJAN
(Argentina, 1916-1976)

SAINT-BENOÎT-DU-LAC
(Quebec, Canada, 1912)

OOSTERHOUT (Saint-Paul)
(Holland, 1920-1966)

MEXICO
(1902-1969)

KERGONAN
(Sainte-Anne)
(France, 1897)

FARNBOROUGH
(England, 1895-1947)

SAINT-WANDRILLE
(France, 1894)

PARIS
(Sainte-Marie)
(1893)

CLERVAUX
(Luxembourg, 1890)

SILOS
(Spain, 1880)

SERVANTS OF THE POOR
(France, 1873)

WISQUES (Saint-Paul)
(France, 1889)

LIGUGÉ
(France, 1853)

MARSEILLES, then Ganagobie
(France, 1856)

PARIS (Saint-Germain)
(1842-1845)

ACEY
(France, 1853-1856)

SOLESMES (Saint-Pierre)
(France, 1833)

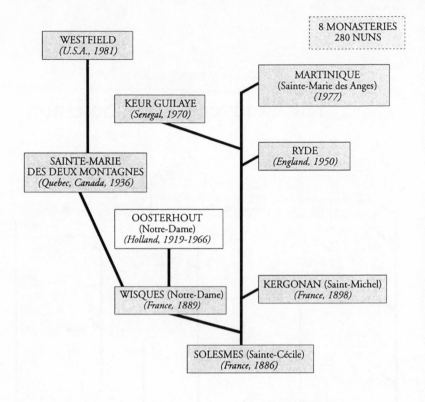

The location of the monasteries (except when this is the actual name) is indicated in italic type. The date mentioned is that of the foundation. This is sometimes followed by the date of closure (as in the case of Saint-Germain at Paris, Acey, and Saint-Jerome, Rome) or the date of transfer to another congregation (boxes in white). Ryde, of Belgian origin (1882), was aggregated to the Congregation of Solesmes in 1950. The full extent of Solesmes' influence is not entirely represented by this diagram. Monks and nuns of the Congregation have participated in many other foundations, as far away as India and China. Two other institutes have sprung from the Congregation of Solesmes: the Servants of the Poor, founded by Dom Camille Leduc of Solesmes, and Croixault, a monastery opened to the handicapped.